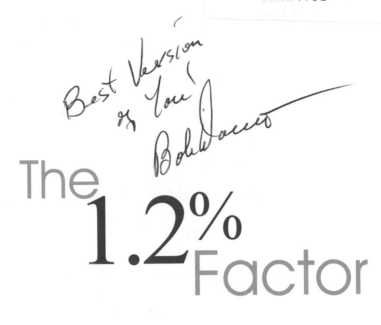

Best Version of You!

Bob Davies

The 1.2% Factor

The science of how the small change of accountability leads to large results!

NLP Based Into

The 1.2% Factor

The science of how the small change
of accountability leads to large results!

By Bob Davies

Published by:

Motivated Publishing Studios

Copyright © 2008 by Bob Davies

ISBN: 978-0-9820086-0-7
Printed in USA

First Edition: August 2008

Edited by: KG MPSP
Cover design by: RAS
Book layout by: RAS

Acknowledgements

The creation of this book has spanned over three years. My first two books contained information that I taught in my seminars. They simply required setting aside the time to write. This book captures three years of scouring through tens of thousands of pages of research in the fields of science. Seeing the finished product was truly a source of pride and accomplishment.

I want to thank my wife Jenifer. She put up with my long hours in the office, my overnighters, and my weekends away from the family — all in the name of this book. Jenifer kept the kids entertained when I made the tough choices to go to the office and write. She was patient, loving and understanding.

It is with great pleasure that I acknowledge the significant contributions of the over 100 research studies that I have cited. I want to thank Rod Schulhauser, of Motivated Publishing Studios, for a very high standard of excellence in editing and formatting. I am impressed.

I'd like to thank my coaching clients who continue to be willing to be guided by my intense questions and challenges. Their continued commitment to excellence is an inspiration to me.

I want to thank all of the organizations that have had confidence in selecting me to speak at their functions. I truly appreciate their trust in myself and bringing in my message to their audiences.

I'd like to thank Select Family of Staffing Companies who has had me as their corporate coach, speaker and trainer for over ten years. I've learned from you as you grew from a 500 million to a 1.5 billion dollar company.

Finally, I'd like to thank you the reader. It takes a special mind set to be open to improving the results you experience in your life. We're a team. Let's compete together!

Table of Contents

Introduction

Welcome to the journey you and I are about to have. I hope you find it fascinating, challenging and of immediate use to you in designing and living the life you are committed to. As you can tell by the title, I'm going to be asking you to make one small change in your habits. This entire book will show you why this one request is in your best interest and will support you in making that change and having it stick.

I'm going to be discussing the problem, giving you a solution, and then the proof. This book is designed to be a format for further research if that is of interest to you. Feel free to be a student of this information and look up my references to take you further into the data if that suits you. Also, please do read the footnotes, because in many cases there is learning and new information contained within them. One more nuts and bolts note. I'm going to take liberty with my pronouns and primarily use the male, "he", to mean him or her. So I'll thank you in advance for bearing with me.

I don't know about you but I'm a bit tired of reading a book and then a month later not remembering what the book was about. What would it be like to pick up a book and have it actually make a difference, an impact in your life? Is this possible? The answer is yes.

One small change reminds me of what is referred to as the butterfly effect.

The **butterfly effect** is a phrase that is a technical description of a *sensitive dependence on initial conditions* in chaos theory.[1] Small variations of the initial condition of a nonlinear dynamic system may produce large variations in the long term behavior of the system. This can be exhibited by very simple systems: for example, a ball placed at the crest of a hill might roll into any of several valleys depending on slight differences in its initial position.

The phrase refers to the idea that a butterfly's wings might create tiny changes in the atmosphere, that ultimately cause a tornado to appear in a distant place on the planet, (or prevent a tornado from appearing). The flapping wing represents a small change in the initial condition of the system, which causes a chain of events leading to a large-scale phenomena. Had the butterfly not flapped its wings, the trajectory of the system might have been vastly different.

Can something as small and insignificant as a butterfly have an impact on the larger scale? Can the small influence the large? What does this mean to you? How can small changes in habits, attitudes, perspectives, and actions have a major impact on the results in your life? That's what this book will explore. This book will offer you one small change that you can make, that has a high predictabilty of creating the results you may be seeking. Have you ever read a book before that was more then entertainment or just information? This book is designed to be the beginning of a long-term relationship. You'll see why and how as you continue to read on.

Let me set the tone or the mindset for your reading. I'll ask you to keep in mind an area in your life where you are not satisfied with the results that you are currently experiencing. Please keep in mind as you begin, where you may want to have some serious changes going on. Perhaps it's your health, maybe business, even personal or all three.

Bear with me as you read this book. Don't get bogged down when I get into complicated brain or mathematics theory. The specifics are not important. The reason for the inclusion of the complicated science is to expose you to that information. Don't get overly concerned with the human desire to "understand" everything. I am following a very precise adult learning process in this book. The only thing that is important is what you do during and after reading the book. Every word has been carefully selected and there is an accumulative impact from one sentence to the next, so stay with me.

Let's look at the 1.2% part of the title.

Chimps Are US!

"Study: Chimps, humans more closely linked." By Mike Tonner of the Atlanta Journal Constitution. This story caught my attention. "Scientists have long thought that humans and chimps split off from a common ancestor around 6 million years ago and continued to evolve separately, gradually acquiring the traits that distinguish each species today."

Scientists published the complete genome of the chimpanzee in August of 2006 in the journal Nature. They found only a 1.2% difference in the coding genes of chimps and humans, but there are of course significant differences in the two species.

That article is what led me to that portion of the title of this book, the 1.2% Factor. It's the small differences or changes that generates the significant results. The intention of this book is to take a look at what science has revealed and relate that to you in such a way that you will gain new perspectives of what you are capable of accomplishing in your life.

I will look to the newest discoveries in the fields of physics, mathematics, biology, psychology and even a dose of philosophy for this information. It will then be simplified and presented to you in a way that will make sense and hopefully generate a spark that ignites a small change in your life habits, which of course over time will result in the magnificent improvements or even the small improvements that you seek. Either way, my objective is that something happens because you have this book.

The "small change leading to significant results" idea is not a new concept. What is new however, is how I am presenting this to you, backed by scientific evidence. What is also new and very unique is that when you have finished reading this book you will be a part of a community. You will essentially be in my coaching program. This means that you are eligible to join my free monthly live telephone conference coaching call starting now.

Send an e-mail to info@bobdavies.com to receive the bridge line number, access code and the date of the next call. I personally lead this 45-minute call. The first 15 minutes is a presentation on the latest discoveries in behavioral excellence and the next 30 minutes is an actual live coaching demonstration with a volunteer which could be you, for free!

You can also join my weekly on-line coaching program. This is a low cost ($19.95 per month) internet based system of coaching and accountability that is so unique, that I am the only one offering this type of a system world-wide.[2] More about this later. The bottom line is that this book will not simply dump you at the end.[3] You will have options for an ongoing relationship with me. There is no reason for you not to experience the changes that you say you are looking for.

Imagine for a moment, that you had a clear picture of where you wanted to be in the next twenty years and that you could make it happen exactly as you wanted. It's your imagination so you can direct it any way you would like! So imagine with all of your senses what your life would be like.

What would you look like physically? What type of health and energy would you have? What would your relationships with family and friends be like? How would your finances look? What could they look like? What types of investments would you have? Where would you live? What types of hobbies would you have? How fulfilling would your life be? Would you have a life of struggle or significance? What are you continuing to build? What impact would you be having on others?

These are all great questions. Now, imagine that you know, or could find out, exactly what you would need to do to make this vision a reality, starting with actions today. That's why this book was written. There is clearly a difference between what you say you will do versus what you actually do. I know there are reasons, stories, circumstances, excuses, priorities and limitations on time. All of that was covered during the explanation of rationalization in my first book, "The Sky Is Not The Limit—You Are!"

I have been in the speaking and training business since 1983. I have constantly been intrigued by observing people who have attended conferences, taken live training, purchased books, cd's and dvd's, and still have not made changes in their lives.

This is the case with all, and I mean all, training. Regardless of the speaker, they all face the same problem. Creating lasting change in their audience is a daunting task! For the most part, most speakers have been reduced by human nature to the realm of entertainers.

When I speak to an audience I love to start out with this question; "What do you think the probability is, that what you will experience from me today will have a significant and long-term impact in your life?"

Most of the time the audience cheers and shouts that it's a high probability. They are almost shocked when I tell them that actually it's a low probability that this presentation will be anything more then entertainment. Look at the graph below. Essentially this graph states that training doesn't matter. It concludes that you will be about where you started after a training program. So why bother? Entertainment?

Entertainment or Impact

Anticipated Results
Post-Training

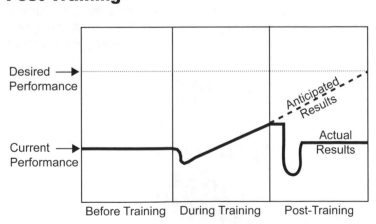

I don't leave it there however. I continue to explain that although it's not highly probable, it is possible to go beyond entertainment into the realm of lifetime impact. That's what we are going for, that possibility. That's what I'm going for with you, impact.

There's nothing wrong with being an entertainer. They are highly paid and very needed. What I'm essentially saying is that taking a training course, reading a book or attending a meeting is mostly entertainment.

However, you can have long-term change if you apply the basic principles that I will reveal in this book. You need to be willing to look at the truth however. The topic of the truth could be another book! I'm fond of saying the truth is not relevant! It's what you choose to pay attention to that matters.

Consider the following: I ask the audience who is afraid of snakes? A woman in the front row raises her hand and graciously accepts my invitation to come up on stage after I assure her that what I'm about to do is safe and I don't have any snakes.

I show her an envelope with a picture of a rattlesnake on the front and I tell her that I have rattlesnake eggs. She opens the envelope and there is a popping sound and movement, she screams in fear!

Then I show her what she just responded to. I show her a wire in the shape of a V with a rubber band stretched across it. There is a small washer in the middle that is wound tight and when you open the envelope it will unwind making the noise and causing the movement.

This is a classic case of expectations and perception versus reality. Psychologists call this **"confirmation bias"**, selective thinking whereby we seek out information that confirms our beliefs and expectations, while ignoring or simply not seeing evidence that challenges them. This is an example of poor human observation colored by expectations.

Next, I repeat the exact same sequence but this time I show the volunteer the wire, the rubber band, the washer, the picture of the rattlesnake on the front of the envelope and I set up different expectations. She opens the envelope and there is no scream, no reaction at all. What was different? It was the exact same set of circumstances as the prior event that produced a scream not only from my volunteer, but also from the entire front row of the audience. The difference was that she had new information that affected her "bias". She was "predisposed" to experience something different. Her expectations were now dramatically changed and she got what she expected, no danger just a loud noise and movement, and therefore no scream!

I constantly emphasize that your ability to influence what you pay attention to is directly correlated to your degree of success or failure. Would it be in your best interest to be able to do this? Would it be of value to you to be able to just eat a small bite of a piece of pie and then push the rest away and yet be totally satisfied with that small bite? Not hungry at all. No fighting with yourself. No issue with willpower. Would it be of value to you to be able to make a decision on what habits either no longer serve you and get rid of them, or decide what new habits you need and then instantly have them? If yes, you're in the right place.

This illustrates the purpose of this book. **The purpose is to influence the way that you think and what you do, by revealing to you some ideas that you would most likely not have been exposed to**.

Charles Darwin's[4] dictum holds that if observations are to be of any use they must be tested against some view, thesis or hypothesis, theory or paradigm. The facts that we measure or perceive never just speak for themselves, but lend themselves to interpretation through the colored lenses of my years of experience in the field of human excellence.[5] I bring my experience as a college football coach and as a professional personal certified business and life coach to bear on these interpretations.[6]

I have taken complicated research in mathematics, physics, and neurobiology and simplified them to suggest their implications on your life. The objective of this book is because of this information you make one small change in your life, one small new habit that will have a significant impact on your life. I will give you my recommendation and coaching on that one small change. If you do this, then you will be living the 1.2 % factor. If you do take action on my coaching, then there is a high probability and predictability that you will experience more results and fulfillment then ever before.

I'm not talking about massive change here. Massive change is possible but large changes have a different and more challenging effect on the brain. My recommendation is to make small changes and let the law of accumulative effect take hold.

Consider this example—increasing the length of a side of a square increases its area exponentially. So little changes have big results.

Exponential Growth

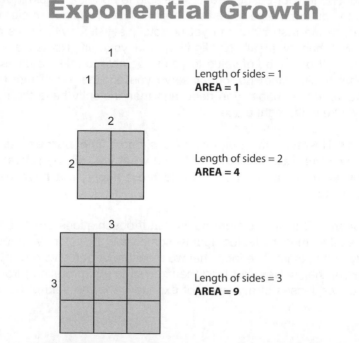

1

1   Length of sides = 1
AREA = 1

2

2   Length of sides = 2
AREA = 4

3

3   Length of sides = 3
AREA = 9

Here's an example of a little change having a big result, and I'm a pilot so I can identify with this. A tragic accident happened on a commercial airliner. The cause of many accidents begins before the engine starts. The flap warning light was disabled on the inbound flight when the warning horn circuit breaker was pulled and was not reset before departure. The pilots were interrupted during their taxi check and did not set the flaps to the takeoff position. The takeoff flap warning horn did not sound as the pilot advanced the thrust levers; resetting the circuit breaker would have saved many lives. A little thing, yet no matter how experienced you are, making small mistakes and not following established procedures can make you a dangerous amateur.

A small lapse like a basketball player not coming off of a screen properly enabling the opponent to have an open shot to win a game has a big impact.

The average baseball player hits .250 and earns about $1 million a year. Hitting .250 means three hits every twelve times at bat. Now lets look at the superstar. The superstar hits .333. That is a significant difference, but how did he get there. The average salary for the super star is $24 million. Is the super star 24 times better then the average? The answer is no. The super star is just a little bit better. The super star just gets one more hit every twelve times at bat. Small inputs create large exponential results like the butterfly effect.

In 1962, the Venus bound spacecraft Mariner 1 had to be destroyed because it strayed off course during launch. An error caused by the omission of a hyphen in the mission's computer programming. This single punctuation mark cost taxpayers $18 million.

It is my hope that your appreciation for small inputs will grow as you read this book. As we progress, it will be powerful for you to see the parallels of the human nervous system to mathematics and physics, and then see those parallels related to a theory of what you do or need to do on a daily basis. By having this revelation, you may have a renewed belief in your purpose and meaning. You will hopefully have a renewed passion and belief, and a consistent surge in activity, as you blast through one previously perceived barrier after another. Knowing that the laws of the universe and Mother Nature are on your side, working for you, every moment of every day! You will have the knowledge that these laws are the same for everyone and you cannot fail!

There is a principle of physics referred to as "Occam's Razor". This states that we should always take the simplest possible path and ignore more clumsy alternatives, especially if the alternatives can never be measured. This book looks to take the complicated and reduce it to the simple and then make suggestions as to its applicability to your life.

Urban legend has it that once during rush hour in New York City, a tractor-trailer became stuck in the very busy Holland Tunnel. The truck was too tall to move forward and wedged too tightly to move backward. The police called the fire department and were about ready to engage in what seemed like the most logical solution, sawing off the top of the trailer and then towing it out of the tunnel.

Then a car drove by and a little girl asked her father why don't they just let the air out of the tires? Her dad asked the police. They scratched their heads, let the air out of the tires and within minutes they had the truck cleared from the tunnel. This young girl was just too naïve to look for difficult solutions. Keep that in mind the next time you're facing a problem.

Observation will be a key. We all start out as poor observers. Test this concept for yourself. How many times have you handled a penny in your lifetime? Which side does President Lincoln's head face, left or right? I'll even give you some pictures to choose from. Which penny below is correct?

Which Penny is Correct?

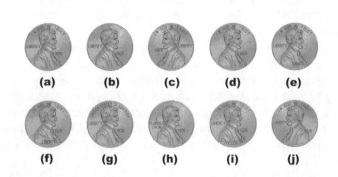

(a)　　(b)　　(c)　　(d)　　(e)

(f)　　(g)　　(h)　　(i)　　(j)

Penny (a) is correct but is seldom recognized. Pennies G and J are popular wrong answers. You'll never forget this phrase and you'll always remember which direction Lincoln is facing, "Lincoln got it right everyone else was left out." This is referred to as encoding failure; the memory was never formed in the first place. Few of us ever encode the details of a penny. We are basically casual observers even of the smallest circumstances in our own lives.

Consider this familiar object, a telephone keypad. How many phone calls have you made using this all too familiar keypad? Probably thousands.

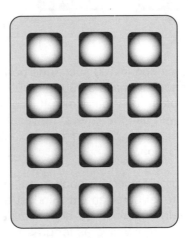

Now label the above keys with the correct numbers, letters, and symbols. Yes, letters and symbols too. Take 60 seconds to do this — that should be sufficient time since the telephone keypad is so familiar to you. When you are finished compare to the picture below:

Less than one person in 100 succeeds perfectly, although all of them use the telephone to make 3,000 to 5,000 calls per year. Think about this. How often do you look at the telephone keypad? Occasionally you even use the letters, however you no longer think about what you are doing. You are able to accomplish your task without close observation.

A necessary ingredient for this book to make a difference for you is your willingness to let go of an old mindset and form a new one. Consider the following exercise as an example. Take six pens or pencils, matches, six of anything as long as they are all equal size. Form four triangles with each leg of the triangle equal in length to each pen or pencil. In other words, all of the triangles are the same size and that size is equal to the length of the pen, pencil or match.

As I walk around a room I see some interesting attempts. I see folks putting three pens on the table in a triangle and then laying the rest of the pens on top. They tell me that they have four triangles. I ask them to show me one of the triangles, and then I ask if each leg of the triangle is the same length as one of the pens. Of course it is not. As I walk around the room, I keep repeating that the way you are attempting to solve your problem will not give you a solution. You need to approach it differently. You need to change your mindset.

Eventually someone will figure it out after they hear me state enough times that they need to approach this differently. The solution is to think in the third dimension, to form a tripod and you can see, four triangles, all the same size.

The point that I make is to paraphrase a statement made by Albert Einstein, "you cannot solve your problems with the same state of mind that you were in when you created them." It will take a new mindset to generate different results in your life. In fact, one of the points that I'll make now is to replace the phrase "I can't" with this new phrase, "At my present level of thinking a solution does not exist".

So reading this book is an experience. I am now your coach. Imagine putting on blinders as you read this book, as if you and I are having a one on one conversation. I am coaching you. My first coaching point is to challenge your way of thinking. Be open to a new mindset, to new habits and to new results.

Lets begin...

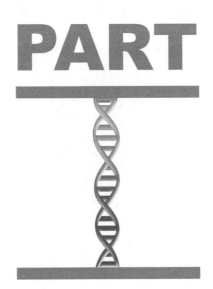

The Problem and the Solution

Chapter 1

Problem #1:

The Human Hard Wired MindSet

"If there is no wind, row"

I have previously gone into great detail about the genetic coding of the human brain regarding our automatic instinct to recognize the highest level of perceived pain and avoid it.[7]

This is a human instinct. Let's look at the concept of instincts. The dictionary defines an instinct as "the innate aspect of behavior that is unlearned, complex, and normally adaptive. A powerful motivation or impulse."[8] Instincts are very powerful. Consider the origination of the flight or fight response.

Walter Cannon first described the **fight-or-flight** response, also called the acute stress response, in 1927.[9] His theory states that animals react to threats with a general discharge of the sympathetic nervous system, priming the animal for fighting or fleeing. This response was later recognized as the first stage of a general adaptation syndrome, that regulates stress responses among vertebrates and other organisms.

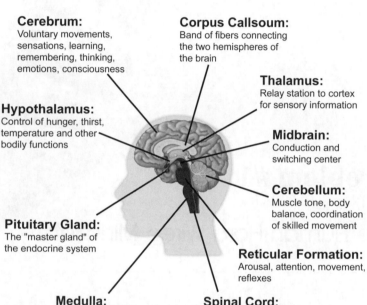

Cerebrum:
Voluntary movements, sensations, learning, remembering, thinking, emotions, consciousness

Corpus Callsoum:
Band of fibers connecting the two hemispheres of the brain

Thalamus:
Relay station to cortex for sensory information

Hypothalamus:
Control of hunger, thirst, temperature and other bodily functions

Midbrain:
Conduction and switching center

Cerebellum:
Muscle tone, body balance, coordination of skilled movement

Pituitary Gland:
The "master gland" of the endocrine system

Reticular Formation:
Arousal, attention, movement, reflexes

Medulla:
Centers for control over breathing, swallowing, digestion, heartbeat

Spinal Cord:
Conduction paths for motor and sensory impulses, local reflexes

Main Structures of the Human Brain

Biology of the Stress Response

Normally, when a person is in a serene, unstimulated state, the "firing" of neurons in the locus ceruleus, the arousal area of the brain, is minimal. A novel stimulus (which could include a perception of danger or an environmental stressor signal, such as elevated sound levels or over-illumination), once perceived, is relayed from the sensory cortex of the brain through the thalamus to the brain stem. (What is important here is not to understand these brain locations, but to appreciate that scientific specific knowledge of them is already established). Route of signaling increases the rate of activity in the locus ceruleus, and the person becomes alert and attentive to the environment. Similarly, an abundance of catecholamines at neuroreceptor sites facilitates reliance on spontaneous or intuitive behaviors that are often related to combat or escape.

If a stimulus is perceived as a threat, a more intense and prolonged discharge of the locus ceruleus activates the sympathetic division of the autonomic nervous system. This activation is associated with specific physiological actions in the system, both directly and indirectly, through the release of epinephrine (adrenaline) and to a lesser extent norepinephrine from the medulla of the adrenal glands. This release is triggered by acetylcholine, released from preganglionic sympathetic nerves. The other major player in the acute stress response is the hypothalamic-pituitary-adrenal axis.

Physiology of the Stress Response

A stimulant occurs, such as a cave man looks up and sees a mountain lion. The cortex taps into the limbic system and a response is initiated long before the cave man is even consciously aware that a danger is present. Catecholamine hormones facilitate immediate physical reactions associated with a preparation for violent muscular action. These include the following:

- ✦ Acceleration of heart and lung action
- ✦ Inhibition of stomach and intestinal action
- ✦ Constriction of blood vessels in many parts of the body
- ✦ Liberation of nutrients for muscular action
- ✦ Dilation of blood vessels for muscles
- ✦ Inhibition of lacrimal glands (responsible for tear production) and salivation
- ✦ Dilation of pupil
- ✦ Relaxation of bladder

Psychology of the Stress Response

A typical example of the stress response is a grazing zebra, calmly maintaining homeostasis. If the zebra sees a lion closing in for the kill, the stress response is activated. The escape requires intense muscular effort, supported by all of the body's systems. The sympathetic nervous system's activation provides for these needs. A similar example involving fight is that of a cat about to be attacked by a dog. The cat shows accelerated heartbeat, piloerection (hair standing on end, normally for conservation of heat), and pupil dilation, all signs of sympathetic arousal.

Behavioral Manifestations of Fight-or-Flight

In prehistoric times when the fight-or-flight response evolved in humans, fight was manifested in aggressive, combative behavior and flight was manifested by fleeing potentially threatening situations, such as being confronted by a predator. In current times, these responses persist, but fight and flight responses have assumed a wider range of behaviors. For example, the fight response may be manifested in angry, argumentative behavior, and the flight response may be manifested through social withdrawal, substance abuse, and even television viewing.

Negative Effects of the Stress Response in Humans

Although the emergency measure of the stress response is undoubtedly both vital and valuable, it can also be disruptive and damaging. In most modern situations, humans rarely encounter emergencies that require physical effort, yet our biology still provides for them. Thus we may find our stress response activated in situations where physical action is inappropriate or even illegal. This activation takes a toll on both our bodies and our minds.

Disruption of the sexual response and the digestive system are common negative results. Diarrhea, constipation, and difficulty maintaining sexual arousal are typical examples. These are functions that are controlled by the parasympathetic nervous system and therefore suppressed by sympathetic arousal. Prolonged stress responses may result in chronic suppression of the immune system, leaving the sufferer vulnerable to infection by bacteria and viruses. Repeated stress responses can be caused not only by real threats, but also by mental disorders such as post-traumatic stress disorder, in which the individual shows a stress response when remembering a past trauma, and panic disorder, in which the stress response is activated apparently by nothing.

From an evolutionary standpoint, the brain is one of the most unusual organs in the human body. Our other organs, the heart, liver, intestines are so well developed that they have remained consistent through millions of years of human evolution. For the last four or five hundred million years, the brain has continued to develop and change. Today we have three separate brains that came along in intervals of about one or two hundred million years. Dr. Robert Maurer has a very simplified description that I'll share with you.[10]

"At the bottom of the brain is the brain stem. It's about five hundred million years old and is called the reptilian brain (and in fact it does look like an alligator's whole brain). The reptilian brain wakes you up in the morning, sends you off to sleep at night, and reminds your heart to beat. It is responsible for the regulation of such fundamental activities as breathing, temperature and the circulation of the blood.

Sitting on top of the brain stem is the midbrain, also known as the mammalian brain. Roughly three hundred million years old, this is the brain possessed in one form or another by all mammals. The midbrain regulates the body's internal temperature, houses our emotions, and governs the fight-or-flight response that keeps us alive in the face of danger. The midbrain processes automatic activities such as walking, which operates without our conscious interference.

The third part of the brain is the cortex, the top most level, which began to develop about one hundred million years ago. The cortex, which wraps around the rest of the brain, is responsible for the miracle of being human. It mediates conscious awareness, intentions and personality. Civilization, art, science, and music all reside there. It's where our rational thoughts and creative impulses take place."

The first problem we have is that although we want to change, we see change as a threat to our homeostasis, or "staying the same", and we resist it. Our entire genetic make-up is designed to keep us safe, recognize and avoid threats, and pass on our genes. Anything in the way of our survival is to be avoided. It doesn't matter if the threat is real or imagined, your avoidance mechanism will be activated and you will be compelled to avoid.

This instinct doesn't ask you to comply with the avoidance. The human instinct compels your avoidance. You don't have an option here. You are coded to recognize the highest level of perceived pain or threat and avoid. Period! This is the first problem to deal with in regards to performance excellence. For the main goal of survival and the passing on of our genes, our brain is coded to find the highest level of perceived pain and compel us to avoid taking that action. However, our brain is not coded to analyze the truth of the threat. Our brains circuitry simply recognizes the possibility of pain or a threat and instinctively initiates the avoidance mechanism.

This is going to be a problem if you want to lose weight with exercise and diet. Why? Because the brain is going to do a neurological search and then look for any previous patterns or links of exercise and dieting to pain. That's the stimulus. The response is the avoidance and rationalization. Rationalization is a justification of avoidance that effects perception. You'll never even think that you're avoiding. You'll instead perceive that you're just "too busy".

If you want to make more money and the necessary action is prospecting, the same neurological firing occurs. Your brain remembers a previous negative past experience when you were rejected and holds prospecting as a threat, triggering the avoidance mechanism. Without an intervention it will be very difficult, if not impossible, to rise past your comfort zone, rationalization and mediocrity.

Chapter 2

Problem #2:

Our Limited Mindset of Perceptions

*"You can either complain that the rose bushes have
thorns — or rejoice that thorn bushes have roses."*
— Alphonse Karr

The second problem that we need to deal with is a continuation
of our physiological limitations and the addition of our limited
perception because of the limits of our senses. Let's examine this
from a scientific perspective.

It is widely understood that humans have very limited perceptual
abilities. We have very limited vision for example.

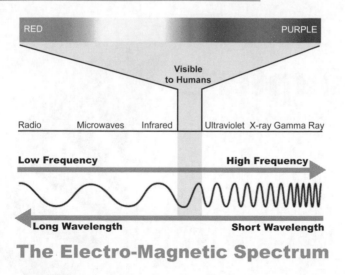

The Electro-Magnetic Spectrum

This chart illustrates how little light is actually visible to humans — the small band in the center. All of the other frequencies of energy vibrations are realities, but humans just don't have the perceptual acuity to see them.

Birds for example, can see dimensions that are unknown to humans.

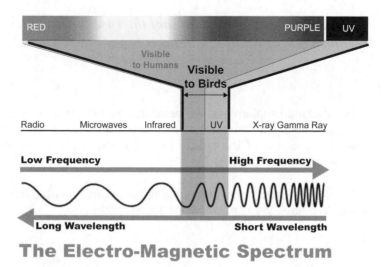

The Electro-Magnetic Spectrum

This is what a flower might look like to a bird:

A UV World

How a Human Sees it

How a Bird Sees it

Which picture is real? Are they both? Is reality that subjective? Is reality influenced by the limitations of the observer? More of this type of a conversation will follow later, when we look into the quantum aspects of reality.

It is well known that dogs have a sense of smell and hearing that is far superior to that of a human. Here's a quick story to that effect. I happen to have two poodles, Sophie the bad one and Zorro. I think Sophie has a species identity conflict issue. At least I have never seen a dog that lies on a couch like her — she thinks she's a cat!

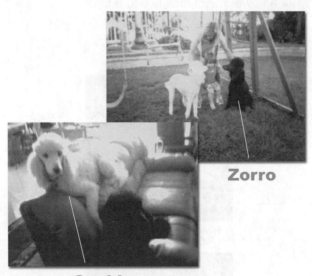

Zorro

Sophie

One night I'm sitting on the couch watching educational TV, (*Family Feud* re-runs), and Sophie is on one side and Zorro on the other. All of a sudden Sophie starts barking. I look at Sophie and yell "what's wrong with you?" A few seconds later the front doorbell rings. I look at Zorro and say "what's wrong with you? Why didn't you hear the people on the front porch?"

Sophie heard some noises that were not perceptible to humans. Perhaps you are aware that dogs can detect cancer in humans before any other known medical test.[11]

5 dogs pass smell test to find cancer

Dogs can smell small amounts of alkanes and benzene derivatives not found in healthy tissue. They are able to detect differences in the breath of cancer patients.

Humans have very limited perceptions. Experience this from a visual perspective.consider the following, what is the distance from the ground to the wingtip of this airplane?

Your brain searches for the patterns that you have stored of the known, namely an airplane. But look what happens when I add a different element or frame of reference to the same picture;

13

What is causing you to change your interpretation of the same question? The facts haven't changed; it's the same plane. What is different? What you are in reference to is different. You are comparing to a visual reference that was absent the first time. What's different is that you are in relationship to something very specific, the men walking past the airplane. Although the airplane is the exact same airplane as the first picture, your interpretation of the facts are different, because your observation is in a different frame of reference to something specific that wasn't there the first time.

This will be very important as I present you with the intervention that will compensate for your limited perceptions. Just remember for now that the key is that you have a specific reference to guide you in forming a perception. That reference is the men walking by. Without that reference your brain searches for past neurological networks that are of known experiences of an airplane and you answer six feet from that reference orientation.

I like to use my piloting examples to illustrate a point. I can recall the first time I was on an instrument flight, by myself without an instructor, in actual instrument conditions, in the clouds.

I was terrified. The problem is that you can't tell what the airplane is doing when there are no visual references. When all you see are clouds, there's no contrast, there's no specific reference from which to judge what the position of the aircraft is. The only things you can rely on are the instruments. The problem to avoid is spatial disorientation. You can't trust how you feel the aircraft is performing. Look at how easy it is to deceive your senses:

I know it looks like these lines are sloping upwards or downwards, however, you can't trust your own interpretation of what you see. The only way you can judge accurately is in reference to something specific. If you draw a straight edge under each of the lines you'll be able to see very objectively that they are a series of straight lines.

The objective references for the airplane are the system of instruments.

This is an actual picture taken in the clouds. Just above the dash is what I see, nothing but white space. Without a visual reference, the only way that I'll be able to control the airplane is by observing, trusting, and responding to the instruments.

These instruments become my system to be in reference to. Let's look at one instrument, the altitude indicator; it's the one in the center. The top represents the sky and the bottom represents the ground. This is a gyroscope, which means rigidity in space. Regardless of the position of the airplane, the gyroscope will tell me exactly what its position is in reference to the ground. If I see this then it means I'm in a descending to level left turn:

15

There would be no way that I could know this based on what I feel or what my senses tell me. I must trust my system of instrumentation. This system of instruments is designed to give me the highest probability of a predictable outcome.

It is the same for human performance. You can't trust your interpretation of your circumstances. We are poor observers. Consider the following; count the black dots.

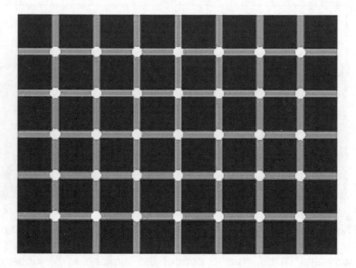

Have some difficulty? Remember, you can't trust your limited perception to reveal the reality. You must have help to compensate for your human limitations. The help is the system that follows.

Chapter 3

The Solution:

A Systems Approach

"If opportunity doesn't knock, build a door."

Because of the limited aspect of our human perception, we need an intervention. We need a way to offset our natural avoidance and rationalization, or at least get those processes to work for us rather than against us. The answer is in a system.

Let's explore the impact of using a system through an analogy. Grab a stop watch and have someone time you for 20 seconds. Starting with the number one, circle as many numbers as you can find consecutively, within that 20 seconds. Here are the numbers:

```
      73    9  49   66    78   62  50
  37      53             46   34
     69       17      38  14        74  18
     41  33
                29           2  70   86
           21  1
               25     10
     13                            22
         81  77  61   58       54  42
  57
        85   45   65    6   30
                               82   26
   79    31    55    32  60         80
          75       63        20  44  76
   23  43      47  51   64
                        88        68
   39    3     11           48      56
      67   87  71    24  36       40
   59                         12
           15    35 28    4          16
   19  7  83      27    84   72   8  52
```

How did you do? When I do this in my live presentations I look for the two extremes, the highest in the group, usually around 12, and the lowest in the group, usually around 4. Those are my elite performers and my poor performers.

Next, I give the group a system. Here is the system and you can try it for yourself. Draw two lines that cut the numbers into quadrants. Draw the first line through half of the numbers vertically and the second line divides the numbers in half horizontally. Next number the quadrants from the top left as 1, top right as 2, bottom left as 3, and bottom right as 4. Now look for the numbers. Look in quadrant 1 for number 1 and circle it, then quadrant 2 for the number 2, then quadrant 3 for the number 3, then quadrant 4 for the number 4, then back to quadrant 1 for number 5 then over to quadrant 2 for the number 6, and so on.

After another 20 seconds I check in with the group. I ask what you think the impact of using a system will be for a poor performer. Most will agree that it will improve performance. I'll ask the low person in the group what their number is now and almost 100% of the time they have had a significant improvement, say from 4 to 12.

Then I'll ask the top performer who had 12 what their number is and they will go to something like 18. Significant improvement was had by all through the use of a system.

A key learning point here is that the facts never changed, the numbers stayed the same, what changed was your approach to locating the numbers. Your observation is what changed. Your relationship to the facts changed, not the facts. You are what changed.

```
      73    9  49 | 66    78   62  50
  37     53       |   46    34
    69      17  5 | 38  14        74  18
  41   33         |
         21 (1) 29| 10 (2)  70    86
    13     25     |
  57   81  77  61 | 58       54 42   22
       85  45     |    6  30      82  26
           65     |
  79   31     55  | 32  60     44  76  80
       75     63  |      20
  23  43  47   51 | 64  88       68
    39  (3)    11 |       48    40   56
       67 87  71  | 24  36     12
  59       15  35 | 28 (4)          16
  19  7  83    27 | 84   72    8   52
```

This is the same application as the miniature airplane. The airplane never changed, you changed. You were different in relationship to the same facts. Your observation was different.

The intervention system for performance excellence has two parts. The first part is to be aware of, and surrender to, human nature. The second part is to use human nature as it was designed to serve us, to compel avoidance. That's right. My recommendation is that you avoid your way to reach your goals. Let's look at the concept of surrendering first.

There is something powerful about surrendering and letting go. There is an old myth about how they catch monkeys in Africa; at least

I think it's a myth, I read about it in Scientific America so maybe it's true.

What the researchers do is tie a goblet to a fence, then place a piece of fruit inside the goblet and leave it out overnight. A monkey comes along and reaches in for the fruit. When he makes a fist around the fruit, his fist becomes too big and he can't get his hand out of the goblet. He is therefore tied to the fence. The monkey won't let go of what's not working.

The question for you is where do you need to let go and surrender. Remember this phrase, "Struggle Negates".

The human performance law states that all humans are wired to avoid pain and seek comfort. This is our instinct, so let's not fight it. Let's accept the fact that we are avoidance machines. It's true.

You are an Avoidance Machine!

Surrender to this fact and stop trying to fight it with willpower and discipline. You are wired to be predisposed to having a confirmation bias, just like the snake eggs example, to perceive the highest level of pain and then avoid it. You are not asked to avoid it. You are compelled to avoid it. The dictionary definition of the word compel is to force, to drive, to necessitate or pressure by force.

You are not asked to comply with the avoidance of your highest level of perceived pain; you are compelled. There is nothing you can do; you can't consciously outwit human nature. Try it. Try running up a flight of stairs and not breathing heavy. I promise you, when you get to the top of the stairs you will be breathing faster. Your brain's survival wiring will override your intentions.

Here's the good news: **You are perfect the way you are!** You don't need to overcome this survival avoidance mechanism, simply put it to use the way nature has designed it. The way that you do this is by influencing your perception. Give yourself a different reference point, so that your brain has a different perception of the highest level of perceived pain. This is where my intervention for you comes in.

Chapter 4

The Solution:

Behavioral Contracting™

"A healthy attitude is contagious but don't wait to catch it from someone else. Be a carrier."

Years ago I had a problem with the mini bars at the hotels when I was traveling. I remember one particular incident back in 1984 where I was starving and when I got into my hotel room I binged at the mini bar. I looked at myself and had a very vulnerable moment. That was the first time that I didn't play victim and blame everyone else for my problems, I simply said to myself that I was a failure. I was a fraud. I thought I had overcome my bingeing and purging (bulimia), but obviously I hadn't. I was overweight, not making the money I wanted to and wasn't in a relationship. I said to myself, "That's it. I surrender. All of my life is the avoidance of pain and the seeking of comfort".

What I did next changed my life and it can change yours too. On my next trip I told five people that if I got into the mini bar on this trip, I'd give them each $250. Tally it up, that's $1,250.

On my next trip I was again starving. I got into the hotel room and my brain searched for its highest level of perceived pain, and at that point it was my hunger. The brain does what is called a cortical-limbic loop. This means that the frontal cortex of the conscious brain immediately starts a cascade of firing neurons that release chemicals and neurotransmitters, which the brain interprets as hunger. Then there is a link to the area of the brain called the limbic system, the emotional system. Not only do I feel hungry, but also my perception is influenced so that all I see is the solution to the pain of being hungry, the mini bar. I am predisposed to scan the environment and tune in to whatever can solve my problem and avoid this pain. I can't help it. I see the mini bar and nothing else in the room is in focus.

As I walk over to the mini bar my brain continues to do what it is designed to do and it continues to search to make sure that I am indeed avoiding the highest level of pain. When I get to the mini bar something new happens. My brain recognizes that there's a higher level of perceived pain, more painful then my hunger, the $1,250 that I will have to pay out and immediately I turn away from the mini bar and don't eat a thing.

What happened? I went from being out of control and bingeing, to having this become a non-issue. My brain sensed the higher level of pain and I did what I am coded to do, avoid. After all, avoidance is not an option, I am an avoidance machine and I will always be compelled to avoid the highest level of perceived pain and so will you.

This was very dramatic for me; I was now able to do something that I didn't think I could do. Are you living your life in resignation, believing that you just can't do something? I had created a dynamic that I never had before; this dynamic is the single most important "take away" from this book. This is a dynamic I would venture to say that you do not currently have in your life. I call this dynamic **Behavioral Contracting™. This is the one small "take away" from this book. This is my 1.2% factor for you. This is the small change that I am asking you to make. I am asking you to participate in behavioral contracting on a weekly basis.**

Consider the following as the formula for performance excellence, the one small intervention that is the reason for this book. This is a system of Behavioral Contracting.

Behavioral Contracting

Specific Declarations + Accountability = Elite Performance

$$\text{Accountability} = \frac{\text{The Check In}}{\text{Enforceable Consequence}}$$

Behavioral contracting has the components of making a commitment; a specific declaration of an activity that you say you will do over the next seven days, and then be held accountable to take that action with a negative consequence, if you don't.

This is the dynamic that is virtually absent for most individuals and most corporations. They may have parts of it in place. You might find an aggressive organization that sets goals, makes commitments and measures, but unless they have the accountability factor present, the results will not be as powerful as they will be with that factor included.

Accountability has two parts and both must be present for maximum impact. The first part is the check in. Someone other than yourself checks to see if you did what you said you were going to do.

You can't hold yourself accountable. You can't trust your own interpretation of how you are doing. (Remember, "count the black dots") It's just like being in the airplane in the clouds; you might think that you're in a right turn and level, but your instruments are showing that you're in a descent. You better respond to your instruments because you can't trust your senses.

It's the same thing here. Someone from the outside must check in with you; however the check in by itself is not enough. Probably the most important aspect of all of this behavioral contracting is also the most controversial.

There must be a negative and painful consequence that will be enforced if you do not do what you said you would do. This consequence must be the aspect that registers as the most painful part of this action.

For example, the perception of the possibility of having to pay $1,250 was more painful then what I perceived my hunger level to be. In fact, I wasn't hungry at all. I had a pattern of neurons that were wired together, a habit, that when I traveled and entered the hotel room with a mini bar, I justified the binge by rationalizing how hungry I was. The bottom line was that I wasn't reaching my health goals or the other goals that I had in my life for that matter.

I looked at the areas of my life where I was not experiencing the results that I said I was committed to having. I asked myself what was the most important activity in business that I needed to accomplish this week. In this instance it was making 100 marketing calls. I then told another person that if I didn't make 100 calls I would pay them $100. At the end of the week they would check in with me to see if I did what I said I would do.

I've been using behavioral contracting for many years now. Every person that I've shared this with, who has used it, has reported that they get more done when they participate with a behavioral contract then when they don't. The most important aspect of this is that you are being held accountable to what you said you would do, with a consequence if you don't. That is a powerful dynamic that will change the world that you see and how you engage it.

A staffing company told me their sales people went from an average of $3,500 per person per week to over $7,000 per person per week, after they began using the 1.2% concept of behavioral contracting. Spread out over 160 sales people, this brings in an additional two million dollars in revenue each month. What is the difference? Steve Sorensen, the owner of the company states that when you are having conversations around accountability production increases.[12]

I've had people tell me that they've doubled their income, improved family relationships, stopped smoking, lost weight and more; all of these results are real and verifiable. The dynamic that's different in each case is the dynamic of behavioral contracting.

I challenge you. Send an e-mail to info@bobdavies.com and let me know what you commit to accomplish over the next seven days, from the time you get up on Monday until the time you go to bed on Sunday. Be specific in your commitment. The commitment must be realistic and doable. You can't go from zero to hero. You and I will have a contract; the consequence for non-performance will be $100. If you don't do what you said you would do, you will owe me $100. You can always send me an e-mail and I will follow-up with you and hold you accountable. Just tell me that you've read this book and you've been avoiding or resisting something. Then state your commitment, plus your agreement to pay the fine if you don't perform and you've just completed a behavioral contract.

I have a lot of fun when I demonstrate this in my live programs. The audience volunteer will say, "I'm not going to pay you $100"! I respond by asking them what are they paying attention to? Are they focused on not doing the activity and owing me $100, or are they focused on doing what they said they would do? If they do what they say they will do then the penalty is not relevant. If they still won't agree, then I'll ask them to lower their commitment level to where they'll agree to either execute the commitment or pay the fine.

Human nature will take over from this point. Something will be different in what they see over the next seven days. They'll be predisposed to see the opportunities to do what they committed to. If they didn't have this dynamic in place, it's most likely those opportunities would never have appeared.

The quantum physics folks would say that they have "conditioned the space". This means that they have put out the "specific intention" into the web of interconnected energy fields called entanglement. This will activate the law of attraction and the opportunities for performance that are always there, but not normally seen, will reveal themselves.

The penalty doesn't always have to be a monetary fine, but it must always be painful. The penalty must be what your brain locks onto — to compel the avoidance of the most uncomfortable and painful aspect associated with the activity commitment.

Years ago I spoke to an organization in Toronto. Six months later they brought me back to deliver a different program to the same audience. After my talk a woman came up to me and said that she had to eat a spider because of me. She explained that she had made a reasonable commitment that she should have been able to do, but just didn't quite finish, and her consequence was to eat a spider. She then told me how she put it between two crackers and I'll leave it at that![13]

I had one financial advisor tell me that if he didn't execute his "promises" this week, then he would have to go into his managers office, take his jacket off, start posing and stating that he was now a body builder.

Another person committed to go into a crowded area and bark like a dog to ten strangers if he didn't do what he said he would do.

You can be as creative as you want to with your consequences. They must be more painful or uncomfortable then whatever pain or discomfort might be associated with the activity it's linked to. Most importantly, it must be enforced if you don't do what you said you would do.

I recommend that you hire a coach. You can hire me but I'm expensive. At the time of this publishing my fee is $3,000 for the first month and $1,500 each month thereafter. My fee very well may have increased by the time you've made contact, or I may be full and not taking on new clients. I do have assistant coaches however that would gladly help you. Let's go back in time regarding hiring a coach...

It was 1995 and I was speaking to 23,000 people at the Memphis Pyramid. Lee Greenwood was performing and the event was spectacular. Fireworks were going off in the arena and the audience went wild! There were large video screens throughout the facility. After Greenwoods entertaining performance the speakers began and I was the second one to go on. The speaker before me was loud and passionate, he ranted and raved. He paced the stage telling his personal stories of moving from poverty to prosperity and told the audience that they could do that too.

I thought for a bit and asked myself what type of an impact this speaker would have on the audience. Was he an impact speaker or was he an entertainer? I asked this without judgment or right and wrong, just to clarify his intention. My conclusion was that this speaker was just an entertainer and would have no real impact on the audience.

The next question would have to be, what is it to have an impact on the audience? My definition is that the audience changes and the changes stick. In my mind, having an impact means that the audience changes an old habit or creates a new habit. If this doesn't happen, then the speaker is an entertainer.

I asked myself what I was. Am I an entertainer or an impact speaker?[14] There is one criterion that is necessary for an impact to happen. It is constant contact. There must be a way to have constant contact with the audience for long-term change to be created and maintained.

Since I am committed to be an impact speaker, I decided to take on clients in a personal one on one coaching capacity. However, if I'm in front of a room of 100 people, how many are going to hire me as their coach? Maybe one, maybe none. Since I served on the board of the International Coaches Federation, as well as on the committee of credentialed coaches, I had access to the talent in the field. One of the toughest areas for coaches is client acquisition. So I had no problem finding less expensive coaches who wanted to be in alliance with my company and coach my lower fee clients. Back to that room of 100 people... How many people would be willing to hire one of my assistant coaches at a much lower fee than my own? This would be the constant contact that is necessary with the weekly calls. The reality is that maybe one or maybe none would hire an assistant coach.

Before I threw up my arms and said, "Ok, I surrender, I'm an entertainer!" I took a close look at how I coach my live clients. I was looking to see if I could duplicate the systematic approach I used with each client in a way that I could recreate the experience automatically, with mass customization, so I could offer this to the masses at an affordable rate, which would include more people in the experience of coaching.

I discovered that I could reproduce the most crucial ingredients of my coaching, making specific commitments with the dynamic of accountability and constant learning. I could create a web based on-line program that would duplicate the way that I coached live. I could support it with personal interaction for a group with my free monthly coaching conference call.

I launched the program several years ago. I'm going to explain my very unique system for influencing what you pay attention to, and what you are in reference to, on a weekly and daily basis. It is designed with the following seven components:

1. **Evaluation of last week's commitments**. Evaluate and score yes I did, or no I did not, accomplish and complete the activities I promised I would do from the previous week.

2. **Authorization to pay any fines that are due.** (Enforceable consequences) One of the biggest issues for organizations and individuals is the actual enforcement of the penalty. People are just hesitant to do the most critical part of the program, the enforcement of the consequence. If you don't enforce the consequence, then the brain will not see it as pain and will instead lock onto the imagined pain associated with the activity you want to accomplish. You are going to avoid pain. You will either avoid the pain of the penalty if it's high enough and will be enforced, or you will avoid the pain associated with the activity.

3. **Specific Declarations for the next seven days.** Step three is to take a look at your goals and to consider the following questions and strategy;

   A. What do I want? Why bother? How much is enough?
   B. What do I need to do to have what I want? Attitude and actions.

  C. What do I need to do over the next seven days?

  D. What will I do over the next seven days?

  E. Make commitments and put them into a behavioral contract with accountability.

4. **Evaluation of last week's homework.** Some calls[15] will ask you to pay attention to certain circumstances over the next seven days or to execute a particular task as homework. An example would be to make a list of what or whom you are tolerating. This step of the coaching program is a discussion of that assignment. If no homework was given then you will proceed directly to step #5.

5. **This week's coaching concept.** In the first year, three of the four weeks per month have some type of coaching concept. These include a variety of topics that are related to human excellence. The weeks that don't have a concept are referred to as "no content" calls and you will proceed right to step 6.

6. **Any additions, deletions, or final changes to this week's commitments.** Particularly if the call was one with a concept, you may want to make changes to your contract prior to final submission. This is your chance to do so.

7. **Final submission and print your agreement.** One of the added features for additional accountability is that you can designate up to three people to automatically receive a copy of your contract. They will see what you said you would do last week, what you did, and what you've committed to for this week.

I'm going to give you a free month's trial on the on-line coaching and accountability program just for buying and reading this book. The program is calculated in 30-day periods from the time you sign on, not according to the calendar. Although the program is free for one month you will still need to enter a credit card because your fines are live immediately. Once the free 30 days has expired you will automatically be charged $19.95. If you don't want to continue using the program, then please cancel by logging on and clicking on "Cancel my account". It's easy.

If you are intrigued and do want to use a free test of a system of behavioral contracting, then go to www.bobdaviescoaching.com and follow the prompts. You will need a code to get your free month. As you log on to the program you will need to enter "Not a registered user yet? Click to set up your new account". Use the following code when prompted for a group code: **10174**. The computer will then recognize you're a book owner and you won't be charged for the first 30 days. If you've already set up your program, then give the code away to someone else for him or her to experience the free trial. Don't adjust the account you've already started. It's only $19.95. This code is not a secret. It is my gift to you. Feel free to share it with anyone you would like to.

This program fills the need for a low cost system of coaching, but, I'd also recommend that you hire a coach. Nothing can be as intense as a live one on one relationship. However, if you are concerned with finances, then just use the on-line program.

If you don't want to invest in the low cost program you can still duplicate the procedures of the on-line coaching and use it in your own way. You will need to make sure you have an outside source for accountability that will be enforced. If you would like to follow my recommendation and automate the process then go to www.bobdaviescoaching.com and set up your account as a new user. Remember to use the code **10174** for your free 30 days.

If you are still a bit unsettled by the use of a negative penalty, a fine, bear with me. I will go over some of the research on "compliance, rewards and punishment" theory after the demonstration of the on-line program.

Here is what a weekly contract looks like:

There are three categories shown in this photo and the fourth category, which is Personal is not shown but follows health.

The Pending category has been called the batters box for commitments. Anything that is on your mind that you haven't made a decision to commit to, would go in Pending. This is the warm up area. Eventually you will get tired of seeing it and will make a decision that you are never going to commit to it and you will get rid of it, or you will decide to move it into either a goal or promise status and place it in the appropriate category of Business, Health or Personal.

Examples of Pending category items might be to do landscaping, clean your garage, take your car in for new tires, learn to play a musical instrument, start research for a new project in business, go skydiving, etc.

You are tapping into a principle of the brain that I call "closure". The brain seeks to find patterns and provide to you incomplete patterns in a whole form. For example, what do you see below:[16] Do you see the dog? Your brain will compare this image to the known and fill in the blanks.

These are blotches of black and white. However, the brain looks for completion. It looks to make meaning and to be congruent. As you pull back from the picture you start to recognize a known and familiar pattern, that of a dog.

When you continuously see the items in the Pending category your brain will subconsciously be stimulated for closure by either taking action or getting rid of the item. Both of these options are movements forward. Your brain does not favor "incompletes".

I have mentioned promises and goals. Since all of this is explained in the on-line program in detail I'll be brief here. A promise is something that you give your word you will do over the next seven days. A goal in the context of the on-line coaching and accountability program is something that you would like to accomplish, but you are not giving your word or being held accountable to complete. All of the focus is in the time frame of seven days.

Here is what the contract looks like completed:

BobDaviesCoaching.com

This is my Behavioral Contract for the week of
Monday, November 11th, 2002 - Sunday, November 17th, 2002

Pending Categories

1. Multi Engine rating ----
2. Learn Microsoft Outlook ----
3. Burt Dublin's cassette course ----
4. Article Submissions-Create own list ----
5. Re-design coaching flyer ----
6. Continue research on Dental Study clubs ----
7. New Book-Health ----
8. market blitz to bureaus ----
9. Find a new coach ----
10. Put voice on web site ----
11. AOL on Mac ----
12. Add for Seminar Promoter ----
13. E mail marketing blitz to data base ----
14. Find video of Deland jump ----
15. Join DSA ----
16. Set telephone apt. for Dec. with Mercon ----
17. Inserts for coaching notebook ----

Business Commitments

	P/G	$ Fine
1. Daytimer Marketing calls: 100 calls	P	10.00
2. Next week: call Marina at Team Staff	G	----
3. E mail Toro in Japan	P	1.00
4. Call American Cash Flow Corporation	G	----
5. Go to Staples: supplies and copies	P	100.00
6. call Hertz re: name and miles 800-654-4173	P	1.00
7. Send bookmark to two bureaus	P	100.00
8. Call Unix re: wireless mouse remote	G	----
9. Call INA	P	1.00
10. Call Saddleback College TV 582-4850	P	1.00
11. Call Polly	P	10.00

You can see the seven-day time frame above, then my Pending categories. You will notice the date of November 11th, 2002; I've been using this program in addition to live coaching for quite some time.

Next you can see the start of my business commitments; I use fines as my consequence. The program is designed to default to a $1.00 fine, yes, one-dollar, for any commitment that you designate as a promise.

You'll notice that goals do not have any penalties for non-performance because you're not being held accountable to complete a goal. You can raise the fine on the promises if you like. The more resistance I anticipate the higher the fine I use. For example, look at number 5; go to Staples. If you look at what I earn per year and break it down into an hourly rate, then you will see that it doesn't make sense for me to personally do this non-productive task, I should delegate it to a $15 per hour person.

That's exactly how I was holding it, except I couldn't delegate it to anyone because I needed to be there to make the decisions on how the product looked, what changes I wanted to make etc. Only I could do that. I kept putting it off. It involved specifically making signs for my books, tapes, DVDs etc., for my display when I'm at conferences.

This started out as a Pending, then was moved to a Business Goal Status, then was moved to a Business Promise with a $1.00 fine, and then I noticed I still wasn't getting it done. My brain saw the inconvenience of traveling to Staples and the time it would take to do this as the highest level of pain. It wasn't until I put a $100 fine on it that it got done.

One note, this is the honor system and it does count on your integrity. However, your deal is that you will either take the action or pay the fine. You still have integrity if you don't complete a promise, as long as you honor your word and pay the fine.

Here is another screen shot of the program:

Edit	37. Invoice Ed Laird for Oct.	P	1.00	☐
Edit	38. send another note (e mail) to people who have signed up for on line coaching	P	1.00	☐
Edit	39. send e mail to support re: auto e mail program	P	1.00	☐

Health Commitments		P/G	$ Fine	
Edit	1. Workout 4 times	P	10.00	☐
Edit	2. Less than or equal to 11,200 (1600) cal for the week	P	25.00	☐
Edit	3. Hit tennis balls once	G	---	☐
Edit	4. Call Mike re: Racquet ball	P	1.00	☐

Personal Commitments		P/G	$ Fine	
Edit	1. Call Washington Mutual re: refund	P	100.00	☐
Edit	2. Call Bill re: Scoots party	P	1.00	☐

[Delete]

Coaching Homework

Get MAD. Please go to the home page and access your Journal. More specifically go to your entry on call #11. This is in response to the inquiry from the previous call, "what decisions are you avoiding?" Update that list.

[Business ▼] _____ ⊙ P ○ G $1 .00

[ADD]

Tip: To delete commitments, click the "Delete" button, NOT the "Add" button.

Click next only when you are finished making changes.

[Prev ←] [Next →]

This shows the program in the stage of editing and making changes, new commitments, or deleting what I will be committing to, for the upcoming week. The on-line program will walk you through exactly how to set up and begin.[17] My objective is for one thing to happen. I want you to begin, and then create, the habit of making one small commitment starting Sunday, on something you give your word you will do and then be willing to execute a penalty (accountability) if you don't. As you can see from my sample, I have multiple commitments in my Health, Business and Personal categories.

If you applied the behavioral contracting principle in just one category and for just one action this week, then I'd consider this to be a success. Remember the 1.2% factor principle, small steps over time lead to significant results.

Another thing to keep in mind is the dynamic that you are paying $19.95 per month after the first free 30 days. Your brain is not going to say it's less than twenty dollars; it's no big deal. Your brain instead is going to take this as if you are paying for performance, make sure that you get your money's worth. You do that by doing what you said you would do.

Chapter 5

Carrot Versus Stick

"Success is not the result of spontaneous combustion.
You must set yourself on fire!"

I have had heated discussions in live programs about this concept. A lot of people don't want to go the negative punitive route and ask me why can't there be a reward if they do what they said they would do instead of a penalty?

I appreciate their concern and I understand it. However, if you follow the science you will clearly see that the "stick" is superior in commanding performance to the "carrot".

Everything has a cost and nothing can be produced without work and sacrifice. There is a whole new branch of behavioral economics that has attracted considerable attention, by combining the insights of psychologists and economists to predict behavior and their most probable outcomes. All performance becomes a ratio of Cost to Benefit comparison. This is consistent with the human performance law of avoiding pain and seeking comfort.

Behavioral economic theory measures the cost of one choice in terms of the benefits of another. Economics starts with one very important assumption: individuals act to make themselves as well off as possible.[18] However, this is offset by human natures coded instructions to predispose the individual to find the possibility of the pain involved in the action, and then to initiate the sequence of avoidance via the survival mechanism. This sequence is to override your desire to take action and compel you to avoid. You will then continue with the illusion, as you justify your avoidance with rationalization, and never realize that you are doing so.

Economists will agree with the findings of the research in this area, by stating that the real cost of something is what you must give up in order to have it. You are more motivated to keep what you already have, rather than acquire something else.

This is a controversial topic. It is more comfortable for people to buy into a reward for a job well done, then a punishment for failing to achieve. People ask me "Why can't I just buy myself a new suit or some other type of reward if I do what I say I will do?" I always respond the same way. You are motivated to keep what you already have rather than getting something else. There is a tremendous amount of research to this point.[19] It is widely recognized that a dollar lost in the stock market will have a much more pronounced effect on the individual than a dollar gained

Economics theory calls this "The Endowment Effect"[20] The endowment effect describes the fact that people require much more to give up an object than they are willing to spend to acquire it. The endowment effect is a hypothesis that people value a good more, once their property right to it has been established. In other words, people place a higher value on objects they own, relative to objects they don't.

In one experiment, people demanded a higher price for a coffee mug that had been given to them, but put a lower price on one they did not yet own. Kahneman, Knetsch and Thaler (1990).[21]

Imagine that the U.S. is preparing for an outbreak of an unusual Asian disease that is expected to kill 600 people. Government officials have proposed two alternative programs to compete with the disease. Under program A, 200 people will be saved. Under program B, there is a 1/3rd probability that 600 people will be saved and a 2/3rd probability that nobody will be saved.

Confronted with this choice, 72% of people choose A, preferring to save 200 people for sure, rather than the risk of saving none

Now imagine that the government presents these two options instead.

Program C, 400 people will die, and Program D, there is a 1/3rd probability that nobody will die and a 2/3rd probability that all 600 people will die.

Faced with this pair of choices, 78% of people choose D, according the results of a study by Nobel laureate Daniel Kahneman, a psychologist at Princeton, and his collaborator, psychologist Amos Tversky.[22]

Of course, these two pairs of options, A or B and C or D are identical; saving 200 lives means that 400 people will die, and in both B and D, taking a one-third chance to save everyone means taking a two-thirds chance to lose everyone. Whichever choice you make, logic would seem to dictate that it should be the same no matter how the options are worded. So why do people statistically prefer A to B, but the reverse when the choices are described as in C and D?

Kahneman and Tversky's research indicates that people respond to choices involving losses, such as deaths, differently from those relating to gains, such as survivors. When choosing between positive outcomes, people tend to be risk averse and want a sure thing (saving 200 people), but are far more willing to take risks when weighing losses.

Risky Choices[23]

People respond differently to options describing gains, than to those that refer to losses. This tendency is called "Prospect Theory" and can result in logically inconsistent decisions.

Objective - Subjective

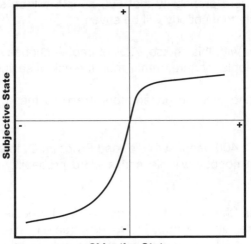

Objective State

The graph above, developed by Kahneman and Tversky,[24] where "X" is the objective state of affairs, and "Y "is the subjective responses to the various objective states, that is, how good or bad these realities make people feel.

The curve in the upper right quadrant captures how people respond to positives, or gains, and its shape portrays the economic principle of Diminishing Marginal Utility. Saving 600 lives will not feel three times as good as saving 200 lives, so people do not want to take a risk to save all 600 people. The lower left quadrant shows how people respond to negatives, or losses, and depicts the Diminishing Marginal Disutility of losses. Because losing 600 lives will not hurt three times as much as losing 200, people feel good about taking the risk to lose nobody. People tend to seek risk more readily when making decisions about losses.

Whether the top right or bottom left part of the curve describes decisions, depends on how the options are framed. Thus, people are unwilling to take a risk if the phrasing emphasizes positive outcomes, but they may flip to a riskier option if the words express the darker side of a picture. Notice that the loss portion of the curve is about twice as steep as the gain portion, meaning that a loss of say, $100 hurts worse than a gain of $100 feels good. The overwhelming conclusion, people will be more motivated to avoid losses than to secure gains.

I'll again restate one of the guiding principles of behavioral contracting:

People are motivated to keep what they already have (avert loss) then to get something else (seek gain).

Here are some practical every day examples of this concept. A Bell helicopter sales person is making a presentation to an executive, attempting to sell a three million dollar helicopter. This sales person is experienced and uses the FAB concept of selling; Features, Advantages and Benefits. For example, the feature is that the helicopter could transport from the executive offices' helicopter pad, to the helicopter pad at a variety of client companies or nearby hotels. The advantage of this would be that the executive would save time and energy by not having to be stuck in bumper-to-bumper traffic. The benefit would be that the executive would have more energy, more status and do better presentations, resulting in making more revenue for his organization.

The executive recognizes all of the features, advantages and benefits, but still says that he can't justify this expense to his stockholders. He'll just have to say no.

The sales person, recognizing the Principle of Endowment, says, "Keep the helicopter for an entire month and just pay for the fuel and the pilot's salary, and see how you like it. At the end of the month I'll come back and if you haven't changed your mind no harm done!"

The executive agrees. For the next month the executive notices how it feels to have his assistant tell their clients that he'll be arriving at the helicopter pad at the top of their buildings. He notices how free he feels not to have to worry about traffic. He notices how effective it is to be able to set an appointment to meet with a client in San Diego, and then have lunch with another client in San Luis Obispo, then dinner with another at the Santa Monica Airport restaurant. He does this consistently over the next few weeks.

Finally the month is over and the sales person calls on the executive again and the executive says, "I've got to have it. I'll authorize the expense".

We are motivated to keep what we already have as opposed to getting something else.

I personally had a very interesting "mindset" shift along the lines of this principle. I fly Delta Airlines. Years ago I just couldn't justify paying a few hundred dollars for the Crown Room Club membership. If you're not familiar, the Crown Room Club is private members only lounge at most of the major airports. I couldn't justify paying for this, so for years I never had the privilege. When I had any layovers, I would just hunt around for an electrical outlet somewhere in the lobby, plug in, and go to work in the public area with everyone else.

Several years ago Delta decided to give free membership to the Crown Room Club to all of its elite flyers. My status at the time was Platinum Medallion so I qualified. For years I enjoyed my layovers. I could have a private booth with an electrical outlet and table in a quiet atmosphere surrounded by other elite flyers.

Although I didn't drink the free alcohol, I did enjoy the complimentary diet soft drinks and other snacks. I also enjoyed the fact that this was an exclusive club and business travelers like me primarily used it, so the likelihood of being around a crying infant or otherwise belligerent person was low.

Then the airlines started to fall onto hard times. Fuel prices escalated and perks were closely scrutinized. It was decided that for now, no level of flyer would have the free Crown Room Club upgrade, and that everyone regardless of status, would now have to pay for the privilege. I pulled out my credit card and paid for the Crown Room Club without giving it a second thought. That was this principle in action. I was motivated to keep what I already had.

I had an interesting conversation with David Dickinson,[25] Department of Economics at Appalachian State University. David has done quite a bit of research on the carrot versus the stick.[26] His intent was to objectively compare the incentive effects of rewarding individuals with a monetary prize, to those of penalizing individuals with a similar monetary fine. As you know, the premise of the on-line coaching program is compliance compelled by the avoidance of the penalty of fines.

His conclusions state that in certain conditions the stick is much more effective than the carrot, in terms of increased performance and motivation. It seems that the highest predictor of improved performance would be a combination of carrot and stick. However, a key finding of his study is that different types of incentives interact differently with performance. When everyone has an equal opportunity to perform, "no handicapping", he found that a monetary fine increased efficiency more than positive incentives such as a cash bonus.

A critical point in the Prospect Theory of Kahneman and Tversky implies that loss aversion would render negative incentives more effective than positive incentives in motivating individuals.

In "The Neural Basis of Loss Aversion in Decision-Making under Risk," in the January 2006 Science magazine, Poldrack, Fox and their colleagues Sabrina M. Tom and Christopher Trepel presented the results of their fMRI studies, in which they offered subjects a prospect of accepting or rejecting a gamble that offered a 50-50 chance of gaining or losing money. As the potential for gains rose, they found increased activity in the mesolimbic and mesocortical dopamine systems, (dopamine is a neurotransmitter substance associated with motivation and reward). As the potential for losses increased, they found decreasing activity in these same reward-sensitive areas. It appears that the loses and gains are coded by the same brain structures, the ventromedial prefrontal cortex, associated with decision making and learning in the context of reward and punishment, and the ventral striatum, associated with learning, motivation and reward.

Individual differences in loss aversion were predicted by how much more the brain was turned off by losses, than it was turned on by gains.

Advertisers know this concept. When advertising a deal or product that is scarce in some way, it is usually more effective to focus the prospective consumer on what they might genuinely stand to lose from not taking the deal, rather than what they stand to gain from doing so.[27]

Let me simplify. There is a case to be made for the use of both the carrot and the stick for maximum performance. However, the research clearly indicates that the carrot has a ceiling for performance enhancement, and the stick will give you a higher ceiling than the carrot. In other words, you will get more performance with the stick than the carrot.

However, this brings up another problem of relationships and trust. Organizations are not in a position to use the most effective strategy to enhance performance, the stick. This must come from an outside source. That's why my on-line program is so effective. It takes the penalty execution out of the hands of the organization and makes it a self-governance issue.[28]

I presented to a network-marketing group years ago[29] and they just loved the concept. They also had the infrastructure to fit the concept of behavioral contracting right into their system. But there was a problem. Here's an example:

One of their principles was "counsel with your up-line". This is a mentoring relationship, where a new team member would be coached by the more experienced person who brought them into the business.

They loved the idea of making a specific commitment to the other person with a negative consequence for non-performance. The new person, full of enthusiasm, commits to showing the business opportunity to new prospects five times over the next seven days, with a consequence of a $100 fine if they don't.

One thing after another happens to this new recruit. Although they meant it when they said it, they did intend to show the plan five times this week, they just didn't get it done.

Now here's the problem. The up-line mentor is in a no win situation. If he enforces the penalty, it looks like an organization that makes money on the misery of the new people. If he doesn't enforce the penalty, then the brain will not recognize the consequence as being more painful than the showing of the plan. So the focus will remain on how uncomfortable it is to show the plan, which of course leads to avoidance and rationalization. This is a "no win" situation.

The enforcement of the penalty must come from an outside source. The penalty also should not have anything positive related to it. The on-line program's penalties come to me and I waste the money. I don't give to my charity, "Angel Flight", nor do I do anything positive with the money. There can be no benefit to your negative consequence.

If there is a benefit, then it will reduce the punitive impact. If the punitive impact is reduced, it may not be positioned as the highest level of perceived pain. Remember, that is what you will avoid. Your intention doesn't matter. Your brain is coded to find the highest level of perceived pain and compel avoidance.

Years ago a famous actress was caught shoplifting at a well-known store with over $5,000 in merchandise. Part of her penalty was paying for the goods. She had her attorney actually ask the judge to donate the merchandise to a charity; after all she had paid for it. The judge applied this principle and declared that there could be no benefit from her actions and denied the request. The property was to be destroyed.

There is a scientific reason for this and I'll get to it soon. This concept is controversial and does upset some people. I always say if your penalty does have a beneficial aspect to it, then it raises a red flag. However, if it works in influencing what you pay attention to, and if it does get you to take the action to avoid the penalty — then go-ahead and use it.

Here are some examples of penalties that might have a benefit. These penalties are supposed to be horrible actions that you want to avoid at all costs. Let's play along, you name the benefit.

1. Take my office out to lunch and pay for it.   **Benefit:**
2. Give my spouse a 30-minute foot massage.   **Benefit:**
3. Wash my neighbor's car.   **Benefit:**
4. Empty the trash in the office for a week.   **Benefit:**
5. Not eat candy every day for a week.   **Benefit:**
6. Will not watch my favorite T.V. show next week.   **Benefit:**

As you can see, there are subtle benefits in the penalties. Remember, your brain does not respond to intentions. Your brain searches like your life depended on it to find its highest level of perceived pain, and again like your life depends on it, compels you to avoid.

There is the benefit of being a good guy, of giving, by taking your office out to lunch and paying for it. Not watching your favorite T.V. show has the benefit of giving you more free time to read, or spend with your family, or even go to sleep earlier. You can't fool your brain. It will sense the benefit and ignore it as a deterrent and latch onto the pain in the activity. You will avoid your highest level of perceived pain and you can't help it.

You can be as creative as you can imagine in your negative consequences. Here are some that I've heard before and notice that there is no benefit implied.

1. A fine of any amount.

Yes, even one dollar will have an impact. Why? Because you already have the dollar and you are motivated to keep what you already have. I ask myself how much resistance do I have related to the commitment? The higher the resistance, the higher the fine. I find that I'm very committed to executing the actions to avoid $100 fines.

2. I will send an e-mail or voice mail message to my entire organization that I am not to be trusted. I don't do what I say I will do.

This is incredible for compliance. The pain in action here is status, embarrassment, and the future projection of how people will take this e-mail.

3. I will donate $100 (or any amount) to a non-reward cause that I don't believe in.

If you are a Republican, then make a donation to the Democratic Party if you don't do what you say you will do.

Here is an example reported by Nurnberger and Zimmerman (1970).[30] A student working on his doctorate had completed all the requirements but his dissertation. Yet for two years he had not written a single page. A contract was drawn up for him in which he agreed to meet weekly deadlines on the number of pages he would complete. To make sure he would meet the deadlines he wrote out post-dated checks. These were to be cashed if he failed to reach his goal for the week. The checks were made out to organizations he despised, the Klu Klux Klan and the American Nazi Party. From the time he signed the agreement until he finished his degree, the student's work output was greatly improved! Behavioral contracting works!

4. I will go to the mall and bark at ten strangers and not tell them why I am doing this.

The pain here is fear and operating outside of your comfort zone. Anything that will be uncomfortable or embarrassing will work. You are motivated to keep what you already have, your comfort.

5. Eat a spider.

It's obvious. Remember the woman who came up to me at a function and told me that she had to eat a spider because of me. I asked her to explain. She told me that she said she would complete a project by Sunday, or the consequence would be that she would have to eat a spider. Just the thought of that makes me cringe. She then went on to explain how she put it between two crackers, etc.

I asked her why didn't you just do what you said you would do. She said she tried but just couldn't quite complete the task.

If you use this one I'll bet you do what you said you would do! It must be enforced however, so I'd read up on spiders so you don't eat a toxic one! (Ugh!)

I once had a person who was involved with the Boy Scouts of America say, that if he didn't do what he said he would do, then he would donate his fine money to that organization. Where's the penalty here? He gives over $5,000 annually to that group anyway. He's the past chairman of their board. Instead, I suggested that the fine money goes to a group such as a Nazi supportive organization. Think about this one. Do you want your fine money going to support an organization that you don't believe in? If no, then make sure you do what you said you would do and you don't have to worry about the fine. That's the entire point of behavioral contracting.

Remember my disclaimer. If your penalty does not meet the criteria of no benefit, it doesn't mean you can't still use it. The prevailing question to ask yourself is did you do the activity because you avoided the penalty? So if you made one more call a day so you wouldn't have to buy your staff lunch, then go ahead and continue to use those kinds of penalties.

The Science

Let's look briefly at some of the science involved. I'm going to get much more involved with the science in later chapters so this is just a warm up.

The purpose of science is to peel back the layer of the appearance of objects to reveal their underlying nature.

The Limbic System

This is the part of our brain that adds an emotional texture to our lives. It allows us to remember events that have taken place. It is an integration system that brings emotion and engagement into our lives.

Our sensory systems allow us to know about the world we are in. Humans primarily use vision and hearing to interpret and gain information about the world.

We also have a somata sensory system, which is how we get information about the immediate world within our touch, and also about the world of our bodies, the surface and the inside of our bodies.

We have motor systems that allow us to have action in the world. We just don't see something; we have emotions attached to it. This system allows us to experience pleasure. It's this system that gives us a unique personality. The limbic system is a system of complexly interconnected nuclei and areas involved in learning, memory, emotion and executive function. Executive function is our ability to make decisions. This has a lot to do with emotion and memory.

In the 1930's a comparative neurologist James Papez (1883-1958), defined a limbic system by identifying particular pathways and structures that underlie the association between memory and emotion. One of these pathways is known as the Papez circuit. The Papez circuit is composed of the hippocampus (memory), anterior nuclei of the thalamus, and the cingulated gyrus (a ring of gray matter just above the corpus callosum). All of these nuclei are interconnected into a feedback circuit or loop allowing for the integration of emotion and memory.

There are two areas of the cortex that are important to the limbic system. One is called the orbitofrontal cortex, right above the orbit of the eye; it is involved with impulse control and the ability to appreciate the consequences of ones actions.

Another area of notice is the dorsolateral prefrontal cortex that is involved primarily in executive functions, contributing to our ability to prioritize behavior and to adapt to change.

A powerful clinical case has lead to the understanding that we have today regarding the brain.

Phineas Gage, a railroad worker in 1848, survived an explosion that blasted an iron bar through the front of his brain. This was a three foot seven inches long, by a one and a quarter inch wide bar. He showed profound negative personality changes after the accident. He went from a kind and considerate person, to one of a horrific personality. His physician, who followed him after the accident for years, gave this description;

"The equilibrium or balance so to speak, in Gage, between his intellectual faculties and animal propensities seems to have been destroyed. He is fitful, irreverent, indulging at times in the grossest profanity, manifesting little deference for his fellows, impatient of restraint or advice when it conflicts with his desires. At times pertinaciously obstinate, yet capricious and vacillating." John Harlow Gage was no longer Gage. He could no longer hold a job; he was homeless, had no friends and at one time was in a freak show in the circus in NY. He died at age of 38. Personality and the ability to guide your actions are linked to functions of the brain. The mind and the soul are linked through the brain. He was no longer a social cultured being who could live in the world. The orbital frontal cortex was damaged.

Gage was honest, well liked by friends and fellow workers on the Rutland and Burlington Railroad. Gage was a young man of exemplary character and promise until one day in September 1848. While tamping down the blasting powder for a dynamite charge, Gage inadvertently sparked an explosion. The inch-thick tamping rod rocketed through his cheek, obliterating his left eye on its way through his brain and out the top of his skull. The rod landed several yards away, and Gage fell back in a convulsive heap. Yet a moment later he stood up and spoke; his fellow workers watched, aghast, then drove him by oxcart to a hotel, where a local doctor, one John Harlow, dressed his wounds. As Harlow stuck his index fingers into the holes in Gage's face and head until their tips met, the young man inquired when he would be able to return to work.

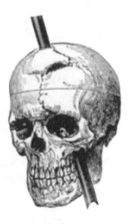

Within two months, the physical organism that was Phineas Gage had completely recovered — he could walk, speak, and demonstrate normal awareness of his surroundings. But the character of the man did not survive the tamping rod's journey through his brain. In place of the diligent, dependable worker stood a foulmouthed and ill-mannered liar, given to extravagant schemes that were never followed through. "Gage," said his friends, "was no longer Gage."

This past year neurobiologists Hanna and Antonio Damasio of the University of Iowa, finally pinpointed what Gage had lost. The Damasios had long been interested in the case; in the intervening century it had become a classic in neurology textbooks. The scientific interest had begun with John Harlow, who on hearing of Gage's death in an epileptic fit 13 years after the accident, persuaded the family to exhume the remains and donate the skull to medical research. Harlow believed that the change in Gage's personality had been wrought by damage to the frontal lobes of the brain. "The equilibrium . . . between his intellectual faculties and animal propensities seems to have been destroyed," Harlow wrote.

But nineteenth-century science had a hard time accepting the notion that a glob of gray jelly could govern something so transcendent as social behavior. "Harlow was never given much credit," says Antonio Damasio. "Some people didn't even believe that Gage's story had ever happened.

So the Damasios decided, 130 years after the fact, to do an autopsy — to track down where exactly the damage in Gage's brain had occurred. Guided by anatomic clues on Gage's battered skull, now preserved in the Warren Medical Museum at Harvard, Hanna Damasio used computer modeling and neural imaging techniques to determine the path the tamping rod had taken through the brain. The most likely trajectory by far, the Damasios found, would have spared the regions of the frontal lobes necessary for language and motor function. But it would have done ruinous damage to a portion of the underbelly of the frontal lobes called the ventromedial region, especially on the left side.

Apparently the loss of that region is what made Gage so antisocial. This did not surprise the Damasios; in present-day patients whose ventromedial region has been damaged by tumor, accident, or surgery, they have observed the same sort of personality change as Gage's. It was gratifying to solve a case that was at the root of so much modern day research and at the same time to pay homage to an under appreciated predecessor. "Gage's story was the historical beginnings of the study of the biological basis of behavior," says Antonio Damasio, "and the location of his lesion had always been a mystery. This was a way to give poor Dr. Harlow his due." — James Shreeve

I can simplify and talk about one region of the brain, the Reticular Activating System, or R.A.S.

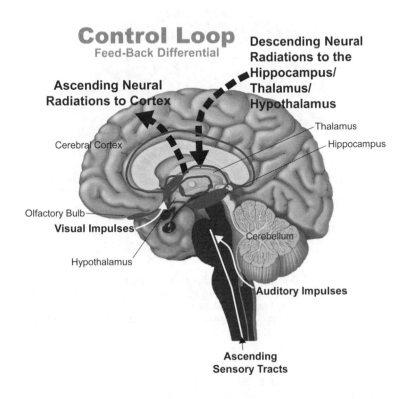

Control Loop Descending Neural
Feed-Back Differential Radiations to the
Hippocampus/
Ascending Neural Thalamus/
Radiations to Cortex Hypothalamus

Thalamus

Cerebral Cortex Hippocampus

Olfactory Bulb
Visual Impulses

Cerebellum

Hypothalamus

Auditory Impulses

**Ascending
Sensory Tracts**

The **reticular activating system** is the name given to the part of the brain, (the reticular formation and its connections), believed to be the center of arousal and motivation in animals, including humans.

53

Reticular Activating System

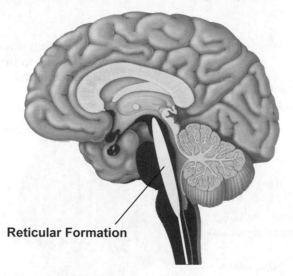

Reticular Formation

The reticular formation is a bundle of densely packed nerve cells located in the central core of the brainstem. Roughly the size of a little finger, the reticular formation runs from the top of the spinal cord into the middle of the brain. This area of tightly packed nerve cells contains nearly 70% of the brain's estimated 100 billion nerve cells-or a total of over 70 billion cells.

The brainstem reticular formation runs all the way up to the mid-brain. As a result, the Reticular Activating System is a very complex collection of neurons that serve as a point of convergence for signals from the external world and from the interior environment.

In other words, it is the part of your brain where the world outside of you, and your thoughts and feelings from "inside" of you, meet.

This Reticular Activating System is very capable of generating dynamic effects on the activity of the cortex, including the frontal lobes, and the motor activity centers of the brain.

We are literally bombarded with sensory images, sounds and goings on all day long. Just imagine what your life would be like if you were aware of every single one of them — it would be mental bedlam! The hair down your neck after a haircut, the clicking sound of your keyboard, the hum of the fan, the voices that surround you,. you are saved from that sort of nerve-racking experience by this wonderful filtering design feature of your brain called the Reticular Activating System.

The RAS acts as the "executive secretary" for your conscious mind. It is the chief gatekeeper to screen or filter the type of information that will be allowed to get through.

Everything else is filtered out. You simply don't pay attention to those other messages, like restaurant noises during lunch while you're reading the newspaper, or the roar of the train that passes by every day at 4:00 pm, you just simply don't hear it.

Only two categories of information are allowed in:

1. Information that is valuable to you to have right now. For example: I have a rental property in Irvine, California. It was vacant one day in the summer and I decided to put an air conditioner in the property and raise the rent. After I made that decision I saw ads for air conditioners on almost every other page in the local newspaper.

Another example: I had a tooth pulled and needed to have an implant procedure. Every time I turned around I was seeing a billboard or television commercial regarding implants.

These ads were there all the time, I just wasn't paying attention to them and I had no reason to do so. This frees up my brain to pay attention to other more essential information. I call this selective perception.

If you are at a party and conversing with an interesting person in a crowded room you are fully engrossed and unaware of any specific sounds, even the din of voices. But if someone across the room says your name, you most likely will hear it instantly. "Why are they talking about me?", you wonder.

That is a prime example of your monitoring mechanism, your reticular activating system at work. You have just tuned in to something specific and useful to you. Although you may think you are giving your conversational companion your undivided attention, the fact is your attention is fragmented and subconsciously taking in the tower of Babel around you, sorting, sorting, sorting, even as you speak. Your name stands out as prominently as a speck of gold in a miner's pan.

> 2. The other kind of information that is allowed in is the sort that alerts you to a threat of danger. If your children are playing outside on your busy street and you hear a sharp horn, you run outside to check on them fearing danger. But if they were still inside you might not even hear the horn.

Your brain has the amazing capacity to filter information.

In view of this, it's easy to see why it is that people so often say, "I'm not interested." They have no need to know that information at the time. Sales people know this very well so the diligent ones seldom throw away a name. They follow up.

Circumstances may change, sparking fresh interest all of a sudden. What a good reason to watch how this censoring device works in people! If you want others to tune in to what you want to get across to them, (think kids, spouses, bosses), answer their question: "What's in it for me?", especially if you're making a request.

The Reticular Activating System plays a significant role in determining whether a person can learn and remember things well or not, whether a person is impulsive or self-controlled, whether a person has high or low motor activity levels, and whether a person is highly motivated or bored easily.

The RAS is the center of balance for the other systems involved in learning, self-control or inhibition, and motivation. When functioning normally, it provides the neural connections that are needed for the processing and learning of information, and the ability to pay attention to the correct task.

If the Reticular Activating System doesn't excite the neurons of the cortex as much as it ought to, then we see the results of an under-aroused cortex, such as difficulty learning, poor memory, little self-control, and so on. In fact, if the Reticular Activating System failed to activate the cortex at all, one would see a lack of consciousness or even a coma.

What would happen if the Reticular Activating System was too excited, and aroused the cortex or other systems of the brain too much?

Then we would see individuals with excessive startle responses, hyper-vigilance, touching everything, talking too much, restlessness, and hyperactivity.

So the Reticular Activating System must be activated at normal levels for the rest of the brain to function as it should.

When you use behavioral contracting you are tapping into this filtering system. You are putting your commitments in writing and with consequences. This sets up the brain to pay attention to the opportunities to take the actions you have committed to, and therefore avoid the negative consequences. This is how you are genetically coded.

The reticular formation is a bundle of densely packed nerve cells located in the central core of the brainstem. Roughly the size of a little finger, the reticular formation runs from the top of the spinal cord into the middle of the brain. This area of tightly packed nerve cells contains nearly 70% of the brain's estimated 100 to 200 billion nerve cells — for a total of over 70 to 140 billion cells.

There must be a reason for so much of the brain's computing power to be concentrated in this area of the brain. It must be very special and very important to survival and it is. It is the Reticular Formation that dictates what we consciously pay attention to.

According to some of the latest research, scientists have demonstrated that the brain processes about 400 billion bits of information every second. Usually however, we are conscious of only about 2,000 of those bits of data.[31] Out of those 2000 bits, the inputs the brain processes pertain only to our awareness of the body, our awareness of the environment, and our awareness of time.

Essentially, in the survival mode in which most people live each day, it is our limbic system that chemically powers the neocortex to function with such awareness on these important cues. Without direct involvement of the frontal lobe, our daily thoughts primarily concern themselves with the survival of the body.[32] There is a huge difference between the brain simply processing information and our awareness of that information. Although the brain processes 400 billion bits of data every second, the frontal lobe enables us to actively select what data we choose to put our awareness on.

As you read this, your brain is taking in information from all of your senses, but you aren't aware of them all because your frontal lobe is filtering them out. If you're wearing glasses it's very likely that you were not aware that you were staring through a plane of glass until I brought it to your attention. Now that's likely all you can think about. You did what is called a negative hallucination, meaning that you did not see something that is there. It's similar to living next to a train station and you never hearing the train that comes by every day at 4:00 pm, it's not important information, so your brain is freed up to pay attention to the important information that can be dangerous to you.

This same process can be used by you to get influence over your R.A.S., to get yourself to pay attention and see the opportunities to do what you said you would do. The frontal lobe is the part of the brain that decides on action, regulates behavior, plans the future and is responsible for firm intention. When you make a decision , a conscious choice or an intention to act in a certain way, you activate the frontal lobe.

Frontal Lobe

The part of the brain involved in planning, organizing, problem solving, selective attention, personality and a variety of "higher cognitive functions", including behavior and emotions.

The anterior (front) portion of the frontal lobe is called the prefrontal cortex. It is very important for the "higher cognitive functions" and the determination of the personality.

The posterior (back) of the frontal lobe consists of the pre-motor and motor areas. Nerve cells that produce movement are located in the posterior and the pre-motor areas serve to modify those movements.

Frontal Lobe

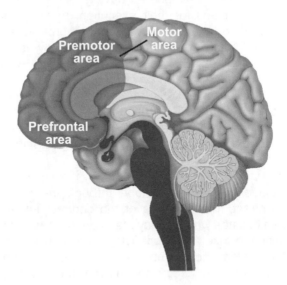

The frontal lobe is divided from the parietal lobe by the central sulcus (spelt with an "s", but pronounced with a hard "c"). The functions of the frontal lobe include:

- Motor Functions
- Higher Order Functions
- Planning
- Reasoning
- Judgment
- Impulse Control
- Memory

However, there is a higher center that overrides your intentions that is housed in the limbic area of the brain. That is our primate area and as previously discussed, before you execute your actions that are in alignment with your intentions, your brain searches to make sure you are avoiding the highest level of perceived pain. That's where the negative consequence comes in.

Science recognizes the prefrontal cortex as crucial to our species ability to activate the highest order of free willed intentional behavior. Thomas Gualtieri, M.D., Medical Director of the North Carolina

Neuropsychiatry Clinics in Chapel Hill, provides an excellent description of the frontal lobe as having: "the capacity to formulate goals, to make plans for their execution, to carry them out in an effective way, to change course and improvise in the face of obstacles and failure, and to do so successfully, in the absence of external direction or structure."[33]

To prevent our intentions from being overridden by our survival mechanism,[34] we must tap into and align the brain's avoidance to the highest level of perceived pain that will be our negative consequence. We avoid the negative consequence by doing what we said we would do. It's that simple.

We influence the frontal lobe through the development of a weekly contract. The specifics of the contract influence the RAS, which then dictates what we pay attention to, so we can then see the opportunities to take action on. The consequences or fines activate the limbic system, so we have now tapped into emotions as we engage in every day circumstances making sure we take specific actions.

With a behavioral contract you are in reference to something very specific that influences everything else. Remember the airplane example and the example of the system for finding numbers? You are the factor that is different because you have the intervention of behavioral contracting. Have you made a commitment with a consequence for non-performance yet? It only takes one to see this in action. What are you waiting for? You don't have to finish this book to begin your application. Do it now! Get online and set up your coaching program. If not, then get online and send me an email with your commitment and $100 fine agreement. Or, give a commitment to a co-worker and explain the consequence and how it will be enforced. Make sure your time frame is for seven days. What are you waiting for?

Chapter 6

The Two Killers of Behavioral Contracting

*"The only good is knowledge
and the only evil is ignorance."*
— Socrates

These two factors will destroy the impact of behavioral contracting. The first is unrealistic commitments. The second is non-enforcement of the penalty.

Unrealistic Commitments

Here is a typical scenario from one of my live audiences. After explaining the concepts of the human performance law, avoiding pain and seeking comfort, along with the intervention of behavioral contracting, I ask the audience to actually make a commitment that will be due coming Sunday night. About 95% of the time I'll get a health commitment. For example, one woman said she would commit to working out five times by Sunday night. She was hearing me speak on Monday late afternoon, so this commitment would be for six days, Tuesday through Sunday.

The first thing I will do is challenge the reality of the commitment by asking, "How many times did you work out last week?" Zero is the most common response I get. "How about the week before that?" "Zero", and "Before that?" "Zero". Then I ask "Do you belong to a gym?" "No". I continue to ask if it would be okay if they worked out only four times or three times, etc. If I get a yes to any of that, then this person is not committed to working out five times and the chances of them doing so are very slim.

I'll also ask the question, "Would you pay me $100 if you don't work out five times this week?" If they say no, then I'll get them to reduce the commitment to the level that they would give their word that they will do it, and pay a fine if they don't complete the promised action.

Many times people just simply don't know what they are committed to. One way to find out is to make commitments with consequences and then look and see what you actually do. If you're not doing what you said you would do consistently, then you're just not committed.

This is very important. No one wants to set him or herself up for failure. Be careful with what you commit to do and do it. If you are setting unrealistic goals you simply won't stay with the concept.

The commitments that a person makes must be short term, seven days, and realistic in comparison to previous verifiable experiences. If the most calls you've ever made on a weekly basis is 200 then you're not going to make a commitment for 400 calls. You can prove me wrong and commit to 200 and then blast through and make 400, but until you actually have a previous history at that activity level you shouldn't be making that commitment.

You are not going to commit to earning $100,000 per year if the most you've ever earned is $50,000. Again, prove me wrong and blast through $100,000, but you can't commit to that level and I can't accept that level of as a commitment until you've actually been there.

Some of you may recall that I've talked about minimum level objectives and stretch level. (Book — "The Sky Is Not The Limit — You Are!" See endnote #7)

One of my first core principles is "I do what I said I would do". Commit to the lowest level — if you give your word you will accomplish — falling short is not an option. You may recall one of the trends of years past, BHAGS, big hairy audacious goals. This is ridiculous. Yes you must have stretch goals, and yes I recommend that you think big, but I also recommend that you get yourself back to the reality of a realistic commitment of action over a short period of time, seven days. The myth of shoot for the stars and if you fall short you are better off then if you aimed lower is just a bunch of nonsense and wishful thinking. Instead, give me the lowest level you give your word you will accomplish and falling short is not an option. You do not fall below your minimum level objectives. Whatever it takes!

This is like my airplane analogy. You might think that the plane is straight and level but in reality your instruments show you are in a descending steep banked right turn. You can't trust your senses without a visual reference.

Likewise, in terms of your commitments, you might think that it's in your best interest to aim higher but it's the "starting" that stops most people. Aiming lower with a minimum level commitment and a stretch to "super star" level, will actually improve performance rather than limit it.

Here's a simple example. Imagine that you said you wanted to make 200 prospecting calls this week. That's 40 calls per day. However, you looked at your schedule, looked at your commitments, business calls, appointments, etc. and decided that although it was doable it was not realistic, so you committed to a minimal level of 100 calls as a promise and a stretch goal of 125.

Here's how this sample day might have unfolded. Let's first start with the higher-level commitment of 200 calls, 40 per day. Here is

Monday. You start off strong and make five calls, then you have some phone appointments with a printer vendor, product manufacturer, lunch, another customer call, then some administration duties, a conversation with your assistant, some long-term planning and it's already 5:00 pm PST, can't reach anyone on any time zone on the mainland. You've made 5 calls total on Monday.

Tuesday comes and you find yourself having to prepare some major proposals for a long-term program you are designing for a customer that takes almost the full day. You had planned to do this a little bit at a time but the deadline was moved up at the last minute.

You've made zero calls for Tuesday. This leaves you at needing to make 195 calls and you only have three days to do so. Wednesday is a focused day, lots of good quality calls and contacts, but at the end of the day you've only made 30 calls for a total of 35 out of 200. This means that you'll have Thursday and Friday to make 165 calls or a bit over 82 calls per day. You look at this number on Thursday and decide you'll never be able to do this, you've failed so why bother, better luck next week.

You make 5 calls on Thursday and decide to take on other projects on Friday and make another 5 calls for a total of 45 calls for the week. You've failed miserably from your commitment for 200 calls.

Now let's look at the same scenario but your commitment is the MLO (minimum level objective) of 100 calls. Look at the shift in your mindset. For the sake of this example I'll repeat the same set of circumstances per day and just plug in the new numbers. However, watch for the difference in your mindset.

Monday comes and you're busy etc., and you make only 5 calls. That leaves 95 calls left. Tuesday comes, again you're busy etc. and you make zero calls. This still leaves 95 calls with three days left. Wednesday is a focused day and you make 30 calls for a total of 35 out of 100. This means that you'll have Thursday and Friday to make 65 calls or a bit over 32 calls per day.

Look at the difference between 32 calls per day and 82 calls per day. You can bear down, handle what comes up and still make 32 calls a day. So you do just that. Something critical comes up in the morning after you've made 5 calls, but you bear down again and make an additional 25 calls for a total of 30 for Thursday, leaving just 35 for Friday, a very realistic number. Friday comes and you can see the finish line.

Your perspective is one of success not of failure. Your thinking has gone from I can't to I can. This is quite a different possibility that you are focusing on now, a totally different potential reality. You bear down, focus, close your door and make 45 calls on Friday for a total of 110. You did more than you said you would do. You feel like a success.

It really is all about mindset. Here is a health example: I've added swimming at the end of my workouts for an extra calorie burn and to tap into the aerobic aspect of my workouts. In other words, this is a higher intensity then I get on the stair master.

I commit to a modest 30 lengths for the week. This can be done in three sessions of 10 and that is my commitment. I can do this any way I want, six sessions of 5, but my commitment is 30.

Monday I swim 10, great, I'm on track. Tuesday — another 10 — fabulous. I take Wednesday off. Thursday I only swim 6 lengths. Here comes Friday. I need to swim 4 lengths to accomplish my promise and avoid my fine.

Here's my mindset; I don't feel like swimming. However, my RAS is stimulated by my behavioral contract. My frontal cortex gets a shot of an electrical discharge which loops to the limbic area of the brain, my amygdala, the emotional area, and I subconsciously wind up with the thought that I can easily do 4 lengths then I'll stop and be done with it, mission accomplished. All I know is that I find myself in the pool, whining, but still in action.

Remember, it's the starting that stops most people. I jump in the pool, the hardest part, and wind up swimming 10 more lengths putting me over my goal by 6. Well done.

What made this happen? Behavioral Contracting. First, I had to care enough to make the commitment. Next I had to have a mechanism to get my attention off of how tired I was how I didn't feel like swimming, the avoidance and rationalization, and shift the attention and energy in the brain. This was accomplished through the use of the behavioral contract. The bottom line, I did what I said I would do.

MLO's generate greater performance then higher commitments, which a person fails in trying to accomplish. My measurable bottom line is 110 calls for the week with a MLO, versus 45 calls with the BHAG. Although this is a sample commitment it is very realistic and I have experienced these numbers personally. I wound up swimming 36 lengths instead of my commitment to 30. Small wins, week in and week out, magnify greatly. The compound interest on the small choices you make will keep you living longer and more fulfilled. Remember the squares example for exponential impact. Twenty years from now you want to be thankful of the choices you've made today.

A big part of this experience is learning how to make commitments. Let me say this a different way. A big part of the behavioral contracting experience is learning what you are really committed to.

Here's some tough love. If you want to know what you are committed, to look at what you have in your life. That's what you're committed to, including all the misery. If you want something different, then you need to have an impact on the cause and effect, action and reaction mindset that creates and your results will be different. Keep reading, as I will be covering all of this in more detail.

Make sure your commitments are specific.[35] I would never accept a commitment that says someone will workout five times this week. I would want to know what specifically the person was going to do, intensity, frequency, and any other specific questions to clarify the exact components of the weekly commitment. I would want that person to answer "What specifically?", "How much specifically?", "When specifically?" where, etc. Precision probing questions.

So, you're with me so far. Your commitment is specific for the next seven days, realistic based on past experiences. Now what could go wrong?

Non-Enforcement of Consequences

It's the second component that causes the failure of behavioral contracting. That is the non-enforcement of the consequence. One organization partnered their team with members that were more experienced and were in the business longer than the committing partner. For the sake of an example let's just imagine that the commitment made to the more experienced "Accountability buddy" was to make five sales presentations over the next week, with a fine of $100 if you didn't do it.

The accountability partner now is at a crossroads. If he or she doesn't enforce the $100 fine, then it will lose its entire pain threshold and the avoidance impact will be lost. Feeling sorry for the person is not doing them any favors. The next time they make a commitment, subconsciously they won't lock in on the pain of the penalty since they know it won't be enforced. Instead the brain will focus on the pain of the commitment and they will avoid the activity. Remember, you are going to avoid either the pain of the commitment or the pain of the penalty; you will avoid the highest level of perceived pain.

That's another reason why the internet based on-line coaching and accountability program is so effective, the internet doesn't hear your stories and excuses, nor does it care about your excuses and circumstances. If you put a $100 fine on doing five presentations this week and you log back on and check the "No" box stating that you didn't do it, the computer will fine you $100! Now that's tough love!

If you are on the receiving end of a commitment make sure that you will accept a fine that you can and will enforce. If your partner has very little money then don't accept a $100 fine. Instead, coach them to some other type of penalty that you will enforce such as washing your car or coming over to your house and pulling weeds, something that you can and will enforce, but will not induce any financial hardship on your partner.

Years ago I presented a full day program for an organization that consisted of residential mortgage lending, appraisal and title insurance divisions. The owner recognized that he was not spending enough time with the divisions outside of lending and committed to a certain amount of time in those divisions over the next seven days. The commitment was very specific and easily verifiable. The penalty was that he would do this or cut off all of his hair, that's right, shave his head. He was a young guy and his hair was important to him.

The mistake that I made was that I accepted a penalty that I could not control and force to be executed. The result was that he did not spend the time in the other divisions and he did not shave his head. He was the CEO of the company, who was going to enforce this other than myself? What leverage did I have since I live in California and he lived in Arizona? What kind of a statement did this make to his company? If the consequence is not enforced the behavioral contracting program will not work. I should have also taken his credit card number and put a $1000 fine on it. At least that is easily enforced.

Have you made your contract for the week yet? By the way, let's do a check-in before continuing on. Do you agree with what I'm saying so far or do you find yourself in feeling a bit of resistance? Check in here without judgment. This is one of my coaching commandments; it's not good or bad, it just is.

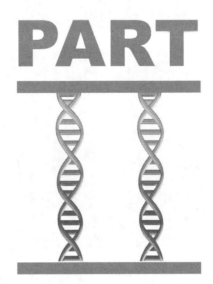

PART II

The Theory of Everything
— The Science of it All

"And that's the way it is."
— Walter Cronkite

Chapter 7

Science — The Millionaire's Mindset

"An open mind collects more riches than an open purse."

If you can recall the seven circles analogy for sales application,[36] it is a conclusion that attitude is a major key ingredient in living the life you love. I am referring to the sales sequence for any type of sales:

The Lesson of the 7 Circles

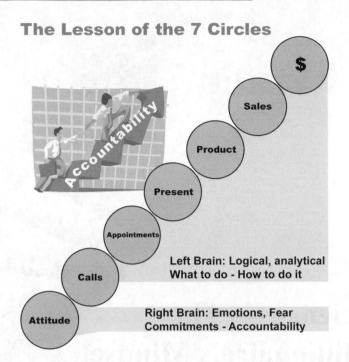

I invite you to do a simple exercise. Think back in your life and identify a particular person who had a major influence on you. Many times it's a best friend, parent, high school football coach or teacher. It could be anyone. Do you have someone in mind? Here is the exercise: make a list of the attributes or qualities that person had. A sample list might look something like this:

Believed in me
Challenged me
Motivational
Integrity
Honest
Caring
Loyalty
Loving
Intelligent
Mentored Me
Prepared

You can make up your own list. Next go to each item and label it as either an attitude or a skill.

Believed in me	Attitude
Challenged me	Attitude
Motivational	Attitude
Integrity	Attitude
Honest	Attitude
Caring	Attitude
Loyalty	Attitude
Loving	Attitude
Intelligent	Skill
Mentored Me	Skill
Prepared	Attitude/Skill

As you look at your own list what you'll find is that almost all of the attributes of a leader, of this person who had such a profound impact on your life are attitudes. If you've heard me speak live or joined the monthly conference calls you've heard me talk about the bell curve. The difference between the top 2% and the rest of the curve is not ability, talent, training, education or opportunity. The difference is attitude.

A very appropriate question for you to ask right now is, "So what? What does this mean to me?"

The application of this leads to another question. If it is true that attitude is the key to success, can you change your attitude to generate the success you say you are committed to? The answer is yes and in fact, you must change your attitude. Let's explore this further.

Dr. Thomas Stanley, author of The Millionaire Mind[37] conducted a national survey of 733 millionaires. He concluded that the foundations of financial success are:

1. Integrity - being honest with all people.
2. Discipline - applying self-control.
3. Social Skills - getting along with people.
4. A supportive spouse.
5. Hard Work - more than most people.

I'd vote attitude for each of these as well. Dr. Stanley continued stating that deca-millionaires, those with net worth of $10 million or more, have the highest incidence of regular exercise. "Keeping in excellent physical condition can be an important tool in dealing with detractors because it helps to hone one's competitive spirit," says Stanley.

Physical conditioning is one of the main sources of extraordinary energy that most multimillionaires possess. That is an attitude.

Dr. Stanley identified actions and thought processes used by millionaires to eliminate and reduce fears and worries.[38] The top twelve were:

1. Hard Work
2. Believing in myself
3. Preparation
4. Focusing on key issues
5. Being decisive
6. Planning
7. Being well organized to deal with big issues
8. Taking immediate action to solve problems
9. Countering negative thoughts with positive ones
10. Out-working, out-thinking, out-toughing the competition
11. Visualizing success
12. Never allowing fears to control my mind

Again, I would vote for these all being attitudes rather than skills.

A few years ago I was invited to attend another trainers program being held over the weekend in Las Vegas. I had met this trainer at a function where we were both speakers and we seemed to be grounded in the same philosophies. I was going to sit in on his training to see what was different and if there might be the possibility of the development of a strategic alliance between our companies.

Unfortunately I was sick. I wanted to cancel. I reasoned however that something would always come up, there would always be other priorities and I wasn't that sick and my calendar was clear so I might as well just suck it up and attend. So I got a flight and made the one-hour trip into Las Vegas.

The next morning the first thing the instructor did was put up 9 dots on a flip chart and challenged the audience to connect the dots with four straight lines without lifting your hands off of the page.

I thought to myself that I had made a big mistake coming out here for this training, particularly if it was going to be a rehash of old stuff like the 9 dots example. I already had that in my book, "The Sky is Not The Limit—You Are!", and although it was new for the rest of the people in the room it certainly wasn't new information for someone in the field. I was disappointed. Then he said something that caught my attention. "If you already know how to connect the dots with four lines, use three."

I didn't know how to do this with three lines. He now had my attention. Sadly I came to the conclusion that it couldn't be accomplished. I have now learned that the correct conclusion to make is the following mindset statement:

At my current level of thinking a solution doesn't exist.

There are several solutions to this. One solution is simply to cut the page, move the dots and use three lines to connect them.

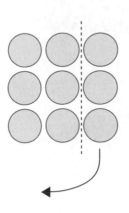 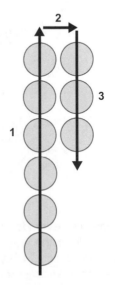

This reminds me of the mindset present during the Wright Brothers. They were ridiculed and thought to be foolish to think that mankind could take flight through a machine. They had plenty of failures and near catastrophes, both financial and physical. A competitor once wrote, "I can't think of anyone who stuck to a plan so carefully, who figured out what he needed to do and just did it."

You could certainly apply the principle "at my current level of thinking a solution does not exist".

On December 17th, 1903, Orville at the controls took flight. He would describe it as the first in which a machine carrying a man had raised itself by its own power.

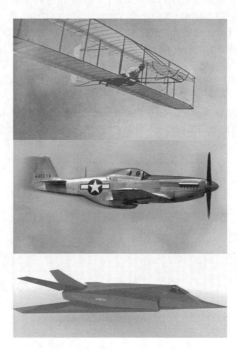

No one had ever done this before. The Wright brothers had to figure it out along the way. They figured out how to go from a glider to a powered vehicle. They had trials and errors with materials and design, but they knew something about the laws of physics and they had faith. They knew the principle of Pressure Gradient and Lift.

How an Airplane Wing Works

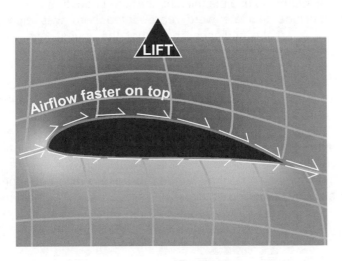

Air flowing over the top of the wing moves faster, creating lower pressure and thus creating lift. The shape and "angle of attack" can impact the lift.

Air flows more quickly over the top of the wing creating low pressure, which in turn creates lift. This is a law of physics. The laws have always been there. Progress is simply man-kind learning to observe and recognize the laws and then use them.

Once the airplane was invented improvement was fast. In a short period of time, less than 100 years, stealth technology was created. However, as the quantum folks would say, the space had to be conditioned first before progress could be made.

To illustrate how rigid we are in our patterns of thought, many times I'll start off a live presentation with the following challenge:

What word does this sequence of letters suggest?

H I J K L M N O

I get very interesting responses. The most common is "alphabet". I'll ask the audience member to tell me how they were thinking to conclude that response. Their reply usually is along the lines that they are letters in sequence from the alphabet. I'll respond with a comment to the audience that they had a very reasonable approach. It was very reasonable to use the thinking that they had, that approach, and then conclude that the word represented here was alphabet. I'll continue to let the audience know that the lowest level of human consciousness is being reasonable.

A few more guesses bring on responses such as "middle". The middle of the alphabet, very reasonable, yet incorrect. Before the replies get too out of hand I'll give the answer:

Water, H2O.

Then I'll show that they needed to have a different approach, a different way of looking at this:

H I J K L M N O

This sequence should suggest one word.

O T T F F S S

These letters form the beginning of an infinite sequence. Find a simple rule for determining any or all successive letters. According to your rule, what would be the next two letters sequenced?

Can you solve the next one, OTTFFSS?

After multiple incorrect attempts, although many very reasonable, the solution is very simple. You simply need to look at this in a different way. The next two letters are E N.Once you uncover the essential element at work, the simple principle in action, then you can predict with absolute certainty far beyond what you can see.

Let me review the principle previously mentioned in physics called "Occam's Razor", which states that we should always take the simplest possible path and ignore more clumsy alternatives. William Occam, "Given two theories that explain the data, the simpler theory is to be preferred." The simpler the theory, the better you understand something.

These letters represent the letters of the numbers in sequence. One = O, Two = T, Three = T, Four = F and so on. So you can see how easy it is to predict once you know the essential element.

Sometimes you can't even trust your own intuition. For example, what is 12 divided by ½? If you said 6, that is not correct. Did you say 6? See how the brain is so quick to recognize a known pattern and fire those neurons without taking the time for closer analysis. The answer is 24. A bit of a math review, take 12 times the inverted ½ or 2/1 and you get 24. Think some more on this. If you have one pie and you divide it in ½ how many pieces do you have? The answer is 2. If you have 2 pies and divide them both by ½ you wind up with 4 pieces. If you have 12 and divide by ½ you wind up with 24 pieces.

And so it is with human excellence. You know the "Occam's Razor" principle. The simple essential element addressed in this book is the simple law of human performance, which states that all human performance is the avoidance of pain and the seeking of comfort. The simple 1.2% (analogy)[39] intervention is Behavioral Contracting™.

Your willingness to be open to a mindset shift is key. If you are not experiencing the result you want in a particular area of your life the first step is to identify your competing mindset, and replace it with a mindset that will support you and compel consistent actions.

There are rather significant mindset shifts happening as we speak. There is new technology that is in direct conflict with current conventional wisdom. The currently held belief is that the central nervous system — the brain, spinal cord and eye nerves — cannot heal in adults.

This thinking no longer holds. Larry Benowitz of Children's Hospital in Boston[40] and his colleagues found a molecule that triggers nerve regeneration. The scientists discovered that a protein, oncomodulin, is secreted in damaged eyes by immune cells known as macrophages. They found that oncomodulin, when given with compounds that enhance its activity, can increase nerve regeneration fivefold to sevenfold in rats with injured optic nerves (below). Benowitz believes oncomodulin could someday help reverse optic nerve damage caused by glaucoma, tumors or trauma and plans to investigate whether the treatment could work to help treat stroke and spinal cord injury.

Regeneration of Nerve Fibers

The photo on the right shows regeneration of the nerve fibers, which occurs in the presence of a protein called oncomodulin, secreted by immune cells.

Once again, the space has been conditioned and new breakthroughs in this area are being launched as you read these pages.

You are exactly where you should be in your health, business and personal life. There are no mistakes. You are where you are because your attitudes dictate your results. If you want to know what you are committed to then just look at what you currently have. That's what you're committed to. If you want to change the results of any of those areas you will need to change your attitude, change your mindset.

Every great transformation, invention or accomplishment has had the same issue of being the pioneer of overcoming an old and accepted limitation and creating an entirely new possibility and mindset. A mindset is a predisposition or mental attitude that predetermines a person's responses to, and interpretation of, situations. It is a great skill to develop the ability to recognize competing mindsets or attitudes, and to rewire or change them.

Let's warm up your brain and see how easy or difficult this is for you. Your previous experiences with the HIJKLMNO and OTTFFSS and even the 9 dots should give you at least a glimpse of what you're in for.

Below six glasses are in a row, the first three full of juice, the second three empty. By moving only one glass, can you arrange them so empty and full glasses alternate?

6 Glasses

The first attempts at a solution most likely involved you being stumped because the directions call for you to only physically touch or move one glass. There may have been a tendency to think that it can't be done. Remember, to replace "I can't" with "at my present state of mind a solution does not exist".

Eventually or perhaps right away, the solution reveals itself and it's simple. Pour the juice from the second glass into the fifth, problem solved.

How about a riddle? A man rode into town on Monday. He stayed three nights and left again on Monday. How is this possible?

Notice your struggle with the usual approach of looking at the days of the week, applying three nights, looking at Monday and getting stumped. You are stuck in a human weakness of making an assumption. That is another coaching commandment, identify and challenge your assumptions. If your starting or seed assumption is incorrect, then you can guarantee that your conclusions will be skewed as well.

My wife walked into my office as I was writing this, so of course I had to give her this one to try. She was stumped, she said, "He stays three nights, but he also stays another four" She was confused. I said, "You are stuck in a mindset that is not serving you. Do you see what I have to put up with? You should call your sister, she's good at these!"

I gave her a clue. "What assumptions are you making?" She said "There are seven days in a week." That was true but not helpful. So I gave her the answer.

He rode into town on a horse named Monday. When I told my wife this she says, "That was stupid!" Well, sometimes the simple solutions can look that way at first.

Here's another one to challenge your assumptions: Two women are playing five games of chess. They each win five games. How can that be?

Answer: they are not playing each other. Do you see the common assumption? This is a very excellent coaching homework assignment for you to notice what assumptions you make for a week, then challenge those assumptions and then to be in choice about taking actions.

Loosen up some of your rigid neurological connections with the following exercise: Three of a kind is the name of this game. Each set of words below has something in common. Can you think of the clever link? Example, hurricane, camera, needle. (Answer: eyes)

1. Barber	Rooster	Beehive	Combs...
2. Bowling Alley	Tailor	Wrestling Match	
3. Telephone	Deck of Cards	Car Trunk	
4. Fishing Rod	Actor	Checkout Counter	
5. Watermelon	Tennis Tournament	Idea	
6. Pelican	Legislature	Person in Debt	
7. Curtain	Fisherman	Nuclear Reactor	
8. Radar	Porch	Basketball	
9. Archer	Violinist	Gift Package	
10. Dentist	Oil Field	Army Camp	

Answers: 1) combs, 2) pins, 3) jacks, 4) lines, 5) seeds, 6) bills, 7) rods, 8) screens, 9) bows, 10) drills.

Think back in time to restrictive mindsets that held back innovation and progress. The world is flat. Man will never fly. You can't stimulate cells to grow into a selected organ. Old established ideas die-hard. Louis Pasteur was born on December 27th, 1822 in Dole, France. His discovery that most infectious diseases are caused by germs, known as the "germ theory of disease", is one of the most important in medical history. His work became the foundation for the science of microbiology and a cornerstone of modern medicine.

His contributions to microbiology and medicine can be summarized as follows: First, he championed changes in hospital practices to minimize the spread of disease by microbes. Second, he discovered that weakened forms of a microbe could be used as an immunization against more virulent forms. Third, he found that rabies was transmitted by agents so small they could not be seen under a microscope, thus revealing the world of viruses. Fourth, he developed "pasteurization", a process by which harmful microbes in perishable food products are destroyed using heat, without destroying the food.

Can you imagine having a conversation with others about something that present day technology would not allow you to see?

It wasn't until his research was presented and from the urgings of Joseph Lister, that finally in the 1880's reluctant doctors were forced to comply with new rules of cleanliness and antiseptic conditions, something as simple as washing their hands before touching patients was resisted.

"Resistance goes beyond all rational, logical boundaries. The parallel in modern times could be made for alternative medicine and its dominant theme, that mind and emotion directly affect health and disease."[41]

Today there are medical discoveries that occur on a moment-by-moment basis. We are in the midst of new mindsets, which are pinpointing the genes involved in cancer that will help chart a new course towards treatments and expectations.

"If we wish to learn more about cancer, we must now concentrate on the cellular genome." Nobel laureate Renato Dulbecco made that declaration more than 20 years ago in one of the earliest public calls for what would become the Human Genome Project. "We are at a turning point," Dulbecco a "pioneering" cancer researcher stated in the 1986 journal Science. Discoveries in preceding years had made it clear that much of the issues with cancers stemmed from damage to their genes and alterations in their turn on turn off cell growth functioning. "We have two options, either try to discover the genes important in malignancy by a piecemeal approach, or sequence the whole genome."

This was a monumental task at the time and one that many thought was just not possible. Over the span of two decades Dulbecco's vision has moved from pipe dream to reality. Less than three years after the Human Genome Project's completion, the national Institutes of Health officially launched the pilot stage of an effort to create a comprehensive catalogue of the genomic changes involved in cancer: The Cancer Genome Atlas (TCGA).

This was new, groundbreaking, and urgent. Every day more than 1,500 Americans die from cancer, about one person every minute. As the U.S. population ages, this rate is expected to rise significantly unless scientists find a way to develop novel strategies for treatment and a smarter war against cancer.

Renato Dulbecco was awarded the Nobel Prize
in physiology and medicine in 1975

DNA Sequencing

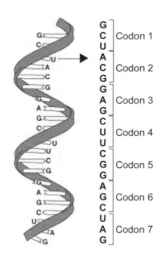

G
C ⎤
C   Codon 1
U ⎦
A
A ⎤
C   Codon 2
G ⎦
G
A ⎤
G   Codon 3
C ⎦
U ⎤
U   Codon 4
C ⎦
G ⎤
G   Codon 5
A ⎦
G ⎤
C   Codon 6
U ⎦
A ⎤
G   Codon 7
G ⎦

This is what one of the 300,000 pages of DNA coding looks like, as collected during the Human Genome Project. Change the letters around, and this could be the coding for a baboon, fly, ant, rose petal, or potato.

An opposite mindset shift had to occur from, it's not possible to do this to, it is possible and it must be done and it is being done. . Notice the shift.

How do you change your attitude and mindset and where do you need to? What areas are you seeking to improve? Here's how — by deciding what you want to have, what you need to do to have it, what you need to do this week, what you will commit to this week and using behavioral contracting to ensure action and align with human nature's driving force of avoidance. You can reinforce the attitudes and beliefs through the use of the technique that you may have already learned, using baroque music to reinforce attitudes and generate neurological patterns.[42] It is not the intention of this book to look at the impact of baroque music on the formation of habits, but that research is readily available and recommended.

This book and the behavioral contracting method of making weekly commitments with accountability, is a system for changing mindsets, behaviors and results.

Chapter 8

The Science of Attitude

"Nothing happens without personal transformation."
— W. Edwards Deming

Since attitude is a high indicator of predicable success, the real question is can you change your attitude and keep the change? The answer is absolutely yes! Now the most important question is how?

The human brain weighs only 3 pounds yet uses 30% of the body's oxygen and 25% of the available blood supply. The brain uses 33% of the available water and 40% of the body's nutrients. There are over 100,000 miles of blood vessels that is greater than the world's telephone system in its complexity. There are estimates that the brain has between 100 to 200 billion neurons. The brain is more complicated than a Donald Trump hair comb over![43]

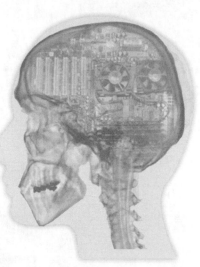

The brain is an electrical chemical organ. An electrical impulse stimulates the release of chemicals. These chemicals have a charge and we attract to ourselves what our most dominant thoughts are.

Your attitude is the sum of your most common thoughts. Thoughts are neurological connections. Thoughts are energy.

With the advent of brain imaging technology, scientists are now able to see the brain in action in real time.

A scanner detects radioactive material that is injected or inhaled to produce an image of the brain. Commonly used radioactively labeled material includes oxygen, fluorine, carbon and nitrogen. When this material gets into the bloodstream, it goes to the areas of the brain that require it. Oxygen and glucose accumulate in brain areas that are metabolically active. When the radioactive material breaks down, it gives off a neutron and a positron. When a positron hits an electron, both are destroyed and two gamma rays are released. Gamma ray detectors record the brain area where the gamma rays are emitted. This method provides a functional view of the brain.

This is called Positron Emission Tomography, or a PET Scan.

Positron Emission Tomography

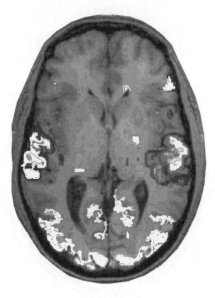

Another type of scanning is called Magnetic Resonance Imaging, MRI.

An MRI uses the detection of radio frequency signals produced by displaced radio waves in a magnetic field. It provides an anatomical view of the brain.

Advantages:
1. No X-rays or radioactive material is used.
2. Provides a detailed view of the brain in different dimensions.
3. Safe, painless, and non-invasive.
4. No special preparation (except the removal of all metal objects), is required from the patient. Patients can eat or drink anything before the procedure.

Magnetic Resonance Imaging (MRI)

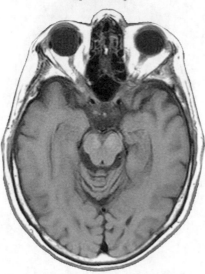

Scientists can see the brain in action. They can see the electrical activity shift from one area of the brain to another with the changing of thoughts or stimuli.

This was recently published by the Orange County Register, a daily newspaper in Southern California:

Implants turn man's thoughts into action

Quadriplegic connected to a computer is able to operate devices.

BY TOM AVRIL
THE PHILADELPHIA INQUIRER

With the aid of electrodes implanted in his brain, a man paralyzed from the neck down was able to perform certain everyday activities - move a computer cursor, open e-mail, turn on a TV set - merely by imagining them.

The patient, whose spinal cord was injured when an attacker stabbed him in the neck, was even able to open and close a prosthetic hand, his thoughts translated into action by a custom-built computer.

For now, the patient must be tethered to a cart loaded with electronics. The system was developed by scientists at Brown University, who say it is just a few years away from commercial use.

The results, reported in today's issue of the journal Nature, offer hope that thousands of people with injured spinal cords could someday regain significant function by simply bypassing the injury. Eventually the team expects patients will have a wireless device implanted in the brain that sends signals not just to computers but to parts of their bodies.

Coincidentally Wednesday, a team that includes Drexel University scientists reported progress toward a similar goal in lab rats, albeit by different means. The researchers removed a nerve from each animal's leg and transplanted it across the injured spinal cord, restoring some mobility to paralyzed forelimbs.

Meanwhile, the efforts of the Brown University team, which included researchers in Chicago and Massachusetts, seem like science fiction.

After implanting electrodes in the brain of Matthew Nagle, the 25-year-old stabbing victim, scientists discovered that the neurons associated with moving his arms and hands could still generate electrical signals - a surprising find, three years after the attack.

They ran wires through his skull to BrainGate, an electronic device that filtered out the noise and learned to interpret the signals. When connected to a computer, Nagle was able to play the video game

"Pong" and also drew a circle using a computer drawing program.

"I just imagined moving the cursor," he said in a telephone interview from his room in a Massachusetts rehab hospital.

The goal is to make a wireless device that could be fully implanted so the patient would not have to be wired to a computer - much like with cochlear implants, the devices that can help deaf people perceive sound.

While the current work involves moving computer cursors and prosthetic devices, the researchers hope someday to transmit electrical signals from the brain to a patient's real hands and arms.

Nagle's parents were somewhat apprehensive about the brain implant, but he was determined to press forward.

The electrodes were removed after the experiment, so he no longer can bypass his crippling injury with the futuristic BrainGate. But Nagle's participation was not just about bettering his own condition, he said, his voice a hoarse rasp because he breathes with a ventilator.

"I knew it would give a lot of people hope," Nagle said.

The BrainGate™ Neural Interface System[44] is currently the subject of a pilot clinical trial[45] being conducted under an Investigational Device Exemption (IDE) from the FDA. The system is designed to restore functionality for a limited, immobile group of severely motor-impaired individuals. It is expected that people using the BrainGate™ System will employ a personal computer as the gateway to a range of self-directed activities. These activities may extend beyond typical computer functions (e.g., communication), to include the control of objects in the environment such as telephones, televisions and lights. Scientists are building devices that help to restore the ability of paralyzed patients to communicate and move by translating neuron signals in their brain into commands that can control computer cursors or robots.

The BrainGate™ System is based on the Cyberkinetics platform technology to sense, transmit, analyze and apply the language of neurons. The System consists of a sensor that is implanted on the motor cortex of the brain and this device analyzes brain signals. The principle of operation behind the BrainGate™ System is that with any intact brain function, brain signals are still generated, even though they are not sent to the arms, hands and legs. The signals are interpreted and translated into cursor movements, offering the user an alternate "BrainGate™ pathway" to control a computer with thought, just as individuals who have the ability to move their hands use a mouse.

Cyberkinetics is further developing the BrainGate™ System to potentially provide limb movement to people with severe motor disabilities. The goal of this development program would be to allow these individuals to one day use their own arms and hands again. Limb movement developments are currently at the research stage and are not available for use with the existing BrainGate™ System. In addition, Cyberkinetics is developing products to allow for robotic control, such as a thought-controlled wheelchair.

In the future, those individuals whose injuries are less severe could use the BrainGate™ System. Next generation products may be able to provide an individual with the ability to control devices that allow breathing, bladder and bowel movements.

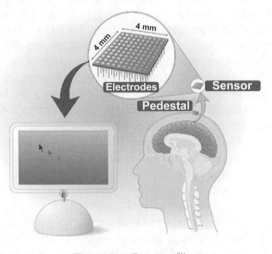

BrainGate™

A direct brain-computer link may provide a way of communicating for people who are paralyzed and unable to speak. An implanted electrode detects activity in the patient's motor cortex, that signal is then amplified and transmitted to a nearby computer. By thinking in certain ways, patients can move an on-screen cursor, thus allowing them to spell out words or select from a list of messages, such as "I'm thirsty."

Matt Nagel, a 26-year-old former athlete, was paralyzed from the neck down as a result of a knife injury. He was the first to use the BrainGate™ System to communicate directly with the computer.

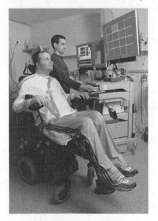

Neurosurgeons implanted an array of hair — thin electrodes into Nagle's brain. The electrodes picked up signals from neurons in his motor cortex, the brain region primarily responsible for movement control. These signals were fed to a computer through a pedestal positioned on top of Nagle's head and then translated into the movement of a computer cursor, a prosthetic hand and a robotic arm.

When Nagle simply imagined performing a movement in a particular direction, the computer, robot or hand prosthesis would respond accordingly. Through this method he was able to open simulated e-mail, perform a "pinching" gesture with the prosthetic hand, and make the robot arm pick up and drop a piece of candy. He has even used the device to make precise copies of geometric figures.

Niels Birbaumer, Ph.D., a German neuroscientist of the University of Tubingen, has developed what he calls a Thought Translation Device, or TTD, that is attuned to a low-frequency brain wave called the slow cortical potential, which people can produce at will. By controlling their thoughts, patients can answer yes-or-no questions, spell out sentences or even surf the Internet. "Anything the brain does, from adding a row of numbers to directing your arm to swat a fly, creates a voltage that an EEG can pick up." Says Birbaumer.[46]

Cleve Backster is a polygraph scientist best known for his controversial experiments in biocommunication, where in the 1960's he would use a polygraph machine on plant and animal cells. The results led to his theory of "Primary Perception." He is currently the director of the Backster School of Lie Detection in San Diego, California.

Backster began his career as an Interrogation Specialist with the CIA, and went on to become Chairman of the Research and Instrument Committee of the Academy for Scientific Interrogation.

His course of study changed dramatically in the 1960s, when he discovered that a polygraph instrument attached to a plant leaf registered a change in electrical resistance when the plant was harmed or even threatened with harm. It appeared that plants perceived human intentions and thoughts, and as Backster began to investigate further, he found that other human thoughts and emotions caused reactions in plants that could be recorded by a polygraph instrument.

He termed the plants' sensitivity to thoughts "Primary Perception," and first published his findings from the experiments in the International Journal of Parapsychology.[47] The article was met with wide criticism of his research methods, however Backster gained the interest of other researchers, and he expanded his experimental range to test for primary perceptions in other life forms such as yogurt, bacteria, and human cells. His work was inspired by the research of Sir Jagadis Chandra Bose, who discovered that playing certain kinds of music in the area where plants grew caused them to grow faster. This was due to the rhythmic nature of the music's energy interacting with the plants cells.

It is interesting to note that Backsters' "Primary Perception" theory was referenced in the Discovery Channel television show MythBusters. The team attempted to reproduce Backster's experiments using a polygraph and an EEG machine. They reproduced the plant experiment and got the results as expected from Backster's work. "They got steadily more stunned, uncomfortable and spooked as the plant they were testing showed inarguable reactions to being 'thought at' threateningly"

The reason I mention this is to emphasize that you can influence the neurons of the brain by your intentions, by your thoughts, on purpose and by design. Thoughts are real. They are energy and they have a real physiological impact on you and your surroundings.

Masaru Emoto born July 22, 1943 in Yokohama, Japan, is an author known for his controversial claim that if human thoughts are directed at water before it's frozen, the resulting water crystals will be beautiful or distorted and unable to crystallize depending upon whether the thoughts were positive or negative. Emoto claims this can be achieved through prayer, music or by attaching written words to a container of water. I have attended training with Masaru Emoto and although his findings are controversial they are very interesting.

Since 1999 Emoto has published several volumes of a work titled Messages from Water, which contains photographs of water crystals next to essays and "words of intent".[48]

Crystals Formed With Positive Words

A bottle of water was wrapped with a piece of paper that had positive words on it. The crystal is as perfect as can be. This indicates that love and gratitude are fundamental to the phenomenon of life in all of nature.

Crystals Formed With Heavy Metal

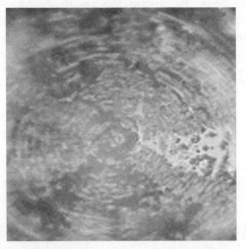

This is the result of loud heavy metal music, full of angry
and vulgar lyrics. The crystals are not well formed at all.

If you've read my first book,[49] then you've read about how by
changing what you think about, changes where the electrical activity
is in your brain. You can go from a negative thought that sends
signals to the amygdala, to a positive thought that sends signals to
the septum and generates a very powerful physiology.

You can cause this shift in electrical stimulation through your
intentional shifting of thoughts and it can be measured through brain
imaging. You have control over a process that was initially thought to
be outside of your control.

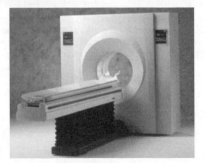

There are no pain sensors in the brain. With local anesthetics doctors are able to have a fully awake patient that they can talk to as they stimulate a variety of areas of the brain. This has enabled doctors to map the brain and to identify which areas are responsible for different sensations and functions with live patient feedback.

Through the use of Positive Emission Tomography, or PET scans, researchers can see in real time the actual areas of the brain that are being active. Below, researchers can actually observe the areas of the brain that are active when the patient is engaged in listening, looking, speaking or thinking. The researchers actually see the activity shift from one side of the brain to the other based on the task being presented to the patient.

PET Images of Brain

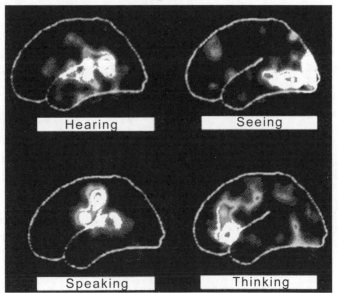

These PET images show scans of the right side of the brain while a person heard a word, saw a word, repeated a word and thought of a word.

The patient has conscious control as well. The patient can determine which area of the brain is electrically and metabolically active by shifting his or her thoughts.

This has tremendous real life applications. You can control your physiology by choosing your thoughts. For example, you can maintain a peak performance zone state by focusing only on positive thoughts and images, rather than giving the negative aspects of a given circumstance any consideration. If you exercise this power then you will keep the electrical activity in the septum area of the limbic system and out of the amygdala.

The Limbic System

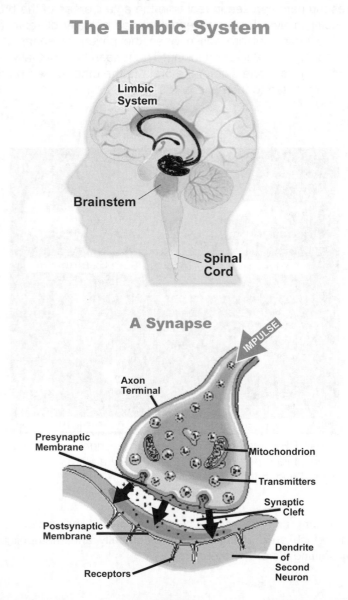

The benefit to you for exercising this conscious control is that you will avoid the negative emotions and physiological release of the destructive stress response. When you keep the activity in the septum, you have open receptor sites for the release of the feel good chemicals, the peak performance chemical dopamine and even the release of endorphins, the morphine like hormone. These receptor sites are blocked when the electrical activity is in the amygdala.

There's been quite a bit of research on positive self-talk. Is your glass half-empty or half-full? How you answer this age-old question about positive thinking may reflect your outlook on life, your attitude toward yourself , and whether you're optimistic or pessimistic. In fact, some studies show that these personality traits, optimism and pessimism, can effect how well you live and even how long you live.

I wasn't a fan of the "Polly Ana" life is great and wonderful positive thinking club until I did research on the power of manifestation. When I learned how thoughts are energy and that they carry an electrical charge with the power to attract like thoughts, I then became a believer. I became very careful with the nature of my thoughts because they are so powerful and will attract the exact nature of the thoughts. Your thoughts are the beginning of the reality. It's thoughts that are real; the outside world is the illusion!

By the way, one researcher showed that using positive self-talk helps increase your physical power and therefore, lift more weight in the gym.

Power Talk

This Graph shows the increase in power that athletes experienced when using instructional or motivational self-talk compared to no self-talk methods.

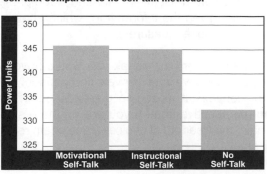

The first graph shows the increase in power that positive motivational self-talk has, "I lift this weight easily and effortlessly", or positive instructional self-talk has, "I explode up on every rep." The second graph below illustrates that positive thinking can have a dramatic impact on both your physique and your health.

Power of Suggestion

This Graph shows the percent decrease in blood pressure and body weight in the group of maids who were told their work was good exercise.

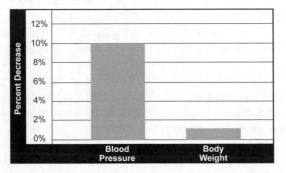

In this experiment the idea was to test whether exercise and health are moderated by one's mindset. Researchers measured several health factors in 84 female maids. Half of the maids were told that the work they did (cleaning hotel rooms) was good exercise. The other half wasn't given this information.

Although actual behavior didn't change, the informed group perceived themselves four weeks after the intervention to be getting significantly more exercise than before. They showed a decrease in bodyweight, body fat, waist to hip ratio and blood pressure, compared to the group not given the information, which showed no significant change in any of those measures.

If you've ever heard me speak you would have heard about the analogy of the concave and convex comparison. What is the line, concave or convex? It of course depends on which side you are taking your perspective from. If you are on the A side it's a concave line. You have the freedom of choice. Once again reality is in the mind of the observer.

Both potentials to be either concave or convex exist, but the other collapses once you make your choice. Your truth then becomes the choice you made. You have the ability to select your perception, just as you have the ability to shift your physiology by carefully allowing or disallowing certain thoughts to persist, either positive or negative. There are psychological effects to the choices you make.

Concave or Convex?

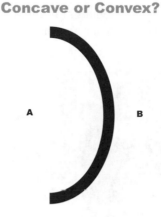

Another example of applying the knowledge of the brain wave activity as real electrical activity that can be manipulated is the case of Jessie Sullivan.

Jesse Sullivan is best-known for operating a fully robotic limb through a nerve-muscle graft, making him one of the first non-fictional cyborgs.

His bionic arm, a prototype developed by the Rehabilitation Institute of Chicago, differs from most other prostheses in that it does not use pull cables or nub switches to function, and instead uses micro-computers to perform a much wider range of complex motions. It is also the first prototype which enables him to actually sense pressure.

As an electrician, Jesse Sullivan accidentally touched an active cable that contained 7,000-7,500 volts of electricity. In May of 2001, he had to have both his arms amputated at the shoulder. Seven weeks after the amputation, Jesse Sullivan received matching bionic prostheses from Dr. Todd Kuiken of the Rehabilitation Institute of Chicago. Originally, they were operated from neural signals at the amputation sites, but Jesse Sullivan developed hyper-sensitivity from his skin grafts, causing great discomfort in those areas. Sullivan underwent neural surgery to graft nerves, which originally led to his arms, were grafted to his chest. The sensors for his bionic arms have been moved to the left side of his chest to receive signals from the newly grafted nerve endings.

While the prototype is being strengthened, Jesse Sullivan does day-to-day tasks using an older model.[50]

Jesse Sullivan

Let's examine the concept of "thoughts are real" on a cellular basis. It is widely noted that neurons that wire together, fire together. All of us have patterns of neurological networks that are instantaneously fired to produce behavior. For example, think back to my example of the hungry volunteer rat in the V-shaped container that is going to attempt to press down on a lever to get food. By placing a scanning device on the rat's skull we can actually measure the brain patterns that occur.

We place the rat in a box and open the doors giving it a choice to proceed to the right for food or the left for rags. Since the rat is hungry it smells the food, sees the food, and runs to the right.

Rat Brain Patterns

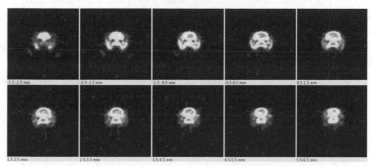

Rat Maze

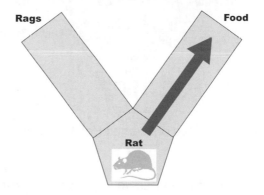

Next we put a shock on the metal grid. The rat doesn't know that there is a shock and once again focuses on the food and runs to the right. The rat experiences the shock on the metal grid and immediately runs off to the opposite side and will not press the lever again for food.

We take notice and record the brain scan of electrical activity, the network that is activated when the rat experiences the shock and avoids the grid. We see an initial firing in the outer cortex and then upon receiving the shock we see the amygdala light up. The next time the rat is introduced to the metal grid with food at the end it has the same neurological firing, the exact same brain scan of networked patterns as it did when it was shocked. It won't even try to test out the grid, it will avoid even if there was no shock on the grid. This is nature's protective mechanism for survival.

The rat remembers the previous trauma and avoids it. This is called "learned helplessness". It doesn't matter what the truth is, in this case that we took the shock away, the only thing that matters is what the rat pays attention to.

Rat Maze - Survival Mechanism

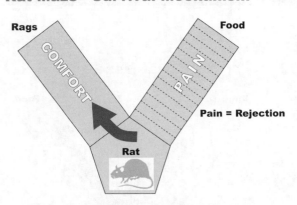

The Science of Learned Helplessness

This is relevant to you. If you are avoiding taking an action the reason is because your brain had accessed a neural network that has that action associated with pain or danger. Remember the statement of my law of human performance, "All performance is either the avoidance of pain or the seeking of comfort".

We are coded to avoid pain and to seek comfort. We do not have a choice in this regard. This is a human instinct. This is evolutions' best move to guarantee that individuals will survive and be able to pass on their genes. We are not asked to obey this rule, we are genetically coded to obey and we are compelled by our life force to comply.

Why is it so difficult for millions of American's to lose weight and keep it off? Is it because they don't know what to do or how to do it?

No, that information is readily available, you diet and exercise. I had one person stand up in a live program once and reveal that he was on two diets at the same time. I asked him why and he told me that there was more food that way![51]

The reason that it is so difficult is because the individual has the thought of losing weight and intends to engage in the activity of diet and exercise. Before the individual takes the actions however, the brain goes through an instant search of prior patterns, stored networks of previous actions and results, and instantly finds the network that says that dieting and exercise is hard, painful, dangerous and to be avoided at all costs.

The outer layer of the brain or the cortex, is the housing for intentional thought, it is looped to the limbic system or the amygdala, the housing for fear and avoidance. The cortex influences the reticular activating system, which directs what you pay attention to, with the result being that you avoid the actions of diet and exercise, and have a reason for doing so, rationalization. The real key here is that this is an illusion. Most of the time you can't tell that you're in avoidance, you think the truth is that you're just too busy.

I have said this many times:

"Your ability to influence what you pay attention to is directly correlated to your degree of success. "

When you apply this to business, the concept of "learned helplessness", you will immediately see that it relates to the fear and avoidance of the number one problem in commission sales, call reluctance.

Quite simply, rejection is viewed by the brain as a threat. Here is an example that I witnessed personally.

One of the ways that I am building for my retirement is through real estate investing. Years ago I was sitting in a realtor's office when I witnessed the following:

A new mortgage broker, a young lady, was trained to call on real estate agents to create relationships and to hopefully have them think of her when they had buyers who needed financing for their deals.

She was trained how to approach the realtor, how to present the rate sheets, how to create rapport, even how to recognize their personality style be it Dominate, Inspirational, Supportive or Cautious and to adjust how she interacted with each style.[52]

What she didn't know was that this particular real estate office had an in-house lending company, owned by the broker. Although his agents were independent contractors and could use any mortgage source that they wanted to, the broker wanted to keep the deals in-house so he could make revenue from that side of the transaction as well.

When he saw this young lady come into the lobby he ran out from his office, took her card, ripped it into pieces and threw it at her and said, "This is how much I want to see you in our office." The young lady ran back to her car in tears.

Here is the science of what happened.

A trauma occurred, the rejection plus the ripped and thrown card. This trauma triggered the amygdala (1 opposite page) to release stress hormones (2), which enhance memory formation in the brain. The memories of the trauma are first stored in the hippocampus (3). Then a chemical reaction encodes them into neurons in the cerebral cortex, cementing them into long-term storage. When the victim recalls the trauma, when this young lady intends to prospect again, the memory transfers back to the hippocampus, where it can trigger the release of more stress hormones.

Propranolol, (4) blocks the effects of the hormones and softens the victim's perception of the trauma. The brain re-stores the newly edited memory.

Propranolol Brain Effects

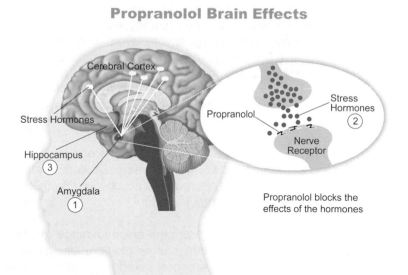

Propranolol blocks the effects of the hormones

The intervention of behavioral contracting has nearly the same effect as the experimental drug Propranolol. When you have a stated activity such as prospecting, the brain will initiate the search for a previous pattern that it will recognize as a threat, such as the rejection, unless there is an intervention, a switch is that is turned in the railroad tracks to change the direction as an analogy.

This switch is the negative consequence that will be enforced if the individual does not complete the activity. Suppose the fine was $1,000 if this young lady did not call on that same real estate office. That is the intervention of behavioral contracting, the specific declaration, call on this real estate office, and if she doesn't the consequence will be a $1,000 fine..

If this was the circumstance, the commitment and the consequence for non-performance, this sales person would think, "I'm not going to pay $1000 I'll just suck it up and go into that office." Almost always, by the way, the fear turns out to be an illusion and it turns out to be a pleasant experience.

As soon as the person declares the intention, calling on the office, the brain does its search looking for the negative previous pattern and it finds it. This happens in less than a second, nearly instantly with the coritical limbic loop already established. However, before it can compel this young lady to avoid and rationalize, it instantaneously also finds a higher level of perceived pain, the $1,000 fine. It immediately locks onto the highest level of pain and compels the avoidance. That's what the brain does! This avoidance is already initiated before she is even conscious of it. The question is what is she avoiding.

The avoidance in this case is to avoid the fine and to call on the office. The focus has shifted as to what is being avoided. The pain of the fine is now being avoided. Purposeful action occurs. Talk about positive manipulation of the nervous system!

Avoidance is not an option. Humans are avoidance machines. We are all coded to recognize the highest level of perceived pain and then compelled to avoid. We are not asked to comply with this avoidance. Our permission is not needed. Our intentions don't matter. Our intentions will always be over ridden by our genetic coding.

Try this yourself. Intend to sprint up a long flight of stairs but keep your breathing at a normal pace. You can intend all you want but when your body senses that the oxygen uptake is not sufficient, your breathing rate will dramatically increase whether you want it to or not.

It's the same thing here. You can want to be successful all you want. You can intend to take the right actions all you want. However, if your survival instinct senses danger you will avoid it. You are an avoidance machine. You should be avoiding uncomfortable activities. You are coded to do so. You will always avoid the highest level of perceived pain. By using behavioral contracting and manipulating the avoidance instinct, you can avoid your way to the top! Without an intervention, the individual is doomed to participate until it becomes uncomfortable and then to avoid and justify the avoidance with rationalization.

Without an intervention, the best you can have is mediocrity and rationalization. There is a range here however. You may be at the high end of the "average" on the bell curve and there may be a tendency to view yourself as successful. However, remember my warning, you can't trust your own interpretation of your circumstances and results. Ask the questions, successful compared to what? How can you be more successful? How can you have a larger impact in the lives of others and live a life of significance? You will never arrive. Arrival is an illusion. You will be striving until you die. Growth is constant, you are either growing or decaying; there is no middle ground.

I love the statement from astronaut Buzz Aldrin, who walked on the moon in 1969, "We need to have inspiration and goals, not be satisfied with just maintaining what we have."

In 1921, Dr Lewis Terman of Stanford University began a landmark study of 1,528 gifted children. The objective was to better understand the relationship between human intelligence and human achievement. This study became world famous and it was Dr. Terman who popularized IQ testing in the United States.

The most remarkable learning from his study was that IQ is not the most important ingredient for success. Instead, Terman's study found that three factors are far more important than sheer intelligence when it comes to achievement. They are:

1. Self-confidence
2. Perseverance
3. A tendency to set goals

The most important of these is the tendency to set goals. Setting goals directly influences the cortex and regulates what you pay attention to. You will see a different world if you set goals then if you don't. When you have goals and you reduce them to weekly commitments, you influence the RAS system in your brain that predisposes you to pay attention to and see the opportunities to execute your "promises", particularly the ones with the highest negative penalties for non-performance.

There is a remarkable study conducted by Dr. Daniel Simmons of Cornell University.

In 1999, Dr. Simmons had two teams of three passing a basketball back and forth to each other while moving in figure eight patterns. One team was wearing white shirts and the other black shirts. You are instructed to count the passes that the white shirt team makes. About half way through this exercise a black gorilla walks to the middle of the screen, beats its chest and walks off, all in clear view. Dr. Simmons reports that one half of the viewers did not see the gorilla. He calls that inattention blindness. My experience with this is that the percentage is much higher, with at least two thirds of my audiences not seeing the gorilla.

This is a startling reminder of how we can be so focused on our priorities, distractions, interruptions and challenges, that we just don't see opportunities that are right in front of us.

Chapter 9

Brain Plasticity —
Good For You!

"At the boundaries, life blossoms."
— Gleick, Chaos

Let's continue to look at the science and relate it to your everyday life. We'll start with brain plasticity. What is **brain plasticity**?[53] Does it mean that our brains are made of plastic? Of course not. Plasticity, or neuroplasticity, is the lifelong ability of the brain to reorganize neural pathways based on new experiences. As we learn, we acquire new knowledge and skills through instruction or experience. In order to learn or memorize a fact or skill, there must be persistent functional changes in the brain that represent the new knowledge. The ability of the brain to change with learning is what is known as **neuroplasticity**.

Neuroplasticity

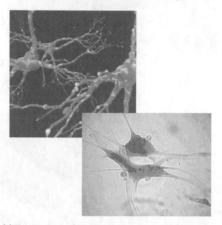

New connections are made with learning

To illustrate the concept of plasticity, imagine the film of a camera, pretend that film represents your brain. Now imagine using the camera to take a picture of a tree. When a picture is taken the film is exposed to new information, that of the image of a tree. In order for the image to be retained, the film must react to the light and "change" to record the image of the tree. Similarly, in order for new knowledge to be retained in memory, changes in the brain representing the new knowledge must occur.

To illustrate plasticity in another way, imagine making an impression of a coin in a lump of clay. In order for the impression of the coin to appear in the clay, changes must occur in the clay. The shape of the clay changes as the coin is pressed into it. Similarly, the neural circuitry in the brain must reorganize in response to experience or sensory stimulation.

Developmental Plasticity: Synaptic Pruning

Gopnick et al. (1999) describes neurons as growing telephone wires that communicate with one another. Following birth, the brain of a newborn is flooded with information from the baby's sense organs. This sensory information must somehow make its way back to the brain where it can be processed. To do so, nerve cells must make connections with one another, transmitting the impulses to the brain.

Continuing with the telephone wire analogy, like the basic telephone trunk lines strung between cities, the newborn's genes instruct the "pathway" to the correct area of the brain from a particular nerve cell. For example, nerve cells in the retina of the eye send impulses to the primary visual area in the occipital lobe of the brain and not to the area of language production, Wernicke's area, in the left posterior temporal lobe. The basic trunk lines have been established, but the specific connections from one house to another require additional signals.

Over the first few years of life, the brain grows rapidly. As each neuron matures, it sends out multiple branches (axons, which send information out, and dendrites, which take in information), increasing the number of synaptic contacts and laying the specific connections from house to house, or in the case of the brain, from neuron to neuron.

Neuron

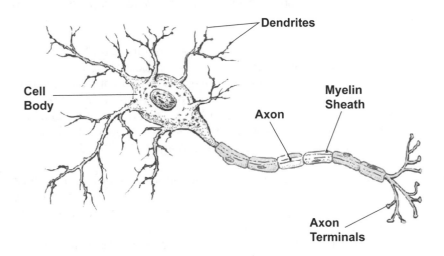

At birth, each neuron in the cerebral cortex has approximately 2,500 synapses. By the time an infant is two or three years old, the number of synapses is approximately 15,000 synapses per neuron (Gopnick, et al., 1999). This amount is about twice that of the average adult brain. The adult brain has around 100 billion neurons. Each neuron may have up to 100,000 dentrites. The connections between our neurons are connected by the dentrites, which are the "maps" that guide our thoughts, behaviors and actions. We each have more than 300 trillion constantly changing connections. There are unlimited numbers of different ways the brain can store information, unlimited options for how experience, learning and information might be encoded into the brain.[54] As we age, old connections are deleted through a process called Synaptic Pruning.

Synaptic Pruning eliminates weaker synaptic contacts while stronger connections are kept and strengthened. Experience determines which connections will be strengthened and which will be pruned; connections that have been activated most frequently are preserved. Neurons must have a purpose to survive. Without a purpose, neurons die through a process called apoptosis, in which neurons that do not receive or transmit information become damaged and die. Ineffective or weak connections are "pruned" in much the same way a gardener would prune a tree or bush, giving the plant the desired shape. It is plasticity that enables the process of developing and pruning connections, allowing the brain to adapt itself to its environment.

This is the reason that I give the recommendation to constantly be learning. Constantly read. Always be passionate about what you are building, until the day you die. The breakthrough of brain plasticity tells us that humans can continue to generate new nerve cell connections throughout life and that we don't lose that capacity as we age. But you've got to be in action for that to happen. If you're not engaging the brain it will deteriorate with age.

It was once believed that as we aged, the brain's networks became fixed. In the past two decades however, an enormous amount of research has revealed that the brain never stops changing and adjusting. Learning, as defined by Tortora and Grabowski (1996)[55], is "the ability to acquire new knowledge or skills through instruction or experience. Memory is the process by which that knowledge is retained over time." The capacity of the brain to change with learning is plasticity. So how does the brain change with learning? According to Durbach (2000), there appear to be at least two types of modifications that occur in the brain with learning:

1. A change in the internal structure of the neurons, the most notable being in the area of synapses.
2. An increase in the number of synapses between neurons.

Initially, newly learned data are "stored" in short-term memory, which is a temporary ability to recall a few pieces of information. Some evidence supports the concept that short-term memory depends upon electrical and chemical events in the brain, as opposed to structural changes such as the formation of new synapses. One theory of short-term memory states that memories may be caused by "reverberating" neuronal circuits, that is an incoming nerve impulse stimulates the first neuron, which stimulates the second, and so on, with branches from the second neuron synapsing with the first. After a period of time, information may be moved into a more permanent type of memory, long-term memory, which is the result of anatomical or biochemical changes that occur in the brain (Tortora and Grabowski, 1996).

What does this mean to you? You can intentionally control neuron growth. Here is a very exciting example

Think about something that frustrates you, or makes you angry. Get a clear and precise image of the last time you felt this way. As you know by now, emotions are chemicals. Candance Pert has reported the findings from her research in this regard.[56] She states that there are molecules for every emotion. Depressed people typically have a high level of stress steroids. In fact, depressed people are in a chronic state of ACTH activation because of a disrupted feedback loop that fails to signal when there are sufficient levels of the steroid in the blood. She states that the level of CRF-ACTH in the cerebrospinal fluid of those who killed themselves, compared to those who died from other causes, is tenfold higher. CRF is the depression peptide. It is a disruptive feedback loop.

Pert continues to state, "We must take responsibility for the way we feel. The notion that others can make us feel good or bad is untrue. We are making a choice of how we feel at every single moment. The external world is in so many ways a mirror of our beliefs and expectations. Why we feel the way we feel is the result of the symphony and harmony of our own molecules of emotion that affect every aspect of our physiology, producing blissful good health or miserable disease."[57]

Science is telling us the same thing that psychologists like the late Albert Ellis have been saying for years, and this has become one of my core principles:

"I am the source of all that I experience, versus going victim and blaming others."

Let's get back to the frustration example and I'll share a specific one of my own. I had a trip scheduled for a series of speaking engagements and I was going to be out of town for about eight days. I didn't want to park my car at John Wayne Airport for that long and I had an early morning departure. I asked my assistant to be outside of my office at 6:00 am to take me to the airport. She would take me in my car and after dropping me off she would park the car back at my home. This way I wouldn't have to take a taxi or disturb my wife and small children. Plus I didn't want to pay a high fee to have my car sitting at the airport for that long.

I had planned to stay on my routine that consisted of a 3:50 am wake up, gym, and then a short breakfast. I would swing by the house at 6:00 am and pick up my assistant who I expected to be waiting outside, and drive to the airport.

Everything went according to plan until the part about picking up my assistant. She wasn't there! It was now 6:15 am and still a no-show I couldn't reach her on her cell phone, I kept wondering where was she? It was now 6:30 am and I still had to get to the airport. I'd just have to bite the bullet and pay for eight days of airport parking. As I reached the corner she arrived.

She was in a panic and was not sure of how I was going to react. There was unexpected traffic from an accident on the freeway, (an excuse), and her cell phone battery went out, (an even more pathetic excuse). She was about ready to burst out in tears.

Instead, what happened next protected our relationship and endeared her to me. It just about guaranteed that I would be the beneficiary of her best efforts forever! My response, I laughed! I told her how fascinating she was, but we better hurry to get me to the airport on time! She laughed as well and off we went. I did make it to my flight in time.

My reaction would make a nice topic for a group discussion. My response protected our relationship and was the best possible response I could have had. What good would have being right and getting angry have done? Would it have changed anything? Would it have changed the behavior of my employee? The answers to all of these questions are NO! All a negative reaction would have done is made the situation worse.

However, I want you to know that I didn't respond the way that I did because I am a nice guy. If anything I tend to be more on the aggressive and non-empathetic side. I responded this way because I listened to the likes of Candace Pert, Albert Ellis, Bruce Lipton, Joe Dispenza, Robert Sapolsky, Michael Starbird, Richard Wolfson and others, whose expertise in the fields of mathematics, physics, biology, psychology, and more, have influenced my beliefs and shaped my behavior. When I am told by a credible scientist who has proof, that I have the power to: shape my behavior, to change or create my automatic habits and rewire neurons, and that in order to have a life of excellence I need to exercise that power, then I will do so.

You can do this as well. Let me first visit the psychology that shaped my response. There were two principles in operation that kept me calm. These two principles kept the electrical activity out of the emotional area of the amygdala and in the area of the septum. This enabled me to remain calm and avoid the destructive fight-or-flight response.

An emotion is a complex reaction pattern of connecting neurons that arises without conscious effort and is either positive or negative. Emotion is related to the group of structures in the brain known as the limbic system. I've mentioned the limbic system so much that it might be a good idea to give you a more detailed description of the parts of the brain that compose it. Again, remember, if you're not interested in the details don't worry, it's the design of this book to expose you to the details and your success with using the one "take away" that I have, Behavioral Contracting, it does not require your remembering or understanding the details.

The following brain structures are currently thought to be most involved in emotion:

Amygdala - two small round structures located anterior to the hippocampi near the temporal poles. The amygdalae are involved in detecting and learning what parts of our surroundings are important and have emotional significance. They are critical for the production of emotion and particularly so for negative emotions, especially fear.

Prefrontal Cortex - this term refers to the front of the brain behind the forehead and above the eyes. It appears to play a critical role in the regulation of emotion and behavior by anticipating the consequences of our actions. You read that right. This is a "pre-conscious" function. The prefrontal cortex plays an important role in delayed gratification by maintaining emotions over time and organizing behavior toward specific goals.

The Prefrontal cortex is our "executive decision maker". It is what stops you from shouting out to your boss, "You're an idiot" when you're really thinking that.

Anterior Cingulate - (ACC) is located in the middle of the brain, just behind the prefrontal cortex. The ACC is thought to play a central role in attention, consciousness and the initiation of motivated behavior.

Ventral Striatum - a group of subcortical structures that play an important role in emotion and behavior. One part of the ventral striatum called the nucleus accumbens is thought to be involved in the experience of goal directed positive emotion. Individuals with addictions experience increased activity in this area when they encounter the object of their addiction.

Insula - bodily experience of emotion. It is connected to other brain structures that regulate the body's autonomic functions like heart rate, breathing, digestion, etc. This area also processes taste information that is thought to play an important role in experiencing the emotion of disgust.

The first great and simple psychological principle that will give you control of where electrical activity is directed in your brain, is that of staying in the NOW[58]. This is such an old concept that most people have already heard about it, however most people are not using it.

Focus in the here and now is a moment of peace and tranquility. This is nonjudgmental awareness, moment-to-moment perception. There is no emotion in the now. There is only bliss.

Ask the question, what am I doing right now? Right now I'm sitting in my car at 6:29 pm waiting for my assistant. A thought such as "she is not reliable" is only found in the past. A stressful thought such as "I can't depend on her", can only be found in the future or the past. There is no destructive thought in the now. Getting angry is the result of flipping back and forth from the past to the future.

This doesn't mean that I don't take corrective or even punitive actions like firing her. What it does mean however is that I don't get myself upset in the process.

The second psychological principle I used here is a mind trick, or a phrase. It's simple, and it's powerful. Get your yellow marker out and highlight this statement:

Turn Frustration into Fascination.

This is what the psychologists would refer to as "cognitive therapy". In other words, I am applying a thought intervention to stop the cortical limbic loop that generates the physiology of frustration, the release of a cascade of chemicals throughout my nervous system and the release of hormones directly into the blood stream.

"Isn't it fascinating that you are 30 minutes late to pick up the boss for a trip to the airport?" Or, "Isn't if fascinating that your sales person continues to blame the client rather than take responsibility for a failed result?"

Look at the difference in heart rate patterns between the disruptive state of frustration versus the powerful state of fascination:

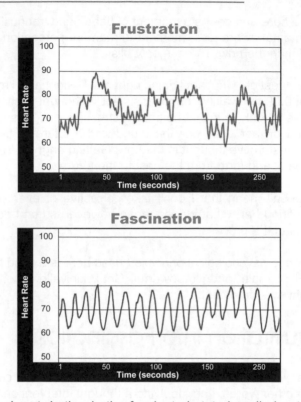

Frustration

Fascination

The heart rhythm in the fascinated state is called entrainment. I did that by using the two mental tricks of staying in the now and simply having the intervention of being fascinated instead of frustrated. It is not what my assistant did that dictates my physiology. Once you realize this and stop giving away your power then you will be very much in control and centered. It is all about you and how you choose to respond that matters. Keep in mind however, that your nervous system is going to resist having you use these two interventions, that's because if you do you will change your neurological wiring and create a new pattern. Remember, you're brain resists change. The way to compete is to make a commitment. Then note how many times you use "stay in the now" and "turn frustration into fascination", and assign a hefty fine as a penalty if you don't make a note for one week.

This simple intervention on your part will pay many dividends back to you. Here's another study for your consideration. Researchers studying 313 healthy Vietnam veterans have found that anger and hostility may increase the risk for cardiovascular disease, diabetes and high blood pressure.

Over a period of 10 years, the men had regular physical examinations involving a variety of medical tests. They also had psychological examinations to determine their levels of hostility, anger and depression.

The researchers measured blood levels of a protein called C3, a marker for the inflammation that is a risk factor for cardiovascular disease.

After controlling for other variables, the scientists found that those in the highest one-quarter in hostility, anger and depression showed a steady and significant increase in C3 levels. Those in the lowest one-quarter had no increase.

"This may put those men at increased risk for hypertension, diabetes and coronary heart disease," said Stephen H. Boyle, the lead author of the study and a researcher at Duke University Medical Center.

Although the exact reasons for these changes are unknown, the authors speculate that anger in hostile and depressed men initiates a series of chemical responses in the immune system that leads to inflammation.

It is essential to take steps to control hostility. "There are interventions that appear to be useful in lowering levels of anger," Boyle said.

Now let's let the neuroscientists have their say as well. Take a look at the following brain cell slices:

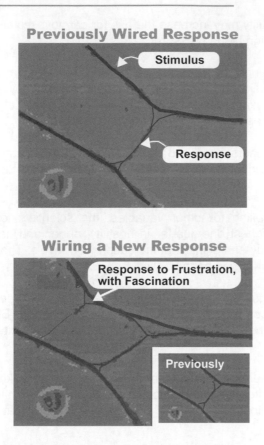

The first slide shows a neuron that gets excited by a stimulus and has an already wired in response. Something happens and you automatically respond in a habitual way. Remember neurons that fire together, wire together. Most people are addicted to being victims and blaming others. It's not good or bad, it's just the way that they have become wired over the years. Now they can't help it. Something happens and they have this well-worn path that leads to the three R's, resentment, resistance, revenge. There is no win to this type of response however.

However, consider the second slide. You have made a decision that you will no longer let others be the source of your emotions. Something happens and this time you have a conscious intervention, "I respond to frustration with fascination". You say this to yourself and you have created a new neurological pathway. You are teaching your brain a new way to respond to an old "trigger". Over time with repetition this new pathway will become stronger and will be reinforced, while the former pathway will deteriorate and eventually be absorbed and disappear. You have now conditioned yourself to respond automatically in a new way.

That's exactly what happened to me with my assistant. It wasn't that I was just a nice guy. It was a result of my commitment to excellence and my understanding that I could influence my own neurological connections, and that I must control what I can control. After several trials of the conscious intervention this became a wired pattern that now happens automatically. I have changed the way that I am wired and so can you. In fact, you must if you are to commit to excellence.

The way that you make this type of a change is to decide to do so, then put it into a behavioral contract by committing to catching yourself becoming frustrated and then shifting to being fascinated and pay a fine if you don't. You can also make a recording of this statement over baroque music, "I respond to frustration with fascination!" Now you'll start to have the same principle as television advertising, forming new neurological pathways of your desired habits instead of "Please don't squeeze the Charmin" or "Fly the friendly skies of United".

Here is another simple explanation of forming new neurological pathways. Imagine that you have a garbage can on the right side of your desk. When you think about throwing something away, (stimulus), you automatically turn to the right without thought. You already have the neurologically wired stimulus response of turning to the right. When you get the stimulus to throw something away you do not need to take up any brainpower to figure out how to do it. You simply subconsciously turn to the right.

Next, move the garbage can to the left side of your desk and notice what happens. Once again you get the stimulus to throw something away and you will automatically fire down the wired pathway of turning to the right to that stimulus. When you do so this time you will become conscious. Your neocortex will fire, the outer most layer of the brain, your conscious mind will be stimulated because the garbage can is not there and you say to yourself, "Oh, I've moved it to the left!" at which time your brain fires the beginning of a new pathway that says turn left to throw something away. You have interrupted a known neuron pattern that is no longer appropriate. That makes you become conscious to the stimulus of "throw something away". After several repetitions of falsely turning to the right at some point in time, you will have atrophied the previous pathway and reinforced the second, turn to the left pathway and the behavior becomes automatic and your brain has rewired itself.

You can create any habit you want. Here are the steps.

1. Make a decision. What do you want?
2. What do you need to do to have what you want?
3. What do you need to do this week?
4. What will you do this week?
5. What attitude or mindset do you need to have to be successful and consistently in action?
6. Put the specific weekly actions into a behavioral contract.

As long as you have a realistic commitment and the consequence for non-performance you will have a high probability of being naturally stimulated and compelled to take the intended actions.

Another question to ask yourself is what habits do you not currently have that would be beneficial to you?

This is all very exciting and confronting however, you don't get to go victim and blame others. You are completely responsible for your own state of mind.

Your current wiring may say otherwise however. You may very well be wired for and addicted to going victim and blaming others. It may very well be your natural default system. The knowledge and scientific proof that you can rewire should be very exciting new information.

Here's an analogy. Imagine that you fly to Las Vegas to play blackjack. This one particular casino is kind enough to label your chances of winning. One table has a sign that says 0% and the other table says 30% to 100%. Which table would you sit at?

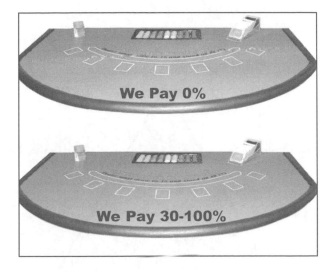

Would you ever sit at the 0% table? Of course not. That's what it's like when you play the victim. There is little to no chance of "winning" when your perspective is to blame someone else or to blame a circumstance or situation. Keep in mind however; that you may have the wiring that releases peptides, dopamine and other feel good chemicals that also draw you into being in the victim mode. However, it is always in your best interest to rewire and to create a more positive addiction, that of taking responsibility and being the source of all that you experience. That's when you'll be at your best.

Ok, let's shift gears and look at performance through another set of eyes. One analogy that I constantly refer to is the triangle of coaching. Essentially, I am your coach as you read this book. My intention is to have the following interaction and impact with you:

Triangle of Coaching

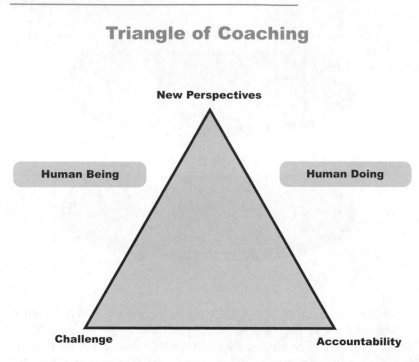

You and I are in an interaction, a conversation if you will, with your reading this book. Out of this conversation arises new perspectives, new ways of looking at yourself and your life because you are engaged with me in this reading. It is also my intention to challenge you and to hold you accountable as best as I can through this book. That is the promise of coaching. This unique relationship will impact you as a human being, your life fulfillment, as well as your "Human Doing", your actions.

At the end of this book I'll have a list of "coaching commandments" or "inquiries". These are statements or questions that I will list for you that I've made or asked throughout the book. These are designed to have a long-term impact for you. They are designed to challenge your thinking on an ongoing basis.

Let's continue our journey and now proceed to look at life through the filter of mathematics.

Chapter 10

The Joy of Thinking
Through Mathematics

*"If one advances confidently in the direction
of his own dreams and endeavors to live the
life which he has imagined, he will meet with
a success unexpected in common hours."*
— Henry David Thoreau

Mathematical thinking is easier then you may believe and it can
also be fun. Familiarity with the concepts that I am about to expose
you to here will expand your power — making your intellect stronger.
I've done all the work of the research and sifting through the
irrelevant, to come up with a simplified version and then relate that to
your everyday life.

Math is a system of conceptual control that allows you to operate more effectively. It's a lot like the concept of time. It allows you to capture an idea, manipulate it, experiment with it, and learn new previously hidden meaning.

Mathematics is an agreed upon language. It's a more precise form of communication however. If I say to you that I'm cold you don't know what I mean. Cold to you if you're on the east coast in the winter might mean 20 degrees, but what I really mean is it's getting down to 60 degrees today in California. This is not the case with the language of numbers. The square root of 4 is 2 in the United States, Russia, and China and on Mars. Math is the unifying language.

The following mathematical insights come from a variety of research in books, articles, and other sources. The applications to human performance are my contribution. The main source of the mathematical concepts comes primarily from two individuals, Professor Edward B. Burger, a professor of Mathematics and Chair of the Department of Mathematics and Statistics at Williams College, and Professor Michael Starbird, a professor of Mathematics and a University Distinguished Teaching Professor at the University of Texas at Austin. These two individuals are absolutely stunning in their ability to take the complicated and make it simple.

Let's begin this journey to increased life fulfillment with this study of Math. Math crosses cultural barriers and transcends the test of time. Math today is the same as math centuries ago. Math ideas just don't age. Most importantly, math provides a way of thinking, a way of understanding and creating ideas, a mindset. Mathematical thinking is about ideas themselves and the way of creating them. Math opens up new perspectives.

In order to understand the world, we measure it. We can see more detail, structure and beauty through a numbers approach. We measure; we count the world to make sense of it. To measure, we developed the concept of the number. To understand the shapes we see in the world, we developed geometry. To face the unknown, we developed the concept of probability.

One of the standard mathematical processes of discovery is to find and identify essential features in the world, and then to think about these ideas in the abstract through the language of math. This process often leads to new ideas, insights and perspectives that in turn reflect back into the real world and make us see things in a way that we hadn't seen before. Math is the great revealer.

Regardless of the area you may want to improve, health, business or your personal life, it will come down to measurement and measurement means numbers! The most successful organizations on the planet embrace measurement. One such company, Select Family of Staffing has this mantra: Measure, Report, Review, Reward. Measurement is king!

"There is no inquiry that is not finally reducible to a question of numbers; for there is none that may not be conceived of as consisting in the determination of quantities by each other, according to certain relations.
— Aguste Comte, 1798-1857, Philosopher

The Study of Numbers

Life is full of numbers and measurements. From the moment we were born the measurements began. The nurse measured our height, weight, time of birth, our parents counted our fingers and toes; numbers have meaning for us throughout our lives.

It is through the observation of numbers that helps us to uncover hidden patterns and structure. When we see the beauty in nature what we are responding to are the subconscious patterns of the hidden structure and order. Our world conforms to the same kind of logical designs that underlies the abstract mathematical reasoning. In fact, it's the other way around. The world was first; our inventions leading to the tools for understanding came next.

One of those tools is calculus. Calculus is all around us. When you throw a baseball and watch where it lands, that's calculus. When you look at the planets and see how they orbit the sun, that's calculus. During the last 300 years when you look at how differently we live now then people did then, most of those differences come from technological differences, and most of those were based in fundamental ways on calculus.

Calculus comes from everyday observations. The fundamental ideas of calculus come from looking at what happens in our lives and thinking about it very clearly. It can be used in a mechanical way. If you follow certain steps, you will get the answer you expect. Engineers and scientists can use the mechanics of calculus to do things that they need to do. Calculus comes from the Greek word calculae, which means stones. Stones were used in the ancient world to count things.

Let me emphasize the statement about the fundamental ideas of calculus.

"If you follow certain steps you will get the answer (result) you expect."

This will be a fundamental theorem of the application of these concepts to your life.

The whole structure of calculus is simply the exploration of two ideas. Calculus deals with change and motion. Calculus allows us to predict what will happen. The Greek philosopher Zeno (c. 495 - c. 430 B.C.) wrote "Paradoxes of Motion" about 2,500 years ago, addressing the paradox of the arrow. Zeno asked the question in what sense is it moving? At every instant, the arrow is at just one place.

Skipping ahead a few thousand years, the person who is most associated with calculus, Isaac Newton (1642-1727), invented the foundations of modern day calculus. His invention was an attempt to put structure to the unknown.

Let's start with the simple concept of counting. Counting is one of the most powerful ideas ever conceived of by human beings. The natural numbers are the building blocks for understanding mathematics and the mysteries in our world. Our premise is to take the complex and break it into the essential smaller, simple components and to observe what you have. This is called reductionism, going from the complex to the simple.

The natural numbers are 1, 2, 3 etc. and the basic properties are that each number is followed by a "next higher" number that is one larger, to infinity.

Numbers have been with us all of our lives. One is the loneliest number. Two arms, eyes, feet, etc. Three, dimensions of space we live in. Four, legs on a dog, table, tires of a car. Five, the number of fingers and toes on each hand and foot. Six, there are six sides of a die. Seven days in a week, etc. Ten is a basis of our number system. Twelve, a dozen eggs, 24 hours in a day, 365 days in a year, these numbers are familiar to us because we see them all the time.

Most natural numbers do not have human association. The universe is 13.7 billion years old. There are 365 days in a year, 24 hours in a day, 60 minutes in an hour, 60 seconds in a minute; these are more familiar uses of numbers.

The universe is about 13,700,000,000 x 365 x 24 x 60 x 60 seconds old. This equals 430,000,000,000,000,000 seconds old. That's 430 quadrillion, or a 43 with 16 zeros. This number has 18 digits.

How does the human mind handle large numbers? What can we do to make the number one million meaningful? One way is to think in terms of familiar collections like the number of people in a large city. The number of pixels, mega, measured in millions.

How much would a million dollars weigh? How would you estimate the weight of a million dollars? Take something familiar, like a ream of paper, each piece of paper is the weight of about 5 one-dollar bills, 1000 pieces of paper = 9 lbs x 200 = 1,800 lbs, almost a ton.

Billions, 6.3 billion people on earth. The age of the earth is 13.7 billion years, 1 gigabyte = 1 billion bites. Here's a quantitative question to put billions into perspective. I love the analogy that Professor Starbird uses about Bill Gates. It is said that during a good year Bill Gates increased his worth by 20 billion dollars. So, if he passed a $100 bill on the street, should he stop and pick it up?[59] Let's figure it out. Consider a 40 hour work week, times 50 weeks, that's 2000 hours, so $20,000,000,000 divided by 2,000 hours = $10,000,000 per hour. $10,000,000 divided by 3,600 seconds in an hour = $2,800 per second, so Bill Gates earns $100 every 0.036 seconds. He should just keep working and not take the time to pick up the $100! I'd pick it up myself!

Let's move on to trillions. Very few numbers are measured in trillions; however, one is the US national debt. Several years ago the national debt was 6.6 trillion dollars. How can we understand this enormous number? It is so large and so far out of our everyday lives that most of us simply don't attempt to understand it.

Taking the trouble to count puts matters into perspective. If we want to experience the world with more precision, more detail, asking "how many" is an excellent strategy to employ. If you are committed to excellence, then not counting is not an option.

Life Application: Everything Counts and Count Everything!

There are lessons from sports that apply to all of our lives.. I may be biased in this area since that was my background, participating in and then coaching college football and wrestling. Many of my fundamental ideas and recommendations had their originations from my mentors in athletics.

Everything is counted! I looked in the sports section of the daily newspaper today and was amazed to see how much is actually measured. In a football game, the score by quarters, the attendance, first downs, rushes-yards, passing, completes, attempts, interceptions, return yards, punts-average, fumbles-lost, penalties-yards, time of possession, individual stats, rushing, passing, receiving. You name it, it's measured!

Most people don't count. They do not and will not measure because they don't want to know the reality of how pathetic their performances really are. They don't want to be "found out". They would rather hide behind excuses, reasons, stories, and rationalizations. It is easier to be a victim than it is to be accountable. Notice that the word itself has "count" in it. Numbers are accountability! The strongest coaches, leaders and managers include "inspect and verify" in their coaching and leadership. They have their clients or employees measure and then report their numbers.

In my personal coaching I start with numbers. I ask the client to rate where they are in terms of results, not compared to someone else, but compared to where they want to be. I have the client place a mark where they rate themselves and then just give me the number, not the story, just the number.

Personal Ratings

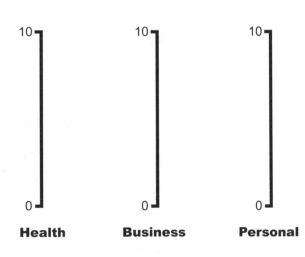

Suppose the client rates themselves as a 6 in health. Then I'll ask the question, "What is the gap from where you are to the next higher number. More of a challenge would be to ask what is an 8?" I'll stay with health as an example of the mathematical application of numbers.

There are some irrefutable numbers associated with an individual making changes in their lives in the area of health. The client tells me that they are committed to lose weight. My first question might be, "How do you know? Do your actions reflect your commitment?"

Our discussion around weight control will start with numbers. There are 3,500 calories in a pound of body fat. Research tells us that the following formula will work for most people:

Your body weight times 10 = the amount of calories you can have on a daily basis without gaining or losing weight. Since there are 3,500 calories in a pound, divide this by 7 days. Subtract that number (500) from the first calculation and that's how many calories you can have as a net total on a daily basis, and you will lose one pound per week. Your net can either be from reduced intake or from intake minus exercise.

Example:

Body weight 190 lbs. X 10 = 1900
3,500 cal/lb divided by 7 = 500
Amount of calories to lose one pound per week: 1400

This sets us up coach and client, for the mathematics involved that we will track. Next comes the system, which is a calorie count form. I'll have the client record every food that they eat and I mean everything. This is counting and accountability. The client will keep a running total of their calories daily and they will know where they are compared to their goals.

One of my coaching commandments for those committed to excellence is "You don't get to not know". People who are committed to excellence don't get to not know. How is your weight control program coming along? You should be able to be very precise in your reply. How's business? Again, how precise of a response can you give? If you are measuring then you can be very precise and you don't get to not know.

It's not my purpose to coach you on weight control in this book however. For that agenda, I'll recommend my Healthy Living album on my website www.bobdavies.com, and then go to Motivational and Learning Tools.

I'm simply using this as an example of the numbers as they are linked to excellence. Regarding the coaching commandment, "You don't get to not know", people of excellence do not tolerate vague generalities. Ask someone who is committed to excellence how they are doing and they can tell you specifically how they are doing and they can document it with numbers.

Any successful business owner is going to know the numbers of their business. They will have a plan and know where they are versus where they forecasted and planned to be. Likewise, any company looking to acquire another company is going to closely scrutinize their financials. Numbers count!

The applications of measurement are widespread and mandatory. As a football coach we measured everything! Take a look at your local newspaper's sports section. You'll see that everything that can be measured — is measured!

Application:
Everything that can be Measured Must be Measured.

Here is another coaching homework assignment that I give to clients who may be stuck in their performances, or simply tell me that they just don't have time to do something. I ask them to measure and track every action that they take for a week. They simply have a calendar and they log in their start time, what they are doing, and their stop time. Their stop time will always be followed by another start time, even if they are sitting in front of the television or in the car on the way to the gym. Even going to bed will have a start and a stop time. Every activity that the person does will be recorded.

This is easy to do and doesn't take much time. However, again, most people will stay as far away from this exercise as they possibly can, they just don't want to know how much time they actually waste.

Here's a fun play with numbers. I received this from an organization that I serve as their corporate coach:

What Is Your Attitude?

IF- A B C D E F G H I J K L M N O P Q R S T U V W X Y Z

Equals 1 2 3 4 5 6 7 8 9 10 11 12 13 14 15 16 17 18 19 20 21
22 23 24 25 26   *(as in a=1 b=2 c=3 d=4 etc.)*

Then:

K+N+O+W+L+E+D+G+E
11+14+15+23+12+5+4+7+5 = 96 %

H+A+R+D+W+O+R+K
8+1+18+4+23+15+18+11 = 98 %

Both are important, but the total falls just short of that 100 % figure.

HOWEVER:

A+T+T+I+T+U+D+E
1+20+20+9+20+21+4+5 = 100 %

What is your attitude?

REMEMBER ...WE CREATE our own reality, with the way we think, speak and act. Make sure your ATTITUDE is correct... As it WILL Design your Life!

Chapter 11

The Concept
of Limitations

*"There is no failure except in no longer trying.
There is no defeat except from within, no really
insurmountable barrier save our own inherent
weakness of purpose."* — Elbert Hubbard

Human beings are poor observers. You and I have no idea of what our true limitations are so we make it up and believe our stories as true.

Consider the normal number line:

Number Line

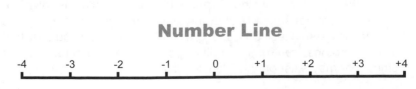

There is the center at zero and the line extends to infinity in two directions, positive and negative. Let's look further at a small segment of the line, the distance between 0 and +1.

Mathematical Concept of Limits

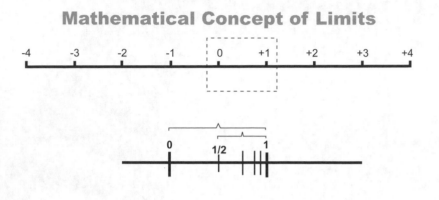

0.99999999999999999999999999999999999999999

You can take one half of the distance from zero to one, and then one half of that distance and one half of that distance to infinity and theoretically never reach the number one.[60]

Chopping the micrometer into a thousand nanometers, and the nanometers into a thousand picometers, and those in steps of a thousand fold into femtometers, attometers, zeptometers, and yoctometers. At this point, 10 to the minus 24 meters, about one-billionth the radius of a proton, the roster of convenient Greek names runs out. But you can still go ahead and keep dividing, again and again until you reach a length of only a hundred-billionth as large as that tiny amount: 10 to the minus 35 meters, or a decimal point followed by 34 zeroes and then a one.[61] Then you would have almost hit bottom. This is a span called the Planck length, the shortest anything can get.

According to recent developments in the quest to devise a so-called "theory of everything", space is not an infinitely divisible continuum. It is not smooth but granular, and the Planck length gives the size of its smallest possible grains. Even the tiny quarks that make up protons, neutrons and other particles are too big to feel the bumps that may exist on the Planck scale.

More recently though, physicists have suggested that quarks and everything else are made of far tinier objects; superstrings vibrating in 10 dimensions.

In the 1950's, the physicist John Wheeler suggested that the Planck length marked the boundary where the random of quantum mechanics scrambled space and time so violently that ordinary notions of measurement stopped making sense. He called the result "quantum foam". "So great would be the fluctuations that there would literally be no left and right, no before and no after", Dr. Wheeler recently wrote in his memoir, "Geons, Black Holes and Quantum Foam" (Norton, 1998). Ordinary ideas of length would disappear. Ordinary ideas of time would evaporate.

Half a century later, physicists are still trying to work out the bizarre implications of minimum length. Suffice it to say that humans with our limited perceptual abilities cannot comprehend this level of measurement and we can't understand the concept of infinity. Therefore, in our attempt to give meaning to our world and to function without noticing this gap in understanding, we use agreement.

Agreements

Agreements are everywhere. As you are driving the light turns green. You look off to the left and a car is still approaching the intersection which you know now has a red light. You continue to drive on because you live in a society that agrees that the car with the red light will stop and the green light means go. If someone breaks this agreement then chaos occurs and there are appropriate penalties. Agreements are a part of civil societies.

Back to the number line, and the infinite increments of the taking 1/2 of the distance between zero and one. At some point in time scientists will agree that we have arrived at .099999999 of the number one and we will begin to count towards number two. Is it real? No, but an agreement has been made. Once you reach the Planck scale everything is indivisible and everything is all merged together so the notion of another division is an illusion, but we agree and continue on.

We look at a wall and agree that we will all view it as a solid. Einstein would be the first one to tell you that the wall in not solid. He would say that there is more space in that wall then there is matter. He would say that the particles are in such a fast frequency of motion that goes beyond our perceptual ability that we see it as a solid. We agree that the wall is solid. This agreement is based on a false assumption, but we all buy into it nevertheless. Again, Einstein would tell us that the wall is a collection of particles that are in such a fast constant state of motion, energy, that with our limited perception we see it as a solid.

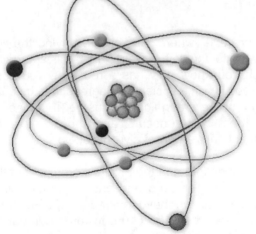

You have no idea of what your limitations are, so you make it up. I do an exercise in my live training. I have the audience partner up, A and B, and A stands about a foot away from the wall with their right shoulder perpendicular to the wall. With their toes pointed straight ahead, they take their left arm and twist across their body, keeping their toes straight, twisting and reaching as far as they possibly can and touch a spot on the wall. Their partner marks the spot.

Next they return to face the front and close their eyes. This time I ask them to visualize twisting again, reaching as far as they can, but I want them to see themselves blasting through their previous spot. People are amazed at how easy it is for them to blast through what they previously thought was their limit.

I can remember when I first experienced this exercise. I twisted as far as I thought I could go. My back hurt. I believed that I was at my limit. Then I visualized and tested again and was amazed at blasting through my spot that I previously accepted as being my true limit and at how easy and effortless it was. Also, my back didn't have any pain on the retest. This has to do with several issues such as the physiology of visualization, the power of intentions, etc., much of which will be covered later.

The question to ask yourself is what limits are you buying into? What lies do you believe as true? Where are you living your life in resignation, believing that you are doing the best that you can? All lies! By the way, do dogs love bones? The answer is no, they love meat but they settle for bones! Don't settle. Read on.

I had a coaching client who was absolutely convinced that he was at the lowest limit for weight control. He charted his intake, exercised consistently and was convinced that he was at the lowest weight that he could possibly be, given the changes in his metabolism, muscularity, etc. That is until his belief was shattered by a root canal!

He had a low calorie ice cream and thought he was going to die. The pain in his lower jaw was so great, he immediately stopped eating. It took a day before he could see his dentist, his root canal was followed by another visit, and the pulling of a different tooth. He went several days with pain and discomfort and noticed a drop in his weight! His belief of what was possible was shattered!

Chapter 12

Math Continued — Some Hidden Secrets of Mother Nature Revealed

If we seek patterns, we will find them everywhere. When we find them, a unique structure emerges, and all of a sudden things that up to this point appeared invisible, come into focus. What I'm about to point out may change the way you shop forever! The next time you are in a grocery store, stop, look, and observe the external patterns of a pineapple or take a good look at the next pinecone you see on the ground.[62]

Spiral Patterns in Nature

A special collection of numbers is around us all of the time. A pineapple has structure, lots of it! On the face of the pineapple you'll see spirals. Look closer and you will see more details of a design; you'll see the spirals go in opposite directions. There are 8 spirals one-way, 13 the other. Spirals are everywhere in nature. A coneflower has 13 spirals one-way and 21 the other. Look at the pattern: 8 13 21

The middle portion of a daisy flower has 21 spirals in one direction, and 34 in the other direction. The pattern continues: 8 13 21 34. I haven't mentioned a pinecone, but we'll add that. Is there a pattern that nature is trying to reveal to us?

5 (pine cone)
8 (pineapple)/(pine cone)
13 (pineapple)/(Cone Flower)
21 (daisy)/(cone flower)
34 (daisy)

You can find spirals in all sorts of things. There are so many coincidences that we start to wonder if there is a hidden structure.[63] Look at the spiral of the human ear. Spirals are everywhere.

Human Ear

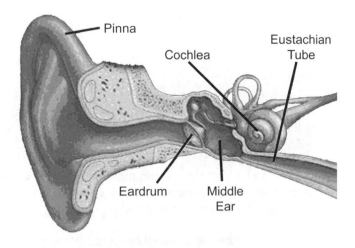

Spiral of a Galaxy

Let's look at the sequence of numbers that we have collected:

5 8 13 21 34

This is the number pattern that nature is displaying. Mathematics teaches us to look for the hidden structure. You start by asking questions about the relationship between the numbers.[64] We start to notice that if you add the preceding number to the current number, the result is the next number in the sequence.

5 + 8 = 13

8 + 13 = 21

13 + 21 = 34

Go from nature to the abstract world of mathematics. If we just continue this pattern we would take the 21 + 34 and add them to get 55, 34 + 55 = 89 and so on.

Once we see the pattern, we can move forwards or backwards in the pattern. The pattern is revealing the structure that has always been there but has been invisible to us.

The number before the 5 would have to be a number that when you add it to 5 you'll get 8, so it must be 3 and what must come before that 3+? = 5

It's a number that I add to 3 to make 5, 2 etc. This is simple I know. Notice the way of thinking however. Also notice the questions that are being asked. Notice how discovery and observations are being made.

5 + 3 = 8
3 + 2 = 5
2 + 1 = 3
1 + 1 = 2

Natures' Number Sequence

1, 1, 2, 3, 5, 8, 13, 21, 34, 55, 89, 144, etc.

Nature is reflecting this simple pattern. Take this abstract discovery and ask how does this relate to me in the everyday world?

You can predict the world in a natural way. You can predict the spiral count patterns of a larger flower than you currently see, perhaps a 34 and 55 pattern. The structure that was there all the time now comes into focus.

Consider composite flowers. Every single component is its own flower, coming together to make a composite flower. Growth occurs from the center and then moves out to the boundary as the newer parts of the flower grows.

Consider this in the familiar vegetable broccoli. If you break a bunch of broccoli in half the remaining half has the same structure of what you just took away. As you continue to take smaller and smaller bits of the whole, what you have left continues to remain a pattern that is identical in structure to the whole.

These numbers in mathematics are called the Fibonacci numbers, named after 13th century mathematician Leonardo de Pisa Fibonacci.

Leonardo de Pisa Fibonacci

It's the Fibonacci Sequence nature has encoded in its spirals. Nature came first, it took quite some time for mankind to see the pattern, but the pattern has always existed.

Not all of the natural numbers are on the list. You don't see, 4, 6, 7 etc.

1, 1, 2, 3, 5, 8, 13, 21, 34, 55, 89, 144, etc.

The Fibonacci Sequence was discovered through observations and noticing the mistakes that were made. The first mistake made by mathematicians was the theory that the numbers doubled. Notice that an observation is made and then tested. The doubling theory held true for 1, but that was it. The theory failed, but that didn't stop the scholars. They kept on failing until they hit upon the true nature of the sequence. Another good lesson about failure is fail until you succeed!

There are real life lessons in terms of thinking beyond mathematics. There is a purpose to making mistakes. Mistakes build insight into what you are focusing on.

1, 1, 2, 3, 5, 8, 13, 21, 34, 55, 89, 144, etc. Fibonacci Sequence

Look at the nature of the numbers themselves, just observe. The first thing you see is that they are getting bigger. How are they growing? They are not doubling. Celebrate and look deeper into the issue. Feel good because you have taken an action or asked a question.

Notice 3 is not quite 2x2= 4 the difference is 1.
The number 5 is not quite 2x3 = 6 the difference is 1.
8 is not quite 2x5=10 the difference is 2.
13 is not quite 2x8=16 the difference 3.

As you look at differences, you see a pattern.

21 is not quite 2x13= 26 the difference is 5.

The differences are the Fibonacci numbers themselves; again, through failure another part of the structure is uncovered. To find the next Fibonacci number you take two times the previous number and subtract the number that comes two before the starting number = the next Fibonacci number...

13 x 2 = 26 - 5 = 21

Making a mistake fuels discovery. The mistake was thinking that the numbers doubled. Take the risk, have a theory, evaluate and observe.

The application that I see here is that failure is a part of learning. It is only through failure that the correct path is discovered. It is through failure that the worlds' greatest discoveries have come to be.

You have to have enough failure to have your successes. If you are not failing, you are not following natures' principles. This means that you need to be able to take action in the face of the projections of your fears. Almost always the fears are not true, but they won't step aside unless you take action.

I know you've heard this a thousand times. However, I like the analogy of nature and mathematics to give this new meaning and application in your life.

I am a speaker. I need to find out the numbers. How many meeting planners need to be contacted until I can find one that is interested in considering me for their convention as a general session or keynote speaker and will request my press kit? The next number in the sequence will tell me how many demo links need to be emailed to meeting planners to have one actually hire me to speak at their function.

Once I know the ratios, then the sequence can be predicted just like the Fibonacci numbers enable you to know the number that you cannot yet see. Once you understand the hidden structure of the pattern, you can apply it to solve your problems.

How much income do I want to generate through the stream of convention speaking? Just for an example, let's say its $100,000. At a speaking fee of $10,000 plus travel, (example purposes only), that would be 10 speaking engagements. Let's say it takes 10 meeting planners to see my materials and videos for one to hire me. It also takes 100 calls to find the 10 that are interested to get the one hire.

100 Calls
10 Demos sent
1 Speaking engagement.

If my goal is 10 speaking engagements then that means that my telemarketer needs to make 1000 calls, or more specifically contacts, where she is actually presenting what I do to the decision maker. This adds another element of measurement. How many dials does she have to make to get 100 contacts? Maybe that number is 10,000 dials to get 100 presentations, resulting in 10 packages being sent resulting in 1 booking. Do the math.

If you've been in a performance oriented field for any length of time I know you've heard this before. However, I find it to be very fascinating to see how math supports the measurement of patterns and numbers. Once you see what the ratios are, then all you need to do is get to work. If my telemarketer needs to dial 10,000 times to talk to 100 people, that's a lot of failure. She has got to have enough failure to reach her targets.

These ratios do follow nature's principles. Every industry has their ratios and measurements. The financial services industry has the ratio that you need to have 10 contacts, to set 3 appointments, to have 1 sale.

Is the person hitting their numbers? Are they measuring? It really is as simple as revealing what the sequence is, seeing the pattern, and then executing the pattern. If you can't stomach the numbers, either hire someone to do it or get out of the business! These ratios must be hit whether it's through your own efforts or someone else's. More on this when we examine the physics application, Action — Reaction!

It is a mathematical certainty that once you reveal your industry ratios, executing the numbers and enough failures will bring you your success!

More interesting information on comparing Fibonacci numbers is seeing how they are compared to each other. Math enables you to look at issues from several points of view and often the different vantage points reveals hidden structure.

Look at how the numbers are growing in relation to each other. This is another life thinking strategy, to look at issues from several points of view. Once you have one perspective, it is very revealing to look at the same set of circumstances from a different point of view to reveal hidden structure. When we talk about multiple realities and quantum physics you'll see that there are a multitude of perspectives available. Why would someone select a perspective that makes them upset? The answer is because it's just as easy to be a victim and blame someone else, as it is to take responsibility.

This is classically illustrated in the conversation of whether a curved line is concave or convex. Of course your answer depends on your perspective, on how you are looking at the line. This concept has helped many people to reduce potential frustrating situations by taking the perspective of the "opposite" point of view.

Back to the Fibonacci numbers, another point of view would be dividing one number by the one that precedes it and look to see if there is a pattern. Again, being curious and looking at the possibilities of new relationships may reveal new or hidden information and essential patterns.

Fibonacci Sequence

1, 1, 2, 3, 5, 8, 13, 21, 34, 55, 89, 144, ...

2 divided by 1 = 2.0
3 divided by 2 = 1.5
5 divided by 3 = 1.6666
8 divided by 5 = 1.6
13 divided by 8 = 1.625
21 divided by 13 = 1.6153846
89 divided by 55 = 1.6181818
1597 divided by 987 = 1.61800344
2584 divided by 1597 = 1.6180338

As you move on the list the numbers converge on the number 1.61803. What is going on with this phenomenon? There is an amazing formula that relates to the Fibonacci numbers.

It won't serve our purpose to go into the evolution of this formula, so let's take it on face value that the Fibonacci sequence of numbers follows this relationship of hidden structure:

$$\gamma = \frac{1 + \sqrt{5}}{2} \approx 1.6180339887 \ldots$$

Phi = 1 + square root of 5 over 2 = 1.618033989...goes on forever. This is a defining trait. This number is called the Golden

Ratio. This is an extremely famous number. It shows up constantly in geometry, art and architecture. One plus the square root of 5 over 2!

The realization is that if you have any kind of recurring sequence no matter which two starting numbers, you will always get the golden ratio. It doesn't matter what the numbers are, it's the process. If you just adopt the process then the results conform. Just like if I follow my instruments in the clouds, I will get the predicted result regardless of my not being able to "see" where I'm going. If I execute the numbers in my business, the results will result in sales and revenue. The pattern performs due to the hidden structure resulting in the Golden Ratio.

There is actually beauty in the Fibonacci numbers.

Sir Francis Bacon said, "Truth comes out of error more easily than out of confusion." There is power in making mistakes.

Let's look at geometry and see if there are reflections of the Golden Ratio there. Consider beauty as a mathematical possibility.

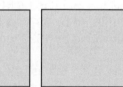

Which one of these captures your attention? For most people, it's the last rectangle on the right. That rectangle is called the Golden Rectangle. This is related to the Golden Ratio. Take the length of the base divided by the length of the height and that will give you the Golden Ratio.

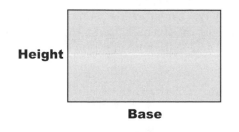

Height

Base

$$\frac{\text{Base}}{\text{Height}} = \text{Golden Ratio} = \frac{1 + \sqrt{5}}{2} \approx 1.61803$$

We see this all the time. The dimensions of an index card 3x5, which are Fibonacci numbers, the Golden Ratio.

Examples of the golden rectangle are seen with the ancient Greeks, the Parthenon is a golden rectangle. Is it coincidence, random, or on purpose? No one knows for sure.

Parthernon

Move ahead in history to the Renaissance, Leonardo da Vinci used the Golden Rectangle in his art. You can see the Golden Rectangle in his paintings. We don't know if this ratio was used consciously or if it just appeared in the art. It doesn't matter. Move forward to modern times, architecture incorporates the Golden Rectangle concept.

Leonardo da Vinci explored the human body involving in the ratios of the lengths of various body parts. He also called this ratio the "Divine Proportion" and featured it in many of his paintings.[65]

The Golden Rectangle is proposed to be the most aesthetically pleasing of all possible rectangles. For this reason, it and the Golden Ratio have been used extensively in art and architecture for thousands of years. The most prominent and well-known uses of the Golden Rectangle in art, were created by the great Italian artist, inventor, and mathematician, Leonardo da Vinci.

"The Mona Lisa," indisputably Leonardo's most famous painting, is full of Golden Rectangles. If you draw a rectangle whose base extends from the woman's right wrist to her left elbow and extend the rectangle vertically until it reaches the very top of her head, you will have a Golden Rectangle. Then, if you draw squares inside this Golden Rectangle you will discover that the edges of these new squares come to all the important focal points of the woman: her chin, her eye, her nose, and the upturned corner of her mouth. It is believed that Leonardo, as a mathematician, purposefully made this painting line up with Golden Rectangles in this fashion in order to further the incorporation of mathematics into art. In the spirit of mathematics in art, it is also worth mentioning that the overall shape of the woman is a triangle with her arms as the base and her head as the tip. This is meant to draw attention to the face of the woman in the portrait.

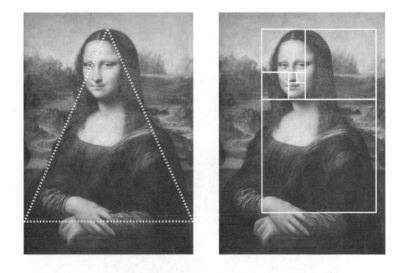

The Golden Section, also known as Phi, is manifested in the structure of the human body. If the length of the hand has the value of 1 for instance, then the combined length of hand + forearm has the approximate value of Phi. Similarly the proportion of upper arm to hand + forearm is in the same ratio of 1: Phi.

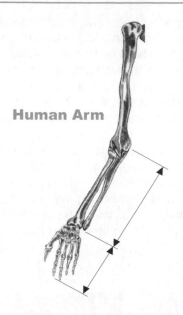

Human Arm

The human face abounds with examples of the Golden Section. The head forms a golden rectangle with the eyes at its midpoint. The mouth and nose are each placed at golden sections of the distance between the eyes and the bottom of the chin. Phi defines the dimensions of the human profile. Even when viewed from the side, the human head illustrates the Golden Proportion.

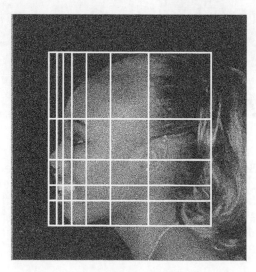

You can build one of these using the techniques of the Greeks. Start with a perfect square; use a straight edge and a compass. Use a compass and make a line from the midpoint to the corner of the square. The specifics of the construction are not what I want to emphasize. My emphasis is that there is a formula that anyone can use to reproduce the ratios of the Golden Rectangle as seen below.

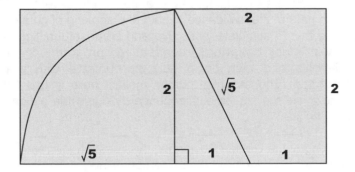

Base over height = 1 + square roof of 5 over 2 (the Golden Ratio)

The triangle in the square is also referred to as the Golden Triangle; the height is twice the base. I won't go into the ramifications of this, other to say that there are further observations that can be made and more hidden patterns that can be revealed. There is a regeneration process here. {Stay with me. Watch your internal dialogue, what you are saying to yourself. Keep reading and don't get bogged down with "understanding"}

Calude Debussy, (sounds like day- bu- cee), was fascinated with the concept of the Golden Ratio and tried to capture this in his musical work. The musical pulses of one of his songs, "Prelude to the Afternoon of Faun", known as Quaver units, display the Fibonacci numbers in action as the ratios of the music conform. It builds in intensity then gradually descends. The buildup in time is 81 seconds; the entire piece is 129 sec, if you divide 129 by 81 you get 1.59259 which is very close to the golden ratio of 1.61803.

Take the complicated issue and whittle it down to find the critical feature. Seeking the essential, will lead to incredible discovery. This also will lead to confidence in making decisions. If I know that I can trust the mathematics of the numbers of my business, then I can make manpower decisions and I can predict the cost to benefit ratios. If business is slow I might first be inclined to cut back on expenses. However, keeping numbers in mind, I might want to hire more people to increase the "output" and get the ratios that I know will be predictors of successful outcomes, regardless of the marketplace.

Math also tells me that if I pay attention to the essential element of human nature, the avoidance of pain and seeking of comfort, then I can use that to stimulate instinctive and purposeful action. This is done with the behavioral contracting program of making commitments and then being held accountable with a painful consequence. (The essential human instinct here is that I will be driven to avoid the fine or consequence by doing the action that is linked to it.)

Looking at the Golden Rectangle, the question still remains as to why we find the Golden Rectangle so appealing.

It turns out that when you extend the perfect square to make the Golden Rectangle, you are actually adding another Golden Rectangle. If you keep cutting it in half what you are left with is still a Golden Rectangle. No other rectangle has this property.

If you keep cutting it in half what you get is a spiral called the Logarithmic Spiral. Look at the Nautilus Shell. Nature conforms to this Golden Rectangle math.

Nautilus Shell

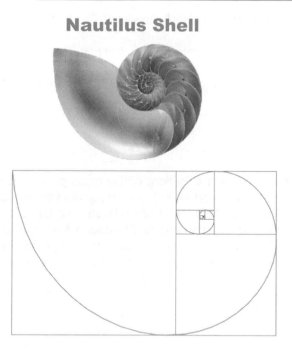

The essential feature of the Golden Rectangle is that is has this regeneration property. If you cut off the largest portion of the square, the remaining rectangle is in fact another example of a Golden Rectangle. An essential feature that only the Golden Rectangle possesses.

The dimensions of the palm of your hand should conform to the Golden Ratio. Nature again prevails![66]

The spirals in nature are very interesting. It definitely gives credence to the philosophy that I have always had, that science and religion start off from different perspectives but eventually meet and are one.

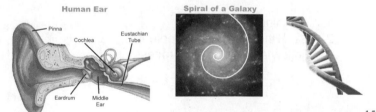

Human Ear — Pinna — Cochlea — Eustachian Tube — Eardrum — Middle Ear

Spiral of a Galaxy

Some mathematical life lessons:

1. Look for the essence of things.
   a. Ask why is something true?
   b. Ask what is the essential feature that makes a property true?
2. Take a complicated situation and first investigate a simple reflection of it.

The business applications of this concept are widespread. I have a desire to use my one-day program as an event for fundraising. The potential marketplace for this is so large it would be paralyzing! "Take a complicated situation and first investigate a simple reflection of it." Rather than even consider the nationwide aspects of this project, the application of this concept would lead me to focus on simply running one fundraiser for one local organization. Once the pattern or sequence is established, then the implementation of it on a larger scale is a simple process.

This is like the Fibonacci numbers. Once you understand the relationships between the numbers, you can predict with absolute certainty future numbers thru to infinity! In other words, once I have the fund-raising formula identified, I can run as many of these as I want to at the same time, with predicable results.

It may seem like an overwhelming task to get all of the new regions of an acquired company up to speed on using your new customer service software programs, but if you find the essential features of the transition, reduce it to the simple, such as one region at a time, an overwhelming task can be made easy.

Look at something you know and see if you can find some unexpected pattern. If you do find it, then you seek a reason.

Mathematics tells us:

1. Try things and fail
2. Seek the essential ingredients
3. Follow a construction process

Chapter 13

The Lesson of
Paper Folds

*"I've had a good life. I would not change
much but, if anything, I think
I would have gone for bigger deals."*
— J. Paul Getty *(On his death bed)*

Strategies of Thinking:

1. Look at simple circumstances.
2. Explore the consequences of a simple repeated process.
3. Look for patterns. (Through repetition structure appears)

Exercise: Take an 8 ½ by 11-inch sheet of regular copy paper and keep folding it in half. Hold the paper in front of you so the 11-inch side is horizontal, and keep folding from the right to the left each time. How many times can you do it? Can anyone do 7? Most likely only 6.

Unfold, a chaotic piece of paper simply wrinkled. What you have looks like a random, chaotic unstructured mess. However, let's take a closer look at this and apply some of the thinking strategies already mentioned. Take another blank sheet of paper 8 ½ x 11-inch again and this time hold it with the 8 ½ side horizontal. Fold about one inch from the right and separate the fold. Now holding it with the 11-inch side horizontal, let's take a smaller, more simplified approach to see if there is structure in the bigger mass of confusion. Fold the one-inch strip once from right to left. Open it up and observe. You will see two types of folds, a downward-valley, and upward-ridge.

Take another one-inch strip and again fold, this time make two folds. Open it up and what do you observe?

Side View of Folded Paper

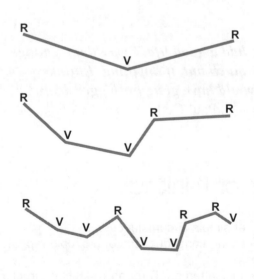

R - Ridge   V - Valley

The paper folding sequence;

- R V R One fold: ridge, valley, ridge
- R V V R R Two folds: ridge, valley, valley, ridge, ridge
- R V V R V V R R V Three folds: ridge, valley, valley, ridge, valley, valley, ridge, ridge, valley
- R V V R V V R R V V V R R V R R Four folds

Structure:

Everything begins with a ridge followed by a valley, everything always starts with ridge, any one level the beginning of that level is precisely the previous level.

R V
R V V R
R V V R V V R R
R V V R V V R R V V V R R V R R

The first half of the next sequence would be exactly what's up top. Once we see structure, other patterns come into focus.

After the previous folds occur, then what follows next is a valley. Another observation is the first new structure you add is always a valley and then some other stuff.

A ridge is just a valley inverted...go to the second sheet and fold it back down over itself showing the ridge becoming a valley, then unfold to go back to a ridge.

Flip the previous layer over, add a center V and flip the front side upside down.

6 fold. Write down what you would have for a 5, put the center V and then flip over the 5 and keep reading.

We can only fold 7 times. Now we can tell what would happen beyond our physical reality. You can tell the precise sequence of folds indefinitely!

We can do that because we found the pattern. Let's look for more patterns.

Another piece of structure is that you have an alternating structure. If you spread it out you'll see that you start with a valley, then it repeats to a valley ridge, and keeps inserting the alternating structure.

V

V   V   R

V   V   R   V   V   R   V   V

V   V   R   V   V   R   R   V   V   V   R   R   V   R   R

Every other fold is an alternating sequence, start with chaos and then see the pattern.

This is not a math book, but I want to expose you to these mathematical concepts for the sole purpose of exposure. It is neither relevant nor important for you to understand the concepts. The only thing that matters is that you get a sense for the complexity and yet the simplicity of the world we live in, and have some new perspectives because you were exposed to these concepts. I want to show you some of the science that underlies my recommendations for improved performance.

That being said, there is a repeating pattern and here is the math:

$F(X) = f1x + f2x2 + f3x3... = Sum fnx$"

An example of what is called a Power Series has a sequence.

Then F (x) = F (x squared) = x over 1 - x fourth

Patterns in Chaos

Valley
Ridge

Out of chaos, order and structure emerge, if you look for them. Patterns enable predictability.

This chaos of a mass of folds that looks like nothing to the untrained eye actually reveals a precise sequence when science and math are applied. There is order and patterns in what looks like chaos to most. The math above may not make any sense to you at all, but to my friends at Cal Tech in Pasadena, it is the language of perfect order.

Strategies of thinking:

1. Look at the opposite of the question that we're actually interested in considering. Remember concave versus convex perspectives.
2. Exaggerate things. Many times the essential element or key structure is revealed through exaggeration.

Looking at the opposite of the question is another way of saying "challenge your perceptions." Exaggerating things is a way of "stretching" your current perception to a new perception.

Probability

The laws of probability are not always in alignment with logic and in fact many times are in direct conflict with logical thought. For example, what do you think the probability is, that within any group of people two individuals will have the same birthday? With 365 days in a year, you might think it would be reasonable to expect the group size to need to be about half of that, 183, to provide a fifty-fifty chance of a birthday match. I'm referring to date, not year. The reality is that you only need 23 people. Now that defies logic.

Try this at your next gathering. Ask each person to state his or her birthday, one at a time. With more then 23 people a match is almost guaranteed. This is another example that you just can't trust human perception.

Here is another mindbender that will also illustrate the clarity from exaggeration. This one gained popularity in the mid-1990's and was a real torment for a lot of math minded folks.

Consider the TV show Let's Make a Deal with Monty Hall as the host. The contestant would be presented with 3 doors. Behind one of these doors is a fancy car. The guest picks a door number, say #1. However, Monty doesn't open the door picked. Instead he opens another door to show a different prize, door 3 had a gag prize.[67]

Then he asks, would you like to stay with your original guess or would you prefer to switch and take door number 2? There are two doors and the car is behind one. What are the probabilities?

That's the circumstance. Now the question: Is the contestant's best move to switch, or does it not matter? How many times would you win the car if you stuck to your original choice, or switched?

Logic number 1: At this moment two doors remain, the desired prize is behind one of them. This would make the chance of either door being correct fifty-fifty. Therefore, it doesn't matter whether the contestant changes or not. Since they would simply be guessing one door is as good as the other. That seems reasonable, right?

Remember my coaching; the lowest level of human consciousness is being reasonable, so when you're turning to reason, be careful.

Consider the alternative perspective. That is my teaching after all isn't it?

Logic number 2: When the first door was selected there was a one-in-three chance of getting the correct door. This means that there was a two-in-three chance that the car was behind one of the other doors.

When Monty opens the goat door, the booby prize, the two-in-three probability went solely to the unopened door that the contestant did not choose. There's still only a one-in-three chance that the first selection is correct. You must conclude that the contestant doubles her chance of **winning by switching doors**.

Both of these thought processes seem to be irrefutable logic yet they reach opposite conclusions and only one decision can be right, stay, or switch doors. When computer programs were run on this dilemma, the results proved that logic number (2) is correct. The contestant will win the car twice as often by switching doors.

Here is another way to gain clarity and insight. Exaggerate the situation by adding three more doors and open them all, check your intuition. Do you still feel that there is an equal chance that the car is behind either door? Let's exaggerate more, say there are 100 doors, pick your favorite, you pick 37, he opens all the doors except for 1 and yours, door 37 the one you picked and 67, the door he still leaves closed. Exaggerate more, one billion doors, you choose a number.

He opens all but one door and yours. Should you switch or stick? Now what does your intuition tell you?

After Monty opens all the millions of doors except for yours and one other, it seems clear you should switch. Can we measure this? Think of the opposite, what is the chance you got the car right on your first guess 1 out of 1 billion? Suppose you were incorrect and you switch, you get a car. Your odds are 1 over 999,999,999 if you switch. Now revert back to the easier case, two doors left, should you switch or stay?

You picked door 1 and Monty opened door 3 showing the gag prize.

What's the chance that you missed the first time? 2 out of 3.

Therefore, if you switch you have a two out of three chance of winning the car. (2/3)

If you stick, you only have a one out of three chance (1/3).

This Monty Hall problem as it has been called, has stumped many a great mathematician. My only purpose for presenting it here is to emphasize the thinking pattern of "exaggerate the conditions" to gain clarity.

A life application is to apply this to making decisions particularly ones that involve change. Let's say you are thinking about changing careers. I'll use the principle of exaggeration in my coaching with you by asking this question; what is the worst possible outcome that can happen if you change careers? Can you live with this? If you can then put it out of your mind and focus on the success.

I personally applied this principle when I quit coaching in 1983 to start my speaking and training company. The worst that could happen was that I would have failed in business. I looked at my options, and yes I could make myself better off with some choices that I had to get back into coaching. Since I could live with the worst that could happen I dismissed it, and focused on being successful and never looked back.

Top 10 List of life lessons[68] from math.

1. Just do it. From where we are, we cannot see a complete solution. By merely taking an action we gain insights that oftentimes become our guide to an imaginative solution. {It's the starting that stops most people}
2. Make mistakes and fail, but never give up. Everyone who does something creative and bold will make mistakes. No one who has ever done anything of great value without making mistakes. The key is to use that insight from the mistake to see more clearly what features that a correct solution has to have.

Fibonacci numbers, doubling, etc. How fast are the numbers growing? That mistake led to the correct formula of the relationship, the Golden Ratio. Mistakes have led to many great products or technologies that have made life easier and more productive, from paper stick-em pads to major medical breakthroughs.

3. Keep an open mind. We must consider possibilities that seem foreign to us. Be willing to consider ideas that lie outside of our initial experience. You wouldn't think of asking the question unless you were open-minded enough to think that the world is a little different than what you would actually expect and currently experience. Explore the consequences of new ideas. The way to think of new thoughts is to see where an idea leads.
4. Seek the essential. One of the biggest obstacles in solving world problems is the noise and clutter of irrelevant issues that surround them. An excellent guide to discovery is to take a complicated situation and ask, what is the essential element that lies right at the crux of this situation? Seeking the essential forces us to focus on the real issue rather than being distracted by debris and clutter. (Remember the

six pens and OTTFFSS examples.)
5. Understand the issue. Know what problem you are trying to solve.
6. Understand simple things deeply. The familiar understood deeply is the best guide to revealing understanding of the unknown.
7. Break a difficult problem into easier and more manageable ones.
8. Examine issues from several points of view. (Exaggerate the representation of the problem —billions of doors in the Monty Hall problem.)
9. Look for patterns and similarities.
10. Explore the consequences of new ideas. Be aggressive and ask the question, what would happen if? This is an ever expanding strategy that results in the possibility of new learning.

The further we travel, the more we see over the emerging horizon. The more we discover, the more we understand what we've already seen.

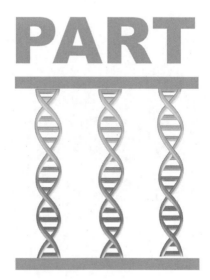

The Theory of Everything
— The Science of it All
— Physics

*"Man sit in chair for long time with open mouth
waiting for roast duck to fly in."*
— Confucius

Chapter 14

Physics

"Happiness lies in the thrill of creative effort and the joy of achievement."
— Franklin D. Roosevelt

We've looked at mathematics and have seen interesting data that enables you to appreciate human nature and human potential from a whole new perspective. Now let's see what meaning we can make from Physics.

Physics (Greek: (phúsis), "nature" and (phusiké), "knowledge of nature") is the branch of science concerned with discovering and characterizing universal laws that govern matter, energy, space, and time. Discoveries in physics resonate throughout the natural sciences, and physics has been described as the "fundamental science" because other fields such as chemistry and biology investigate systems whose properties depend on and are influenced by the laws of physics.

The development of physics as a science that was distinct from natural philosophy began with the scientific revolution of the 16th and 17th centuries, and continued through the birth of modern physics in the early 20th century. The field has continued to expand, with a growing body of research leading to discoveries such as the standard model of fundamental particles and a detailed history of the universe, along with revolutionary new technologies like nuclear energy, semiconductors and more.

Research today progresses on a variety of topics, including high-temperature superconductivity, quantum computing, the search for the Higgs Boson[69] , and the attempt to develop a theory of quantum gravity. Grounded in observations and experiments and supported by deep, far-reaching theories, physics has made a multitude of contributions to science, technology, philosophy and our quality of life.

Physics is the subject that describes our physical environment, from the smallest subatomic particles to the entire universe. Our basic ideas of time, space and what it means to be rigid and solid are all in some way compromised, modified, extended or enriched by the ideas of modern physics.

Physics is the essence of the physical universe. The laws of physics underlie everything that goes on in the world. Physics as a subject divides into two very broad classes. Classical physics was discovered before 1900, which is still applicable to most everyday phenomena such as driving a car, engineering a building, launching a satellite to Jupiter, generating electric power, predicting weather, etc.

Modern physics has been developed in the twentieth century and describes phenomena at a very small atomic scale or when relative speeds approach that of light. There are two big ideas of modern physics, Relativity and Quantum Physics. Relativity was developed by Albert Einstein beginning in 1905, and states that everyone has equal access to the laws of physics regardless of their location and state of motion. It really is as simple as this: the universe behaves the same way for everyone in uniform motion.

Quantum physics is the study of matter and energy. It includes the smallest possible discrete unit of any physical property.

Motion

Motion is the key to everything. Understanding motion, is understanding space and time. Is there a natural state of motion? Everything is moving, electrons, the planets, cars, people, etc.

Isaac Newton was born in 1642; he developed his famous three laws of motion.

Newton's three laws of motion:

1. Objects move uniformly unless acted on by an outside force. Law of Inertia.
2. F = MA Force (F), produces changes in motion, (A) Acceleration, in an object of (M) mass. A larger force produces a larger acceleration: A larger mass is harder to accelerate.
3. For every action there is an equal and opposite reaction. Forces always come in pairs. Exert a force on object A, and then object B exerts a force of equal strength back on A. If you push on a table it pushes back on you.

I'll stop here with this initial conversation on physics to relate to you. I've always maintained that the laws of nature apply to human beings. The law I'm referring to is that you are either growing or decaying; there is no middle ground. I extend this law for your entire life, retirement included. My belief is that even if your activities change and you are no longer in an accumulation and growth phase of your life, you had still better be growing. If you don't, then what's left? That's right, decaying.

Even if you're retired, you still need to be passionate about life. Be passionately learning new challenges, and that is how you will keep yourself sharp and healthy until you die.

Newton's three laws of motion are directly applicable. If you keep on putting out good and ethical efforts, it is a certainty that good results will come back to you. Newton's law that forces come in pairs is evidence of this. As you keep on telling your story, as you keep on prospecting, then not only is it a numbers game that will play in your favor with the law of large numbers, but it is also a law of inertia, a law of momentum and a law of forces that what you put out also responds to you in kind.

If you are in a growth state of mind, then it's a continued sum of the efforts of the individuals in your organization that will generate the momentum of your company.

Constant speed is the natural state of motion. Pushes and Pulls are required only for changes in motion. Unless there's a force, there won't be a change of motion. These three laws describe everything there is to know about motion according to Newton.

I had an interesting coaching call one day on my free monthly call line. The client was in residential real estate sales in a cyclical marketplace where the market was very down and getting worse. This is around the time of the mortgage fall-outs from the sub prime lending that was happening in 2007, 2008.

There was a force that was affecting the natural state of motion. This force was the marketplace. This person was concerned that he was not having the same success that he was when the market was different.

It was an interesting conversation. What was called for was a new perspective. What was called for was the life lessons previously discussed. Remember the paper folds; what looked like chaos, like a market that was running away in a negative direction, was simply a perception. If you look at what was essential you would find that there were still people buying and selling homes. There was still a market. It was a normal market rather then an inflated market, with artificially rising home appreciation that couldn't possibly be maintained, fueled by loans that were unrealistic for the sub prime market.

The resetting adjustable loans and foreclosures were the forces, or push and pulls, on the market that shifted the momentum and caused a correction. This individual thought that some type of new strategy was necessary to be successful. However, using many of the principles we've already discussed, what he realized is that all he needed to do was go to work. Just put out consistent efforts on the activities that he already knew how to do, like advertising and making follow up calls, setting appointments, getting busy.

What he learned was that there wasn't any magic necessary. He had shut down his activity in the name of a bad market, rather than pick it up with consistent applications of the basics and work his way to results. A leader of a billion dollar company once told me you can work your way out of any problem and he was right!

What Can Gravity Teach Us?

Here is a definition straight from Wikipedia, an encyclopedia on the Internet:

Gravitation is a natural phenomenon by which all objects with mass attract each other. In everyday life, gravitation is most commonly thought of as the agency that gives objects weight. It is responsible for keeping the Earth and the other planets in their orbits around the Sun; for keeping the Moon in its orbit around the Earth, for the formation of tides; for convection (by which hot fluids rise); for heating the interiors of forming stars and planets to very high temperatures; and for various other phenomena that we observe. Gravitation is also the reason for the very existence of the Earth, the Sun, and most macroscopic objects in the universe; without it, matter would not have coalesced into these large masses and life, as we know it, would not exist.

Solar System

Gravitation keeps the planets in orbit about our sun.

There is a popular story that as Newton was sitting under an apple tree, an apple fell on his head, and he suddenly thought of the Universal Law of Gravitation. As in all such legends, this is almost certainly not true in its details, but the story contains elements of what actually happened.

What Really Happened with the Apple?

Probably the more correct version of the story is that Newton, upon observing an apple fall from a tree, began to think along the following lines: The apple is accelerated, since its velocity changes from zero as it is hanging on the tree and moves toward the ground. Thus, by Newton's 2nd Law there must be a force that acts on the apple to cause this acceleration. Let's call this force "gravity", and the associated acceleration the "acceleration due to gravity".   Now imagine the apple tree is twice as high, again we expect the apple to be accelerated towards the ground, so this suggests that this force that we call gravity reaches to the top of the tallest apple tree.

Sir Isaac's Most Excellent Idea

Now came Newton's truly brilliant insight: if the force of gravity reaches to the top of the highest tree, might it not reach even further; in particular, might it not reach all the way to the orbit of the Moon! Then, the orbit of the Moon about the Earth could be a consequence of the gravitational force, because the acceleration due to gravity could change the velocity of the Moon in just such a way that it followed an orbit around the Earth.

This can be illustrated with the thought experiment shown in the following figure. Suppose we fire a cannon horizontally from a high mountain; the projectile will eventually fall to earth, as indicated by the shortest trajectory in the figure, because of the gravitational force directed toward the center of the Earth and the associated acceleration. (Remember that acceleration is a change in velocity and that velocity is a vector, so it has both a magnitude and a direction. Thus, acceleration occurs if either or both the magnitude and the direction of the velocity change.)

Newton's Orbital Cannon

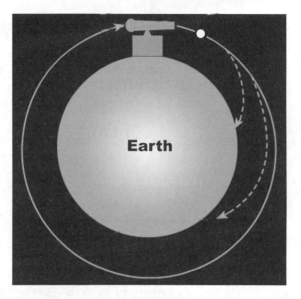

But as we increase the muzzle velocity for our imaginary cannon, the projectile will travel further and further before returning to earth. Finally, Newton reasoned that if the cannon projected the cannon ball with exactly the right velocity, the projectile would travel completely around the Earth, always falling in the gravitational field but never reaching the Earth, which is curving away at the same rate that the projectile falls. That is, the cannon ball would have been put into orbit around the Earth. Newton concluded that the orbit of the Moon was of exactly the same nature: the Moon continuously "fell" in its path around the Earth because of the acceleration due to gravity, thus producing its orbit.

By such reasoning, Newton came to the conclusion that any two objects in the Universe exert gravitational attraction on each other, with the force having a universal form:

Law of Universal Gravitation

Every object in the Universe attracts every other object with a force directed along the line of centers for the two objects that is proportional to the product of their masses and inversely proportional to the square of the separation between the two objects.

$$F = G \ \frac{m_1 m_2}{r^2}$$

The constant of proportionality G is known as the **universal gravitational constant**. It is termed a "universal constant" because it is thought to be the same at all places and all times, and thus universally characterizes the intrinsic strength of the gravitational force.

In the middle of the 20th century we invented the technology to put up satellites to take advantage of this principle. We can now broadcast signals, study the weather etc.

The application to you is all about the intensity of your effort. Are you doing enough of the right activities, for a long enough period of time to produce the desired effect? This is the analogy of exerting enough of a force to put an object into orbit where a constant force, gravity, keeps it in constant motion. Are your actions intense enough to create the orbit, or momentum for constant results?

I'm fond of recalling what is referred to as the S.A.I.D. effect. Specific Adaptations to Imposed Demands.

If you look at athletes they will look like what they do. An offensive lineman will be massive, capable of explosive movements in any forward or sideways direction for about five yards. Look at a wide receiver that consistently runs 40 to 60 yard patterns and you'll see a six foot five two hundred pounder who can run fast, but doesn't have the same power over short distances as the six foot four, three hundred pound lineman.

A long distance runner looks different than a Sumo Wrestler! You will adapt to the demands that you place on yourself. If all you do is sit in a chair for eight hours a day, you will be a candidate to be overweight.

If your business is not making enough calls, contacts, presentations, then you will not have the revenue from sales that you are looking for. So if you put in enough high level sustained effort over a consistent period of time, you will be like that satellite that is in a constant circular motion around the earth. The results will just keep coming. Newton anticipated artificial satellites, showing that an object given enough speed will "fall" around Earth, pulled by gravity out of the straight-line path it would otherwise follow.

I follow my alma mater, Rutgers University's football program. Their head coach has the entire stadium and team embrace the motto, "Keep Chopping". This is exactly what I am talking about. I read about this theme in an insurance industry magazine, Seymour, Sellmore, and K.O.K.O. Translation, see more and you will sell more. Keep On Keeping On. It's about the intensity and duration of your activities.

The laws of motion work exactly the same way for anyone as long as he or she is moving uniformly. My application of this principle to you is that the more consistent action that you take, the closer you come to your desired outcome. Since every "object" or outcome attracts every other object or outcome with a force that depends on their masses and the distance between them, the closer you get to your desired outcome the more it attracts you as well.

The essence of Einstein's theory of relativity is that all of us are equal. Everyone has equal access to the laws of physics regardless of where you are or how you're moving.

My application of this involves the frequency distribution or bell curve.

Percentage Distribution of Cases in a Normal Curve

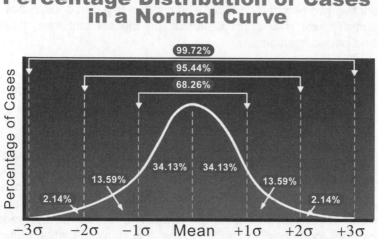

The curve is an example of the central limit tendency, where most of the population is centered between minus one and plus one standard deviation of the norm or mean. The extremes are a very small percentage of the population only 2%. Physics is telling us that everyone has equal opportunity to be in whatever percentage of the performance curve that they want to be in. Science is telling us that the top 2% is not reserved for the chosen few, but for the few who have chosen, since we all have equal access to the laws that govern behavior, performance and results.

The natural state of motion is not to be at rest, it is to move uniformly in a straight line at a constant speed. It winds up at rest because of external factors, mostly gravity. This is the law of inertia. It takes a push to start something and a pull to stop it, but it wants to remain in a constant state of motion.

My application is that the natural state of human behavior is being in action moving towards purposeful goals and to be successful and in abundance. It takes constant activity. The pushes and pulls become our distractions, our competing priorities, our challenges, fatigue, and our attitude

Chapter 15

Electricity and Magnetism

"You see but do not observe."
— Sir Arthur Conan Doyle

The study of motion is not all there is to physics. The ancient Greeks and Chinese knew about electricity and magnetism. It was James Clark Maxwell who, in 1865, finally unified the concepts of electricity and magnetism into one theory of electromagnetism. The force is mediated by the electromagnetic field. The various derivatives of this field lead to the electric and magnetic fields, respectively.

Maxwell showed that changing an electric field would create a magnetic field. He demonstrated the existence of electromagnetic waves, and structures of linked electric and magnetic fields that travel through empty space. He calculated the speeds of these waves that turned out to be the speed of light. Maxwell concluded that light is an electromagnetic wave.

A property called an electric charge is a fundamental state of matter. Benjamin Franklin (1706-1790) actually studied this in some detail and coined the phrase positive and negative for those two kinds of electric charge.

One of most basic properties of matter is charge. One of the most fundamental properties is that like charges repel, opposites attract. If you look at a magnet you will see two poles, a north and south. If you hold two magnets apart with the opposite poles facing each other, the force is very small over a distance but increases as the two magnets come together.

My application is that someone has a need for what you do or produce. Decrease the distance between you through your prospecting and follow up and this will increase the attraction. What you are seeking is also seeking you.

Newton's third law of motion states that for every action there is an equal and opposite reaction, which would mean that those organizations with a need for your product and/or service will seek you out in direct proportion to the degree (force) that you seek (prospecting) them out. This is referred to as "action at a distance".

The interaction being described here is called the Field of Force. The field concept describes electric and magnetic interactions in terms of invisible fields that exert forces on charges and magnets.

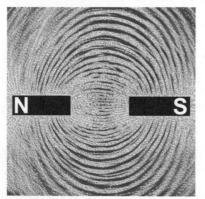

This magnet contains a field of force. You can't see it, yet another magnet somewhere in the vicinity experiences that field of force. Two objects interact creating a field in the space around it and the other object experiences it. The fields have energy. There is a relationship between the aspects of electricity and magnetic fields. If you move a magnet it creates electricity. The atoms in iron are moving and this creates magnetism.

There is a relationship between the electric fields and magnetic fields. If you change the magnetic field in any way, by moving the magnet, shaking it, you create electricity. Once again, there is an example of action and motion changing a state and creating something. You pick up the telephone; you are taking action and therefore changing the state to create something.

A change in a magnetic field makes an electric field. Action creates something. Maxwell also discovered that changing electricity produces magnetism. Once again, a reciprocal relationship — that what you seek is also seeking you.

Maxwell predicted that there could be a structure of changing electric fields then changing magnetic fields, throughout space continuously. Maxwell predicted electromagnetic waves. He calculated their speed and it came out to be the known speed of light. All electromagnetic waves are the same except for the frequency that they vibrate. They all go at the same speed but they vibrate at different frequencies.

In 1887 Heinrich Hertz generated and received electromagnetic waves in a laboratory, and in 1901 Guglielmo Marconi transmitted radio waves across the Atlantic Ocean.

As a planet we are seeing constant movement towards new learning. Things in all fields are being discovered very quickly and there is a constant movement of forward motion in understanding science and its application to improving our lives. This is like the third law of thermodynamics that states in part, that there is a direction of time. A hot cup of soup never gets hotter when left on a table, it cools. There is a direction. We never remain the same, we are always moving forward to new learning.

That is a recommendation that I have been making for years. Constant growth, constant learning will keep you young and healthy. You'll also see later how it will help to grow new neurological connections. Stay tuned!

$$E=MC^2$$

This equation shows equivalence between what makes up the universe. One is matter, and the other major stuff that makes up the universe is energy. Energy is motion. If you lift an object you've given it energy. A light wave traveling from the sun to the earth has energy. If there were no energy everything would stop. Before $E = MC^2$ they were thought to be two different things, energy and matter. They are the same however.

Energy and matter may change forms but are always conserved. This equation says that if you have a hunk of matter, say a tennis ball, and you take its mass, its weight, and multiply by the speed of light squared, then you get the energy equivalent. This is the exchange rate between matter and energy.

There is a tremendous amount of energy in all the matter around us. Also, you can create mass from energy. If you put enough energy out you can create matter. It's not a creation of something that wasn't there; it's a transition of the form of energy into matter. My application of this is again related to action, motion. Taking action will not create something that is not already there, it will just transform the possibility of new business into the reality of new business coming your way. New business is already out there. The question is in which direction is it headed?

Chapter 16

Quantum Theory
— Beware

"Everything you can imagine is real"
— Pablo Picasso

Quantum mechanics is one of the major revolutions in 20th century physics. It may be the closest science has come to a fundamental description of the underlying nature of reality. However, the interpretations I see are bizarre, they fly in the face of all our intuition and common sense and could be hazardous to human performance.

I will examine the scientific experiments and conclusions, and along with my own interpretations, attempt to make sense of this quantum world and in a way that will give you the opportunity to improve your performances.

There is an underlying theme with quantum physics. This theme is that the reality is in the eye of the observer. Nothing is real until you observe it and it is your choice that gives it reality. To take this further let's examine my third core principle, "Accountability — I am the source of all that I experience, versus playing   victim and blaming others."

You create your reality by your choice of observation. When something happens you create how it will influence you by the attitude you have about it. So with your own interpretation you create whether the driver who just cut you off on the freeway is hostile or merely careless, and you react accordingly.

You create your own reality. But you didn't create the driver cutting you off, or did you? Scientists are saying you create all of it, even other drivers on the road. (I'm warning you that a quantum conversation gets weird!) The good news is that you have the power of choice and it all starts with taking responsibility. If you are not responsible then you can't change it. So being responsible and accountable for everything that happens to you is the first step.

You have the power to look at a circumstance from whatever point of view you choose. Is the line concave or convex? Remember, there are no victims, only volunteers.

How real is our world? How solid is it? Perhaps you've seen a model of an atom[70] with the electrons orbiting around a nucleus like the planets orbiting the sun. As it turns out, that model was not correct. The electrons don't orbit the nucleus that way at all. In fact, what makes up most of an atom is space.

Model of an Atom

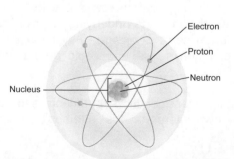

Electron

Proton

Neutron

Nucleus

The atom consists mostly of space, with a nucleus in the middle of a bunch of electrons that randomly move around all the time. It's like a giggling creature. The way nature works inside an atom does not follow Newton's laws. The electrons don't orbit the nucleus that way. Subatomic particles have their own laws that are different than the rules governing everything else. The world of the very tiny and very fast is known as quantum physics.[71] In the quantum world where Newton's laws don't apply, we can't make the same kind of predictions.

The World According to Newton

In 1687, Isaac Newton wrote an article about how the world works. In a paper called "Principia Mathematica", he wrote about his ideas concerning motion. He put forth his observations known as the three laws of motion. With this paper Newton was able to demonstrate that the world is logical and predictable.

Newton taught us that what goes up must come down. This way of thinking is called "determinism", which means that everything is determined ahead of time. In other words, once something has begun it will continue in a way that can be predicted according to natural law.

I am not disagreeing with this. I endorse this principle and include it in my recommendations for consistent high-level activity leading to predictable results, such as making enough prospecting calls, etc. However, a quantum discussion is a different discussion altogether. Remember, at the sub atomic level, Newtonian physics does not apply. This applies to thoughts and manifestation, more about this later.

Newton's fundamental interpretation was cause and effect, and that this relationship would hold up every time with consistent predictability. Regarding exercise, there are 3500 calories in one pound, so if you exercise five days a week and count your intake, when you have a deficit of 3500 calories for the week you will lose one pound. For every action, there is an equal and opposite reaction.

With determinism, everything is inevitable and accounted for. This is very precise, predictable, and pure mathematics. Remember however, this does not apply to the sub atomic world and your thoughts lie in that domain.

Quantum scientists have made startling discoveries that defy conventional experimentation and the way people thought the universe worked. They have shown that simply by making responsible choices and observing certain experiences, a person can change the outcome of what takes place.

A fundamental principle of quantum physics is that we cannot examine anything in the quantum without changing it. Experiments have shown that you get one result when you observe and a different one if you don't observe an experiment. This is like trying to observe a subatomic particle that you cannot see the observation changes the particle. Imagine that the particle is a bowling ball and you can't see it. So you roll another ball to hit it and when you locate it or "see" it, and strike it with the other ball you have now changed it's location. The observation changes the reality.

Scientists acknowledge Werner Heisenberg's uncertainty principle. In this principle, Heisenberg states that one cannot measure both the position and the momentum of a subatomic particle, an electron for example, at the same time. As soon as you figure out exactly where the electron is you cause a change and it is no longer possible to know how much momentum or force it has.

"The universe of subatomic entities and their workings actually support the idea of more than one world or reality."[72]

Newton would have us believe that there is only one true way of seeing anything in life, that there is a single reality that is not influenced by people. As it turns out, the truth is subjective. There are likely to be many versions of the truth.

Quantum physics rules out the old ideas of determinism and instead provides a picture of a world of multiple possibilities. Quantum physics sees multiple probabilities, that the world is overflowing with potential and that it is not determined and pre-set.

Let There be Light!

Scientists will not rest until there is objective and repeatable observations and measurable results. The question was how do you prove quantum theory?

It has actually happened through a series of experiments. Newton believed that light was comprised of a stream of tiny particles. Einstein in 1905 explained the photoelectric effect by declaring that the energy in a light wave is not spread uniformly over the wave, but is concentrated in particle like bundles called photons. In the now famous double-slit experiments done in 1803, Thomas Young discovered that light operates in waves that can bump into or interfere with each other.

What is light?

One of the driving questions of medieval science was "what is the nature of light?" By the end of the 19th century, that question seemed to have an answer. The mathematics (Maxwell's Equations") is a bit complex but the basic idea is straightforward and concludes that light is a wave. The double slit experiments also show that light is a particle. Which is it?

The double-slit experiment contains a lot of the best aspects of the weirdness of quantum physics.

A light shining through a small hole or slit creates a spot of light on the screen. However, light shown on two slits that are close together creates not two spots on the screen, but rather a series of bright and dark lines, with the brightest line in the exact middle of this interference pattern.

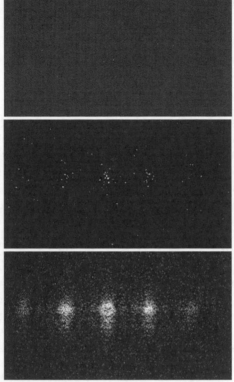

With the acquisition of an intensified CCD camera (ICCD) this demonstration is now possible in the laboratory. Each single photon of light passes through the double slit arrangement and enters the ICCD. Shown in the photos above are successive exposures.

ICCD Camera Images

Wave Interference
Pattern (side view)

Pattern on Back Screen
or Film (front view)

These bands of light are an indication of an interference pattern, which occurs when two waves — like waves in a pool — bump into each other.

Based on this experiment Young concluded that light is not a particle as Newton believed, but rather it is a wave that functions just as a sound wave does.

If light traveled in a simple straight line, you would just see a small vertical bar of light on the back screen. But light actually radiates outward as it travels, so the light goes through the slit, and then starts radiating outward. What you see on the wall is a very bright bar immediately behind the slit and then dimmer light.

ICCD Camera Images

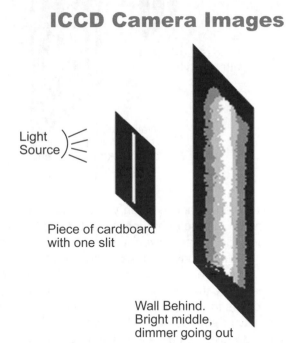

Light Source

Piece of cardboard with one slit

Wall Behind.
Bright middle,
dimmer going out

But what about all of the wave stuff? Well things get very interesting when you add another slit to the cardboard. You might expect to see the same pattern as you saw the first time, only repeated twice; two bright vertical bars, getting dimmer the further you get from the openings. However, what you see is a new pattern.

Bright bars where a lot of light is hitting the wall alternate with dark bars where no light seems to hit at all.

ICCD Camera Images

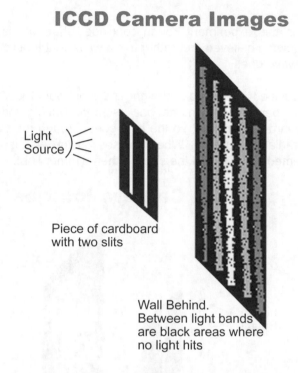

Light Source

Piece of cardboard with two slits

Wall Behind. Between light bands are black areas where no light hits

This makes perfect sense when you consider the wave theory of light. When one beam gets through a slit it immediately spreads out in all directions. So for any given spot on the screen there are two beams of light hitting it, one from each slit. The waves are at different points of the cycle. If both are up or both are down, then you get a very bright patch — the two beams of light constructively interfere, creating more light then either one individually could. If one is up and the other is down then you get a dark patch, the two beams of light destructively interfere, actually canceling each other out.

Particles are things like marbles, molecules and planets. Sometimes a wave is made up of particles such as when you make standing waves by shaking a rope. Regardless of what they are made of, waves and particles act very differently. Some of the differences are:

1. Particles are quantized or discrete. This basically means that they come in little individual chunks. Waves do not come in chunks; they're kind of a big blur over an area of space.
2. Another thing about quantization — there is a smallest unit possible. If you split the matter, let's say an M&M, keep splitting it into half and eventually it isn't an M&M anymore. An individual M&M is the smallest unit of M&M's. A wave however, you can keep cutting the height of the wave in half and it keeps on being a wave.
3. Waves can add constructively, or destructively. But particles always add constructively. Seven M&M's plus one M&M is always 8 M&M's, never 2.
4. Because of the difference in the way they add, they act very differently in a double-slit experiment. With waves, you get bands of darkness, where the two slits cancel each other out. With particles, you do not get any canceling out; you just get two big blurs.

So what does this mean to you? Well, read on. Something very interesting happens when measurement occurs.

When we throw things, matter, particles, through two slits we get two bands. When we throw waves we get interference patterns.

Now, let's go quantum! An electron is a tiny bit of matter. If we shoot it through a single slit we get a band. If we shoot it through two slits we would expect two bands, but what we get instead is an interference pattern.

Electrons

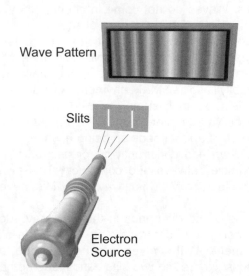

Wave Pattern

Slits

Electron
Source

Scientists fired electrons, tiny bits of matter, through the slits but they got a pattern like waves. How could pieces of matter create an interference pattern like a wave? It doesn't make sense.

The conclusion, the single electron leaves as a particle and becomes a wave of potentials, it goes through both slits and interferes with itself. It gets even weirder. It goes though both slits and it goes through neither. It goes through just one or just the other. All of these possibilities are in superposition with each other. Physicists were absolutely confused by all of this so they decided to measure, to take a look at which slit it actually goes through.

They put a measuring device by one slit to observe. But when they measured, the electron went back to behaving like a particle, and produced two bands and not an interference pattern of many bands. The very act of measuring and observing which slit it went through meant it only went through one, not both. The electron decided to act differently as though it was aware that it was being watched.

(A side note here. This can be applied to the coaching commandment of "inspect and verify". People will behave differently when they know they are being watched and measured, and then when they know they are not.)

What is matter, particles or waves? And what does an observer have to do with any of this? The observer collapsed the wave functions simply by observing. This is not a theory. This is an experimental fact that has been verified many times. Sensible or not, measuring a photon's path changes what it does.

This particular result is so important and so contrary to our classical notions of the world, that it just shatters our neat explanations. In classical physics things are assumed to happen in the world the same way, whether you look at them or not. In the double slit experiment there is no way to separate the experimenter from the experiment. No matter how you do the measurement, the simple fact of measuring which slit the photon goes through causes the interference pattern to disappear.

About 20 years after Einstein proposed his particle theory of light, a French graduate student named Louis de Broglie proposed that all particles have wave functions. If this is true, then the electron wave function shows interference patterns just like the photon wave functions and of course as you have already seen, this is exactly what happened. De Broglie was awarded his Ph.D. for this idea and five years later he was awarded the Nobel Prize. It turns out that you get a wave pattern whether you use electrons, protons, or even entire atoms. In fact, everything seems to do this.

What does this mean to you? It means everything. It means that there is a scientific basis that measurement is everything and that the act of measurement has a cause and effect property. When you observe and measure something you change it. So track every activity that leads to the Newtonian "cause and effect". If you can't measure, you can't manage. You change your reality when you measure. This is readily verifiable at the quantum level that the individual cannot see. However, with time and persistence we are able to see it on the larger scale such as our business results or our health.

This also raises the question about the TRUTH. I say in my live programs that the truth is not relevant. The truth doesn't matter. The only thing that matters is what you are paying attention to. Your ability to influence what you pay attention to is directly related to your degree of success. Does what you're paying attention to compel you to take the actions you need to take or does your attention compel you to avoid? You have a choice. You can observe opportunity or you can observe a desperate market place. I love this analogy, "Opportunity is nowhere". Now observe the word differently, "Opportunity is [now] [here]". See the difference? It's the same word but with a different observation.

It is up to you to choose your perspectives, what meaning you decide to give to everything that happens in your life. Do your choices compel you to take positive actions to reach your goals? It's your power to make your choice of your interpretation. Once you make your choice, then the other potentials or options for truth collapse and your perception becomes the true reality for you! It's just like the double slit. Once you observe, the matter acts like a particle and responds accordingly. Without the observation it acts like a wave, your observation changes it. Your choice changes your reality, or creates it. Confused? It doesn't matter. This is just another example that there is a science underlying my recommendations. Interesting for sure.

By the way, Einstein won the Nobel Prize for discovering that waves of light were actually particles — little bits of light strung closely together in what he called photons. Young's experiment proved that light was waves and Einstein proved that it was particles. Even today this debate continues.[73]

If we don't focus on the subatomic entity, it's a wave. If we focus on it, it's a particle. Since every atom in our world is made up of subatomic elements that behave this way, what does this mean to you?

It means that whatever you pay attention to will happen in your world. The exciting thing about wave-particle duality is you can change what you choose to observe and by doing so, you can change what happens. It is the very act of your observation that produces the results.

Therefore the first fundamental step is to accept and live the third core principle,

"I am the source of all that I experience versus playing victim and blaming others!" I know that I've repeated this multiple times. It is worthy of the attention.

"Our physical reality, our world itself, doesn't appear unless we observe it. Until we manifest it, our universe, like light, exists only as waves of energy, as waves of probability"[74]

I'm about to be controversial. How do you respond to this statement?

"Your life is empty and meaningless"

I've seen a variety of different emotional responses to this, ranging from annoyed to outright angry. I call this coaching concept "Circles of Perception — Living Life Authentically". Here is the analogy.

Something happens in our lives. Regardless of what this event is, it has no meaning it is neutral, empty, without any meaning whatsoever.

Most people are going to hear this phrase and become upset or defensive. This is exactly my point. We are **"meaning making machines"**. This phrase has no meaning. It is up to you and your language to give it an interpretation and meaning.

199

What do you see below and what does it mean?

What was your response? Here's what I commonly hear:

1. We are all one. [Show me where it says that]
2. Love. [Where do you see that?]

Show me the physical aspects of this picture that says anything. This photo is empty and meaningless until you decide what meaning to give it. This photo has waves of possible interpretations. It is your observation, your choice.

I see a black boy and a white girl with her arm on the boy's shoulder, cheek-to-cheek, blonde hair, blue eyes, etc. Everything else is a made up interpretation, or a story made up by the observer.

At the earliest time of mankind, prehistoric man needed to be able to see an event and to interpret danger or safe, immediately! This was such a necessity for survival that our "primitive" brain, or primate brain, still has this mechanism of recognition today. We are meaning making machines. Something happens and our brain searches through all of the past networks that we have, looking to match patterns so we can make an instant decision and recognition of safe or dangerous.

Our meaning is constantly a comparison of our past experiences projected to the future.

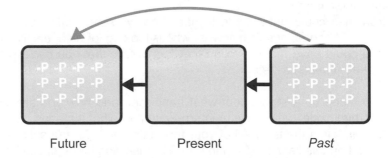

Future   Present   *Past*

Something happens and we immediately tell ourselves a story about what it means. Then we store it in the past. When we want to create our future we don't step into an empty future, we step into a future that is filled with our interpretations about what has happened in the past.

For example, a sales person in real estate learns how to make a presentation to someone who is going to sell his or her own home. They've got it down word for word! Next they pick up the phone and call a for sale by owner ad and the home owner is very rude, aggressive and yells at them that they are the fifth realtor to call them, they are selling their own home and hangs up!

This person now has a negative P to put into their past regarding prospecting to for sale by owners. The next time they want to pick up the phone and create a future for themselves through prospecting, they will not step into a blank future, they will step into the previous negative past experience! Put enough of these together and it will be very difficult to get this person to prospect.

The reality of it is that the rejection had no meaning until you gave it one. The fact was that the homeowner said NO and hung up! You made it mean something about you! There was a wave of multiple interpretations that you could have chosen. When you chose it went from a wave of potentials to a particle of one meaning.

You could have made it mean that you are bothering them, that you are imposing, that you are a bad sales person etc. You might have made it mean that this is tough, that it will never work, that you'll never be successful in sales, that you are a failure and a

disappointment!
You also could have made it mean that you are getting closer to finding that one for sale by owner who is looking for an agent like you. You could have made it mean that this is fun, that you can't wait to make the next call, etc.

You made up a story about what happened and now you are living the third circle, which is your interpretation of what it means. You live this as if it is the truth! All of your thoughts, feelings and actions are based on this lie that you made up. That is living inauthentically!

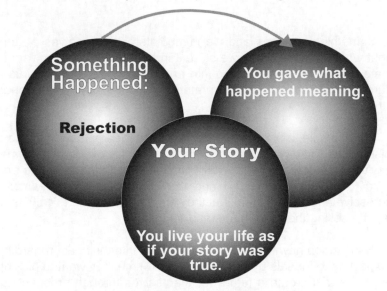

We live in a black and white world. Something happens and you make it mean something. However, most people then live in the gray by living their lives as if their story was true.

This is an example of inauthentic living. You may be living believing that your story is the truth and reacting accordingly. Your story is an illusion. Your story is simply what you made up about what happened in your striving to give meaning and understanding to all things.

The challenge is to take the negative past out of the future. Your goal is to have your future be empty, (of the negative past), and meaningless, (no inherent meaning until you say so).

When you achieve this level of reaction to events, you will be what is called Enlightened. You will now have the freedom to choose fascination over frustration, good over evil, calm over upset. When you step into the freedom to interpret, you can then select to create whatever reality you want.

This reminds me of what some people say about the University of California's football teams recruiting in the 2000's under Pete Carol. The comment was that they don't recruit, they select! You don't have to wait for what the world gives you in terms of the quality of your life; you can create it through the power of observation and choice.

Think about this and try it on. Here is a homework assignment that I often give to my live coaching clients.

Identify the "stories" you have been telling yourself. Do your interpretations serve you? Notice what you say about what has happened and exercise the freedom to choose a different interpretation.

You can manifest anything that you want in your life. The key is to prepare for it and to take purposeful actions. Therein lays my issue with this quantum movement. The prevailing quantum theory would have you think that all things are possible and it's all simply a matter of your choosing. Choose this and it will become your reality. By itself this is a bunch of bull! This is a dangerous trend that I wholeheartedly reject. Don't be a student of the quantum world and think that you can just visualize your way to success, health and happiness.

It is going to take your ability to withstand the projection of your worst fears. It's going to take your ability to consistently implement and execute your plan through consistent daily actions, heavily laced with an accountability system. You've got to have a work ethic. You've got to go out and compete. You compete against the limiting aspects of human nature. You compete against the limiting thinking of others. You need to compete on a daily and moment-by-moment basis.

What I love about quantum physics is that it clearly does show that we don't understand our limitations. We clearly don't have an understanding of human performance. I love the underlying aspects of quantum physics regarding our reality being subject to our choice and we have the freedom to choose. So take my advice, combine the limitless probabilities and possibilities of quantum physics by selecting a mindset and vision of the desired outcome, along with the Newtonian physics of action and reaction, and you will have the highest probable predictable future of reaching your dreams and living the life that you love.

Let's now transition from making choices to taking a look at the effect of your expectations.

Chapter 17

The Science of
Expectation
— The Placebo Effect

I'm sitting on a Delta flight coming home from Atlanta, I've got an aisle seat and I'm people watching as everyone boards the plane. I'm right up front and this is a smaller plane that boards from the cockpit area door, so everyone passes by me.

After about five minutes I notice that everyone is in such a good mood, everyone is smiling, greeting each other and the flight attendants, helping each other and as polite as can be. Then I had an awareness of myself, I was smiling and in a good mood. I was engaged in cheerful conversation.

The quantum folks would say the following:

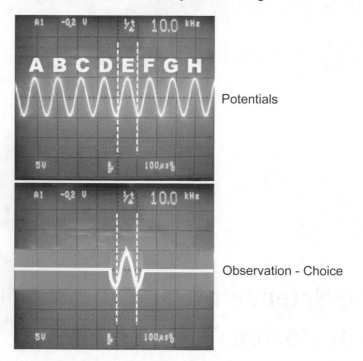

Potentials

Observation - Choice

All of these waves of possibilities exist as potentials, it's only when I choose that everything else collapses and my choice becomes my reality. I chose in this case (E), which just happens to be the reality of everyone being happy, courteous and in a good mood. The moment that I made my choice all other possibilities collapsed and disappeared. However, I could have made a different choice and selected (A), which would have been everyone is rude and impatient and that could have been my realty as well. So once again, reality is in the mind of the observer.

Another key consideration is to examine the impact of expectations on reality. I've already touched on this with the lesson of the snake eggs. Of course that example illustrated a bias towards a particular fear based perception of danger. However, when you changed your orientation, or what I call "in reference to", then of course your expectation was different and your reaction was different as well. This is referred to as "confirmation bias", where you are selectively looking for evidence to support the held point of view (Expectation).

Years ago Tyra Banks was involved with research on expectations. The 31-year old model wore a "fat suit" and went on three blind dates as a 350-pound woman. The result was one of the most heart breaking experiences of her life. "Obesity seemed like the last form of open discrimination", said the five-foot-nine 150-pound Banks. She said she walked down the street and within 10 seconds people would point and laugh in her face. She tried to catch a taxi and someone cut in front of her to steal her cab.

Upon further inquiry it became clear that Tyra expected to be discriminated against as an obese woman. She participated in another experiment, but this time with a different expectation. This time she put on her fat suit but had a completely different attitude and expectation. This time she walked on the streets of New York City and she smiled, she was friendly, and people responded in kind. She went to a hot dog vendor and ordered a hot dog with everything and the vendor was friendly and said "anything for you honey".

Once again, quantum physics will prevail. All possibilities exist, good reactions as well as poor prejudiced reactions. They all exist in a waveform. Once you choose, then the rest of the possibilities collapse and your expectation, your choice of what you believe, becomes your reality. (Wave to Particle, with Particle being the selected reality)

Another human phenomenon at play here is the brains design to recognize a pattern and become susceptible to seeing what is supported by the pattern. Remember the dog and spots earlier. The human brain does not want to operate incongruently, so once a pattern is established; your expectation, then you will be more apt to pay attention to those aspects of your environment that supports the accomplishment of your expectation. I've called this "selective perception".

The Placebo Effect[75]

Researchers have demonstrated that for the first time just thinking that medicine will make pain go away prompts the brain to release its own natural painkillers. Although the placebo effect has long been dismissed as psychological rather than physical phenomenon, scientists have recently spotted specific activity in brain centers related to pain after fake treatments were administered. A new study reveals the brain chemistry invoked by a pain-related placebo. Researchers at the University of Michigan Health System reported their work in the Journal of Neuroscience in 2005. This involved brain scans on 14 healthy men who agreed to let the scientist inject their jaw muscles with a concentrated saltwater solution to induce pain.

The injections were done as the men's brains were being scanned with PET scans. During one session, the volunteers were told they would receive medicine, (actually a placebo), that might relieve the pain.

All participants showed an increase in activation of their endogenous opioid systems after they were told the medicine was coming and the placebo was given. This system naturally acts to stop or slow the transmission of pain signals from one nerve cell to the next, and also reacts to drugs such as heroin, morphine, methadone and various anesthetics.

"This deals another serious blow to the idea that the placebo effect is purely psychological," said Dr. Jhon-Kar Aubieta, an associate professor of psychiatry and radiology at the health system and a research scientist at the university's Molecular and Behavioral Neurosciences Institute.

"We were able to see that the endorphin system was activated in pain-related areas of the brain, and that activity increased when someone was told they were receiving medicine to ease their pain. They then reported feeling less pain. The mind-body connection is quite clear".

"Your expectations can have profound impacts on your brain and your health," says Columbia University neuroscientist Tor Wagner. A Baylor School of Medicine study, published in 2002 in the New England Journal of Medicine, evaluated surgery for patients with severe debilitating knee pain. The lead author of the study, Dr. Bruce Moseley, "knew" that knee surgery helped his patients. "All good surgeons know there is no placebo effect in surgery." But Moseley wanted to know what part of the surgery was giving the patients their relief. The patients in the study were divided into three groups.

Moseley shaved the damaged cartilage in the knee of one group. In the second group, he flushed the knee with a fluid that would remove floating materials that would cause inflammation. Both of these are standard treatment.

The third group received "fake" surgery. The patient was sedated and Moseley made three standard incisions and then talked and acted like he was doing the surgery.

All three groups received the same postoperative care, including an exercise program. The results were amazing. Yes the groups who did receive the surgery, as expected, improved. However, the placebo group improved just as much as the other two groups. This led Moseley to pronounce, " My skill as a surgeon had no benefit on these patients. The entire benefit of surgery for osteoarthritis of the knee was the placebo effect."

In a 2002 article in the American Psychological Association's Prevention & Treatment, "The Emperor's New Drugs," University of Connecticut psychology professor Irving Kirsch found that 80% of the effect of antidepressants, as measured in clinical trials, could be attributed to the placebo effect.

Doctors have found that expecting a benefit or negative outcome, called nocebo effect, can trigger the same neurological pathways of healing as real medicine.

"Our brain really is on drugs when we get a placebo," says Christian Stohler, University of Maryland.

In 1974 a Nashville physician, Clifton Meador, had a patient Sam Londe, a retired shoe salesman suffering from cancer of the esophagus, a condition that was at the time considered 100% fatal. Londe was treated for that condition but everyone "knew" that the cancer would return and he would die. A few weeks later he died after this diagnosis.

The surprise came when the autopsy found very little cancer in his body, certainly not enough to kill him. In fact, there was no trace of the esophageal cancer that everyone thought caused his death. He died because he believed and expected that he would die. He thought he had cancer.

Our positive and negative thoughts and beliefs not only impact our health, but also every aspect of our life. One report says that after thousands of studies, hundreds of millions of prescriptions and tens of billions of dollars in sales, sugar pills are as effective at treating depression as antidepressants such as Prozac, Paxil and Zoloft.[76]

What are your thoughts and beliefs about your future? What are you predisposed to see? What false assumptions are you operating from and holding as being true? What lies are you buying into? How's it going so far? If you don't like what you have in your health, business and personal life, then I'd recommend that you create a new set of expectations and set out to make those come true.

Henry Ford was right when he said about the power of the mind, "If you believe you can or if you believe you can't …you're right!"

The application for you is to prepare for your future. Prepare for the next seven days and then execute using the power of behavioral contracting to engage human nature to compel you to avoid the uncomfortable consequence of non-performance, that is the penalty or fine that you've placed on your activities.

The use of the behavioral contracting on-line program will give you a reference point that is based in precise planning. You will now have preset your expectations for what you want to accomplish over the next seven days. This will precondition you to "see" opportunities to take the actions, or to avoid the penalties and to do what you said you would do. You are tapping into the quantum world by presetting your outcomes and living with accountability.

So many times we all buy into the negative beliefs of others, even authority figures. When we don't buy into these limiting beliefs the impossible is possible. I remember the story Lynn Rogers tells. Lynn (a man by the way) was the head coach of the women's gymnastics team at Cal State Fullerton when I was coaching football there from 1979-1983. At that time the women's gymnastics team was a world-class elite program, in the top five nationally every year. Lynn tells the story about Carol Johnson, All American gymnast. Carol, from Canada, had one hand and a stump; Disney made a movie about her titled "Lefty".

One day during her freshman year, Carol was bugging Lynn to teach her a new trick on the uneven bars. As everyone knows there is no way that a freshman, with one hand, could ever do this difficult trick. Carol didn't know that. She didn't know that she shouldn't be able to succeed.

To get her out of his hair and to free him up to work with the more experienced girls, Lynn told his assistant coach Breck Greenwood, to go ahead and work with her on the uneven bars. Breck, a former football player at the school, was relatively new to gymnastics coaching and also didn't realize that Carol should not be able to perform this maneuver.

Shortly thereafter, to everyone's amazement, except to Breck and Carol, she executed the routine perfectly. It's amazing what you can accomplish when you haven't been taught what you can't do. This gets into the last portion of the book, the biological aspects, but it is certainly appropriate to mention one concept from biology now. This concept is called mirror Neurons.

Mirror Neurons

Mirror neurons were first discovered in monkeys just 15 years ago. In early tests, a neuron in the premotor area associated with hand and mouth acts, became highly active when the monkey grasped a raisin on a plate (diagram, next page). The same neuron also responded intensely when an experimenter grasped the raisin as the monkey watched (second diagram, next page).

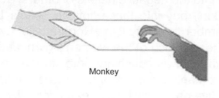

Monkey

Activation Intensity

Monkey Mirror Neuron Responses

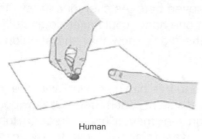

Human

Activation Intensity

Mirror neurons fire when we watch someone else perform a goal-oriented action (grabbing an apple and bringing it to his or her mouth, for instance). They're linked to imitation learning, empathy, and the ability to recognize and predict behavior. Whether we do the activity ourselves or watch someone else do it, mirror neurons fire. Our conscious brain generates an inner simulation of sorts when we follow the actions of another person. Mirror neurons are presumed to be abundant in brain regions responsible for planning and initiating actions, including the primary motor cortex, the premotor cortex and supplementary motor areas. Actions performed by one person can activate motor pathways in another's brain responsible for performing the same action. The second person understands viscerally what the first is doing because this mirror mechanism lets her experience it in her own mind.

Scientists have revealed that mirror neurons reflect not only the actions of other people but their intentions and emotions as well.[77] This discovery is offering new insight into human empathy, language evolution and may help explain certain neurological conditions such as autism.

In 2001 a research team at the University of Parma in Italy, led by Giovanni Buccino, used MRI's to track brain activity in people watching video sequences showing mouth, hand or foot movements. As it turned out, when the subjects watched a mouth move, the part of the brain responsible for controlling their mouth lit up. Likewise, observing hand and foot images engaged the corresponding brain regions.

Emotional Mirrors

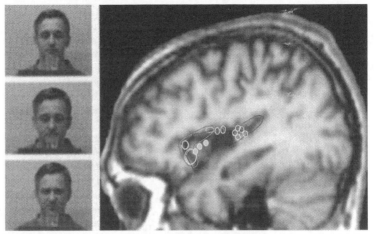

Feeling emotions like disgust, activated similar parts of the brain when humans experienced the emotion while smelling a disgusting odor. The brain cross section shows neurons that were activated by the experience.

An example of mirror neurons is the above example of disgust, a basic reaction whose expression has important survival value for fellow members of a species. In its most primitive form, disgust indicates that something the individual tastes or smells is bad and, most likely, dangerous. Once again using an MRI, studies show that experiencing disgust as a result of inhaling foul odorants and witnessing disgust on the face of someone else, activates the same neural structures — the anterior insula — at some of the very same locations within that structure. The results indicate that populations of mirror neurons in the insula become active both when the test participants experience the emotion and when they see it expressed by others. In other words, the observer and the observed, share a neural mechanism that enables a form of direct experiential understanding.

This data strongly suggests that humans may comprehend emotions, or at least powerful negative emotions, through a direct mapping mechanism involving parts of the brain that generate visceral motor responses. This explains for the first time some of the interpersonal relations on which more complex social behaviors are built.

Imitation

Imitation requires reproduction of actions performed by another person. If mirror neurons underlie the uniquely human facility for imitation, the mirror system may serve as a bridge that allows us to teach and learn new skills.

Application:

Be the change that you seek in others. Others will literally take their cues from the way that you are. If you are in a good mood, they will be as well. If you are hopeful, positive and focus on great opportunity, others will as well. This means that as a leader you have a responsibility to come into the office in a positive mood, upbeat, cheerful and with an expectation of success and possibility. Your co-workers will mirror the image that you project.

I recently read an article on obesity. People are most likely to become obese when a friend becomes obese. It increased a person's chances of becoming obese by 57%. People change what is acceptable by what they are around and by what is said and done.

Researchers from Harvard found that when hotel maids were informed that the work that they did was good exercise and satisfied the surgeon general's recommendations for an active lifestyle, they experienced a decrease in blood pressure and bodyweight after four weeks of work, compared to those who weren't given this information. Remember the graph from page 100?

This data suggests that positive thinking can make a significant difference in how you can influence your environment. Take into account the placebo effect, the mirror neuron effect, and your ability to influence people to make a positive choice, (particle or wave), of positive possibilities and you will see that you must be the guardian of how you think and the choices you make. So come into the office with an enthusiastic and positive approach regardless of what the "truth" is. Make up your own truth and continue to have an impact on others as they join in and match your reality.

Pete Carroll, the coach of the USC Fighting Trojans during their tremendous run of Pac 10 Championships and BCS Bowl appearances and wins, when asked how he created such consistency was quick to point out that he had to be a model of enthusiasm every day. He didn't have the option of not being in an energetic and positive mood. He took responsibility for setting the expectations both on and off the field. Mirror neurons at play again!

Likewise, you don't have the luxury of coming into your office and interacting with others and not be anything other than a stand for excellence, whether you feel like it or not. I love the scene from the movie "As Good As It Gets", where Jack Nicholson is asking the waitress played by Helen Hunt, to go on a trip with him. She remarks something to the effect that she doesn't feel like going and doesn't want to go, to which Nicholson's character replies, "What's that got to do with it?"

Now that you know there is scientific proof that those around you will pick up and take on your demeanor, do you really have the option of not feeling like being in a good mood in the office?

Another application regarding the influence of mirror neurons is related to sales techniques and the creation of rapport. He rubs his chin, you rub your chin. She crosses her legs, you cross your legs. Does he have a southern accent? Talk more slowly and drop the occasional "y'all." While this may sound like one of those games that children play, this adult version of "mirror-mirror" is actually part of a sophisticated negotiation strategy that has helped close otherwise impossible deals. The art and science of negotiation frequently centers on how to build trust. Who are you more likely to reach an agreement with, someone you like and empathize with or someone you don't?

As far back as 1936, when Dale Carnegie published "How to Win Friends and Influence People", business gurus have recognized the power of tiny gestures in creating trust. For example, repeating a persons name and getting them to talk about themselves are two of Carnegie's nuggets for getting people to like you. Engaging a form of verbal mimicry by understanding and speaking a counterpart's lingo can have the same effect as physical mimicking, says Deepak Malhotra, associate professor at Harvard business School and co-author of the 2007 book "Negotiation Genius".

This way of creating rapport by mirroring, matching and pacing is a technique that would put you in alignment with the mirror neurons of your potential client, and increasing the likelihood of making a sale.[78]

Speaking of Expectations —
How About Your Intentions?

Dr. William Teller[79] has conducted some interesting experiments that lends the vote of science to the idea that your thoughts are indeed very powerful and do manifest into reality. Dr. Teller also examines the 20th century viewpoint of quantum physics as the dominant paradigm at the fundamental particle level. The underlying message of his book is that human intention (and I add expectation), acts like a typical potential, capable of creating effects in what we call physical reality. "This significantly broadens the purview of physics, challenges its present perspectives, mindsets and laws, and sets it on a new course toward understanding how physical matter and energy are connected to human consciousness" says Dr. Teller.

I've always stated that all of us need to be very careful with our thoughts because our thoughts are real. They are a system of electrical energy being transferred into a chemical substance that is real and measurable. This chemistry has a charge and we attract to ourselves what we are thinking. This is not just philosophical; it is backed by scientific research.

Dr. Teller, Professor Emeritus from Stanford University, performed three experiments. He wanted to see what affect the power of focused thought and intentions would have in three circumstances. His subjects were four trained meditators.

First, the experimenters would concentrate on raising the ph of a container of water by 1.0 ph units.

Second, the intention was to increase the thermodynamic activity of an enzyme in the liver.

Third, the intention was to influence a living system, Fruit Fly larvae, to increase the ADP to ATP ratio, which would result in the reduction of larvae development time.

All of the controls were in place including what is called a Faraday Box, which would prevent contamination. The results were achieved exactly as intended in all three experiments. All three were statistically significant, meaning valid. Yes, the power of intention actually did "imprint" the results they were looking for.

For more information on this research go to this link,

http://www.spiritofmaat.com/archive/mar2/tiller1.htm

I can't guess as to how long the above link will be in use so you can always refer to his book as well.

I use the following formula:

Intentions + Mechanism = Results

What do you think this means? Usually it boils down to having the want to, the intentions, and adding the how to, the mechanism, will create the result.

Shift your thinking! Eliminate the word Mechanism! What's that leave you?

Intentions = Results

When you intend to have a result you will have it. In fact, all of our current results are exactly what they should be because we are simply living out our intentions.

Here's some tough love. If you are poor that is your intention. If you are sick, that is your intention. If you are in a great relationship, that is your intention!

I know, many of you will take issue with this and not agree. That is also your intention, to be right and to be a victim and blame others.

Don't get mad at me, I'm just a carrier of the scientific research, not the inventor!

Application:

Examine your results and uncover your intentions. If you want to know what someone is committed to, take a look at what they have. That's what they are committed to. This is more evidence for you to be very careful with how you allow yourself to think. The universe doesn't edit your thoughts. Always think in terms of what you want, not what you don't want. This is a "moving towards" versus "moving away" strategy. Always think in terms of what you want because you will move towards that, rather then what you don't want, because you will likewise move towards that as well. So instead of thinking "I don't bite my nails," think instead, "I have long, healthy, beautiful nails."

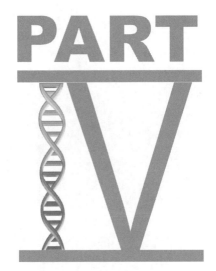

PART

V

Towards a Theory of Everything
— The Biological Perspective

Chapter 18

What Does Biology Have to Say?

Biology is the science of life and of living organisms, including their structure, function, growth, origin, evolution, and distribution. This is the branch of knowledge that treats living matter as distinct from non-living. It is fitting therefore that we look at the biology of what makes us the way that we are, and to consider this body of knowledge to look for applications in your life.

What is the biology of our behavior? An examination of biology will take us through additional looking at how the brain works. Let's first look at the basics, the nerve cell or neuron. Neurons are the body's method of communication.

It all starts with a stimulus, or excitation. Neurons do very dramatic things. They are all about contrasts. This is going from silent or resting or turned off, to an explosion of electric charge or turned on.

Flow of Information Across a Neuron

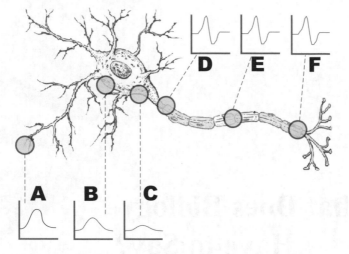

A single dentritic spine is electrically excited, causing a wave at point A. The wave spreads along the cell body, decreasing in strength by the time it reaches B, and is virtually gone by point C.
If there is still enough strength to trigger an action potential at the hillock (D), the action potential is just as strong at points E and F.

Nature has the answers and we don't need to look any further than the human brain for some insights! The above is an explanation of the concept of summation, the accumulative effect of signal strength creating a "tipping point" that generates an action potential.[80] If the stimulation or electrical charge to the neuron is not great enough, then it doesn't meet the threshold at a location called the axon hillock, and it doesn't generate an action potential stimulating the neuron to pass on the signal. It's all about the strength of the input.

Here is how this relates to the concept of Specific Adaptations To Imposed Demands, the S.A.I.D. Principle as previously discussed.

The law of accumulative effect relates to the activities that are necessary for you to reach your goals. For example, every industry has their numbers. In real estate there are a number of calls you need to make, to get enough contacts, to set enough appointments, to get a listing or make a sale.

The insurance industry has their numbers. They are 10-3-1, you need to make ten contacts, to set three appointments and you will make one sale. There would also be a number of how many dials you need to make to get ten contacts. Let's just for the sake of an example say that this number is 50.

What happens if you stop making calls at number 20? This input loses its charge over space and time. (Input = intentions plus the actions necessary to make results happen). It takes a large enough of a stimulus to trigger the area of the nerve cell called the axon hillock to the tipping point. Once the axon hillock recognizes the signal strength, (50 calls), it then creates the "action potential" and sends that down the axon at a rate that does not degrade.

The analogy to you is that there is an accumulative effect of the activities necessary that will trigger an impact of appointments and sales, or weight loss, or improved relationships, etc.

It is important to remember that what you are looking for is CHANGE! It is also important to remember that you will resist the very thing that you want, change! This is a lifetime challenge. Consistency is the key. It is not possible to be executing your numbers and not have change for the positive occur. My apologies to the quantum folks, but this is cause and effect at its best!

Keep this in mind. There is no try in your life. You either do or do not do. Think about the word commitment. I'm committed when I get into the clouds when I'm flying in the Bonanza, or step out the door to go skydiving from the twin engine Otter at 12,500 feet over Perris, California. The question to ask yourself is what are you committed to? What is the stand that you are for the year? What are your intentions? To see what you are committed to just look and observe what results you have in your life. Take a look at what activities you are accomplishing on a weekly basis. That will reveal what you are committed to!

You and I need to fight through circumstances, excuses, obstacles, competing priorities, resistances and whatever else to create extra ordinary results.

Let's revisit the concept of summation. I've also referred to this as the law of accumulated effect meaning that small consistent actions over a long period of time will produce large results.

Looking at the nerve cell stimulation, there needs to be either a very strong centralized stimulus that is strong enough to reach the threshold of the axon hillock, or multiple inputs that would sum up to the effect of a very large concentrated stimulus, referred to as spatial summation. No given single input is enough to pass on the message, so there must be multiple neurons having their input at the same time.

Application:

This is very similar to the S.A.I.D. principle, Specific Adaptations to Imposed Demands. On the cellular level there must be an intense enough input to generate the action potential. Likewise, there must be an intense enough input of actions either by you or from multiple sources, (spatial summation), that will be intense enough to create the action potential (results in your business, health and personal lives).

As we continue to examine what happens in a nerve cell, we see that once the threshold of stimulation is great enough then an action potential is created. This sends a tremendous charge down the axon of the nerve cell to the dendrites, which then release a chemical called a neurotransmitter. This neurotransmitter is a chemical, like dopamine, which then is physically picked up by the dendrites of a connecting neuron completing the communication.

Neuron Communication

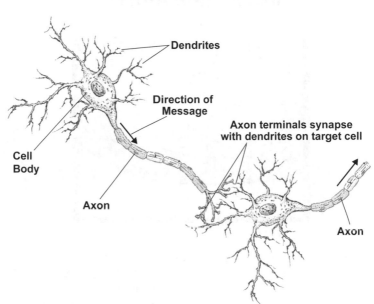

Application:

This seems to be the analogy of constant proper action. Intense levels of the necessary activities, such as prospecting, (reaching the threshold of the Axon Hillock and generating the action potential), and the release of the chemicals (neurotransmitters), would be the information you are putting out to the universe — your database, in terms of marketing materials, articles, links, web pages, proposals and the like — is being received by the prospect with the need for your product or service.

I hope this application doesn't seem like too much of a stretch, just go with it. A diagram of the neurotransmitters is below:

Neurotransmitter

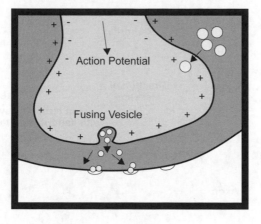

As you can see from the above diagram, there is a gap or space from one neuron to another. This is a microscopic space of intracellular fluid called the synapse. An electrical charge cannot cross this space; it has to translate itself into a different language. It translates into a chemical.

The action potential occurs and this causes the chemical messenger to be dumped into the synapes and there is a receptor on the receiving neuron, like a key into a lock. These chemical messengers are called neurotransmitters.

Application:

Let's say the analogy of the sending impulse neuron is your marketing activity, and the receiving neuron would be the prospect with the need for your product or service. One side note to make. The neurotransmitters that are not used can either be degraded via enzymes, and discarded to your cerebrospinal fluid and eventually into your blood stream, kidneys and then discarded out of the body, or recycled back to the sending neuron where they are reassembled into reusable neurotransmitters, just like recycling plastic!

There are many ways that you can manipulate the amounts of neurotransmitters and the amounts of receptors. One such manipulation is through the use of drugs. This body of research is called neuropharmacology. This is how you manipulate the nervous system.

There are drugs you can take that have almost the exact same molecular makeup as the neurotransmitter, so it takes up the receptor sites as if it were the real neurotransmitter. The postsynaptic or second neuron fires as if the presynaptic neuron had released the chemical.

There are drugs that mimic the neurotransmitter serotonin and when taken they fill up the receptor sites for seratonin and the brain acts like real serotonin has been released and you have a hallucination. There is a message sent that really isn't there (LSD, Mescalin).

The opposite is true as well. You can block the receptor. A neural transmitter called dopamine is one that is quite well known. In one part of the brain the level of dopamine has to do with coherent, logical, linear and clear thinking. If these levels get out of proportion you have the psychiatric disorder of schizophrenia, a pattern of very disordered thought. If there were too much dopamine then antipsychotic drugs would inhibit the uptake of the receptor sites.

Another way to manipulate the nervous system by using drugs is to force the presynaptic neuron to send a message, release a neurotransmitter when it had no intention of doing so.

Mood, pleasure, pain, and other mental states are determined by particular groups of neurons in the brain that use special sets of neurotransmitters and neuromodulators. Mood, for example, is strongly influenced by the neurotransmitter serotonin. Many researchers think that depression results from a shortage of serotonin. Prozac, the world's bestselling antidepressant, inhibits the reabsorption of serotonin, thus increasing the amount in the synapse.

Effect of Prozac

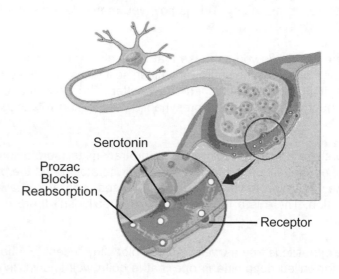

Serotonin

Prozac
Blocks
Reabsorption

Receptor

Learning Theory

Many things are happening on a neurological basis when learning occurs. First, there may be the formation of new neurons. There is brain plasticity which states that the brain can and does form new neurons. Another event that may happen is that the synaptic connection between two existing neurons strengthens during learning.

Let's look at both of these. The common factor is constant excitation over time, which then creates a release of the neurotransmitter called glutamate, which in turn causes calcium uptake to occur and strengthens the impulse connection between two neurons (learning), or the generation of a new neurological connection.

Long Term Potentiation, (LTP), is a synaptic model for learning and is the process of stimulating a dentritic spine in a dense cluster of rapid action potentials, resulting in the synapse becoming hyper responsive or potentiated.[81]

Long Term Potentiation

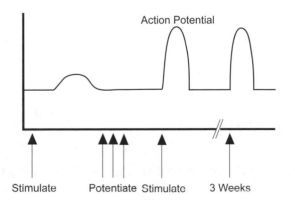

Stimulate   Potentiate Stimulate   3 Weeks

After potentiation occurred, that pathway is stronger and the connection occurs long-term and that is the physiology of learning. These changes are long lasting.

Application

Once again a case is made for a "threshold" of repeated stimulation. Enough action produces the changes in the neuron to create a connection to be made, which is learning. The key concept here is that there needs to be enough of a continuous exposure to the input to create the change. The case for ongoing, high intensity activities to produce the results to reach your goals.

With the introduction of calcium, you have stimulated the neuron to bring buried receptor sites to the surface, so you now have more receptor sites and you've increased the receptivity to the stimulus.

You can change the marketplaces' receptivity to your product or service through identifying more prospects from your increased intensity of marketing activity. I know this is simple, but I find it interesting to see this same principle on a cellular level.

It is the release of glutamate from constant stimulation of the neuron that generates the release and absorption of calcium, which creates the added receptor cites making the post synaptic neuron more excitable and connect faster which is learning.

However, too much glutamate is toxic and will actually kill the neuron. This is called Glutamatergic Toxicity. This is the centerpiece of understanding neurological diseases.

Application:

This relates to the inverted U in terms of the optimal performance curve. This is the relationship between effort and results.

The Peak Performance Zone

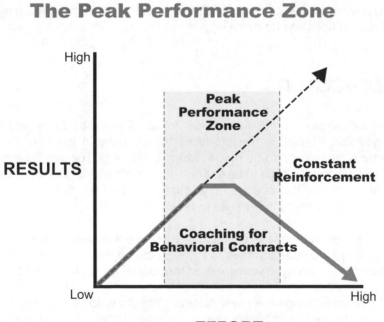

The relationship starts out to be a direct correlation. As you increase effort you get an increase in performance results. However, you will reach a point where an increase in effort will actually decrease performance. There is an optimal level or range, where you will arrive at the highest level of results for your efforts. This range is called the peak performance zone. If you are below this level of intensity then you will not have peak performance, (or action potential to relate this to the neuron), and if you are too intense in your effort (or to highly stimulated), then you likewise will not have peak performance.

The way to keep yourself in the "zone" is by being in relationship to a feedback mechanism. This feedback mechanism is the constant reinforcement and evaluation of your behavioral contract. Your weekly commitments are the "reference system" where you will receive the feedback to know if you are below the intensity level and need to pick it up, or if you are too high and are in danger of "burn-out" and need to back off a bit.

Athletes know this. If they press too hard performance decreases, struggle negates. It's just the right amount of effort that generates the peak result.

Another biology example of the inverted U concept or a performance zone, is how hormones affect neurotransmitter release.

Hormones and Neurotransmitter Release

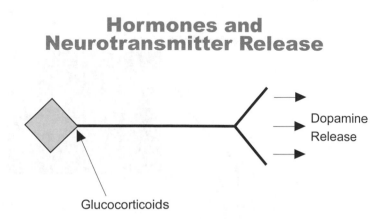

Glucocorticoids

Steroid hormones called glucocorticoids are released during stress. These hormones have an effect on dopamine release. When you are stimulated, your neuron releases the neurotransmitter dopamine, a feel good chemical, this produces pleasurable effects. During long-term stress however, a chronic rise in glucocorticoid levels occurs and the dopamine neurons are depleted leading to the inability to feel pleasure. There is a threshold or duration of stress stimulation that will increase the release of the dopamine until an optimal level is achieved, and then an increase in stress will decrease the release of dopamine, just as in the performance zone.

Networking

The diagram of a single neuron transmitting information to a single dendrite in a linear flow is an oversimplification of how our brain actually functions. The brain is far more then single neurons in a straight line.

Instead, neurons send axons to multiple other neurons, sending branches off in a variety of directions even back to themselves, forming networks.

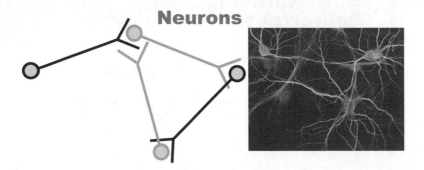

This networking pattern is an example of how the brain works. Our brain does not work in a linear straight-line fashion. Our brains work in a networking pattern. That is why the use of a mind map is the most effective way to take notes, prepare information or even deliver a presentation. A mind map mimics the way that the brain naturally forms relationships and connections.

A **mind map** is a diagram used to represent words, ideas, tasks or other items linked to, and arranged radially, around a central key word or idea. It is used to generate, visualize, structure and classify ideas, and as an aid in study, organization, problem solving, decision making, and writing.

It is an image-centered diagram that represents semantic or other connections between portions of information. By presenting these connections in a radial, non-linear graphical manner, it encourages a brainstorming approach to any given organizational task, eliminating the hurdle of initially establishing an intrinsically appropriate or relevant conceptual framework to work within.

A mind map is similar to a semantic network or cognitive map, but there are no formal restrictions on the kinds of links used.

The elements are arranged intuitively according to the importance of the concepts and they are organized into groupings, branches, or areas. The uniform graphic formulation of the semantic structure of information on the method of gathering knowledge may aid recall of existing memories.

The use of a mind map also engages both parts of the brain. The decision of how to form the mind map engages the creative right hemisphere, and the actual writing of the information, and execution of the thought engages the analytical language centered left brain. Hence, through the use of a mind map you are using both sides of your brain, when without the use of a mind map you may only be activating the left hemisphere. What this means to you is that you will have access to more infromation and more creativity then you would using a traditional list.

A complete mind map may have main topic lines radiating in all directions from the center. Sub-topics and facts will branch off these, like branches and twigs from the trunk of a tree. You do not need to worry about the structure produced, as this will evolve of its own.

Mind mapping is an important technique that improves the way you take notes, and supports and enhances your creative problem-solving. By using mind maps, you can quickly identify and understand the structure of a subject and the way that pieces of information fit together, as well as recording the raw facts contained in normal notes. More than this, mind maps provide a structure which encourages creative problem solving, and they hold information in a format that your mind will find easy to remember and quick to review.

Your mind maps are your own property: once you understand how to make notes in the mind map format, you can develop your own conventions to take them further. The following suggestions may help to increase their effectiveness.

Popularized by Tony Buzan, mind maps abandon the list format of conventional note taking. They do this in favor of a two-dimensional structure. A good mind map shows the 'shape' of the subject, the relative importance of individual points, and the way in which facts relate to one another.

Mind maps are more compact than conventional notes, often taking up one side of paper. This helps you to make associations easily. If you find out more information after you have drawn the main mind map, then you can easily integrate it with little disruption.

Mind maps are also useful for:
- Summarizing information;
- Consolidating information from different research sources;
- Thinking through complex problems;
- Presenting information in a format that shows the overall structure of your subject.

They are very quick to review as you can often refresh information in your mind just by glancing at one. And in the same way, they can be effective mnemonics: Remembering the shape and structure of a mind map can give you the cues you need to remember the information within it. As such, they engage much more of your brain in the process of assimilating and connecting facts, compared with conventional notes.

An Example mind map

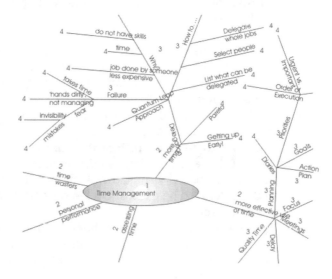

To make notes on a subject using a mind map, draw it in the following way:

1. Write the title of the subject you're exploring in the center of the page, and draw a circle around it. .

2. As you come across major subdivisions or subheadings of the topic, or important facts that relate to the subject, draw lines out from this circle. Label these lines with these subdivisions or subheadings. .

3. As you go deeper into the subject and uncover another level of information, (further subheadings, or individual facts) belonging to the subheadings above, draw these as lines linked to the subheading lines. .

4. Finally, for individual facts or ideas, draw lines out from the appropriate heading line and label them.

As you come across new information, link it in to the mind map appropriately.

♦ **Use single words or simple phrases for information:** Most words in normal writing are padding, as they ensure that facts are conveyed in the correct context, and in a format that is pleasant to read. In your own mind maps, single strong words and meaningful phrases can convey the same meaning more potently. Excess words just clutter the mind map.

♦ **Print words:** Joined up or indistinct writing can be more difficult to read.

♦ **Use color to separate different ideas:** This will help you to separate ideas where necessary. It also helps you to visualize the mind map for recall. Color also helps to show the organization of the subject.

♦ **Use symbols and images:** Where a symbol or picture means something to you, use it. Pictures can help you to remember information more effectively than words.

♦ **Using cross-linkages:** Information in one part of the mind map may relate to another part. Here you can draw in lines to show the cross-linkages. This helps you to see how one part of the subject affects another.

Key points:

Mind mapping is an extremely effective method of taking notes. Mind maps show not only facts, but also the overall structure of a subject and the relative importance of individual parts of it. They help you to associate ideas and make connections that might not otherwise make.

If you do any form of research or note taking, try experimenting with mind maps. You will find them surprisingly effective. An easy topic to practice a mind map would be to mind map your life. There is no right or wrong so be inventive and creative.

More on networking.

The brain recruits multiple neurons that together give you the memory of an event including all of the senses and emotions. Notice that this involves multiple neurons that are fired in a "pattern" to give you the totality of the experience.

Application:

The thought that comes to mind in this regard, is the networking of a variety of experts to give a more complete picture of the business environment to the customer. Let's use a financial advisor for an example. The financial advisor has an expertise in a certain area, or portion of the overall picture and needs of the client. By networking with other experts the financial advisor can better serve the needs of their client then by acting alone, where they are limited to their own expertise and biases.

With this in mind I coach financial advisors, (usually insurance and annuity products), to build a team consisting of other experts such as estate planning attorneys, accountants, perhaps stock brokers, or other people, who will then combined together, represent the totality of the clients needs. This is better customer service and "one stop shopping" for the customer. The client doesn't want to be told that they need to find an estate planning attorney to speak with. The client expects you to have a team that includes all of the expertise they will need for a full financial picture.

Consider the blind man describing the elephant example. There is an old tale from India which tells of a wise man Rajah, who made a study of human nature. The Rajah gathered six blind men together and asked them to describe the animal in front of them. Since all six men had been blind since birth, they had never seen an elephant.

The first man touched the tusk and said, "This animal is like a spear." The second man felt the trunk and declared, "This animal is like a snake." Feeling the ear, the third man exclaimed, "This animal is like a fan." The fourth man stroked the elephant's front leg and announced, "This animal is like a tree." The fifth man, after patting the elephant's side, decided, "This animal is like a wall." Finally, the sixth man grasped the tail and proclaimed, "This animal is like a rope."[82]

The men argued over who was right. The elephant is a large animal made up of different parts. Each of the blind men had knowledge of only one part. To find out the whole truth they must gain knowledge of all the parts and put them together. They must set aside their egos to realize that they may not have all of the knowledge themselves.

This story exemplifies the essence of big picture thinking and co-operation. A neurological pathway may hold just a piece of the big picture recall or experience, but wired together with a pattern of other neurons, creates the total experience.

What business alliances or networks can you create that would generate a more fulfilled expertise for your clients?

Now back to neurons...

Chapter 19

The Biology of
"Turn On - Turn Off"

There is something else to make mention of here regarding how neurons function. Neurons increase their sensitivity to detect signals, by inhibiting themselves and other neurons. The diagram below shows what is referred to as a recurrent collateral projection, which are projections coming off the axon, back onto the cell body, which enables the neuron to give feedback, in this case inhibition, to itself.

Neuron Feedback

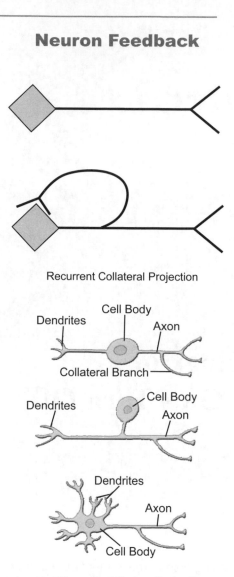

Recurrent Collateral Projection

The neurotransmitters that it sends to the postsynaptic neuron are excitatory and the feedback to the presynaptic neuron is inhibitory. This is a way of sharpening the signal over time. This property occurs all over the nervous system. It is a turn on, turn off feedback system.

Let's look at this type of feedback system regarding the perception of pain.

Let's say that you have a paper cut. Ever get one of these? You're looking through some files, shifting through some papers and you cut your finger on the edge of a piece. Here is what happens in your nervous system:

A neuron that when stimulated, signals through the spinal cord to your brain's outer cortex that something is painful.

It turns out that pain comes in a number of different varieties. You can have a certain type of sharp pain, such as the paper cut; the technical term is epicritic pain. This is very intense pain that goes away very quickly. Here is a pathway that explains it.

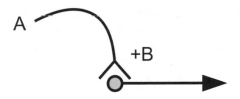

Here you have a pain receptor (A) that sends its signal to the neuron (B), excites it, and you have an action potential and you feel pain as the information shoots up your spine. Notice however that this same pain receptor neuron sends collateral (C) off to this second neuron (D).

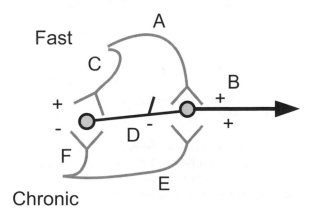

The second neuron (C) inhibits the pain messenger neuron. This collateral (C) stimulates that neuron (D). This is the case of a feedback signal. Your finger is cut by the paper, then an immediate signal (A) is sent to (B) to signal pain, and then a second later it (C) turns it off (D).

Something very different can also occur. A pain signal comes in (E) and stimulates that pain neuron (B) to fire to tell your spine that something is painful, and it sends its collateral off to that local inhibitory neuron (F), but in this case it inhibits the inhibitory neuron. It blocks the ability of that inhibitory neuron to turn off that pain in neuron (B). This pathway, once stimulated, keeps on going. That's throbbing pain. That's a pulled muscle, a burn; it's a very different version of pain.

Here you have two pathways, one is a fast perception that shuts down and the other is a slow, throbbing perception that lingers on. This turns out to explain quite a bit in pain perception. If you have throbbing muscles and you get a massage, that triggers fast pain and it momentarily turns off the chronic pain and you get relief.

Application:

The nervous system has turn-on and mechanisms throughout, as does our system of genes. There is a need for this same mechanism in our daily lives as well. We need to be able to turn off distractions and turn on attention to the required task at hand.

According to some of the latest research, scientists have demonstrated that the brain processes about 400 billion bits of information every second. Usually however, we are conscious of only about 2,000 of those bits of data.[83] Out of those 2000 bits, the inputs the brain is processing pertain only to our awareness of the body, our awareness of the environment and our awareness of time.[84]

A huge difference exists between the brain processing information and your awareness of it. Although the brain processes 400 billion bits of data every second, the frontal lobe has on and off mechanisms that enable us to actively select what data we choose to put our awareness on.

If you are wearing glasses, as you read this page,, you are not aware of the fact that you are staring through a pane of glass until I just pointed it out. You were not aware of how your back feels against the chair until I point it out as well. That is just not important information so you are freed up to pay attention to other items (Selective Perception).

As human beings we have the privilege to choose where to put our attention and for how long. If we don't exercise this choice then our genetic make up will select it for us, and it will have us avoiding and rationalizing all day long.

I have a wonderful on-off technique for you that I will explain now. I call it the Pending versus Current mind map. Here is how it works.

Whenever I start to feel a bit overwhelmed, when I have multiple distractions and competing priorities coming at me at the same time, I grab a piece of paper and begin a pending versus current or now mind map.

Split the paper in half and draw two circles about the size of a quarter on each side. Write Pending in the right circle and Current or Now in the left. The deal is to only have one open item at a time on the left or current side. This is your "on" switch. The "off" switch is the pending side. Here is a sample:

Distracted... Try Mind Mapping

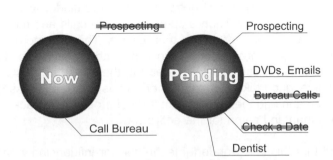

Does the pending item override my current item?

243

The most important activity for me right now lets say is prospecting, that means making the calls that I am prompted to make in my database. So I simply write prospecting on the left side in the "now" mind map. As I'm in the process of my personal prospecting, my marketing director comes into my office and informs me that he has a resume of a promising telemarketer. We are looking to hire additional staff.

Now this is an interruption. It's almost as if I have a collateral neuron to either excite or inhibit my attention. I ask this question:

Does the pending item override what I am currently doing right now? If yes, then I take what I am currently doing and put it on the pending mind map and I put this more important item on the now side. I will always only have one item open or "turned on" on the now side. Everything else will be placed in the "off" position on the pending side.

If the answer is no, the pending item is not more important then what I am currently doing, then at least I have a place to put it so it doesn't get lost. It goes onto the pending mind map.

In between prospecting calls I remember that I need to order some DVD's from my manufacturer for my office inventory. This is another distraction. It's another one of the 2000 bits of information competing for my attention. I put it to the screening process again by asking if it overrides my current priority, and it doesn't, so it gets added to the pending.

Next I hear a new e-mail beep in so it's a reminder to check e-mails, but not right now. Then a speaker bureau calls and they want to submit me to speak for one of their clients. This is a more urgent item and so I take prospecting, turn it off and move it over to the pending and then I add speaker bureau to the turned on position on the now side, and I take that call. When that is finished I cross it out, turning it off and add the most urgent item of prospecting back on the now mind map and so on for the entire day.

I find that this is a wonderful technique for influencing what you pay attention to and to keeping your physiology out of the panic mode and in the peak performance zone. You now have a technique to capture your thoughts and pendings, and at the same time to stay focused on one item at a time. The next time you are feeling pulled in different directions with multiple priorities tugging at you use this technique and appreciate how focused you stay.

PART V

Conclusion

Chapter 20

So What Will You do Now?

That's a question for how decisions are made and how difficult it is for people to change. One thing is for sure; you can't rely on your left-brain to decide for you to make changes and to take on new habits. You will not respond to rational, reasonable and logical reasoning. I tell my clients being reasonable is the lowest level of human existence!

You are not going to start an exercise program because it is good for you. You are not going to stop smoking for the same reason. And you are not going to get on your computer, go to my web site and begin your on-line coaching and accountability program because it will make you more productive.

Professors at Princeton University are using brain scans to try to figure out why people make what appear to be morally inconsistent choices. In one experiment they asked subjects to also respond to a classic moral conundrum known as the Trolley Problem, which is explained below.

In the first scenario, you are at the wheel of a runaway trolley quickly approaching a fork in the tracks. On the tracks extending to the left is a group of five railway workmen. On the tracks extending to the right is a single railway workman.

If you do nothing, the trolley will proceed to the left, causing the deaths of the five workmen. The only way to avoid the deaths of these workmen is to hit a switch on your dashboard that will cause the trolley to proceed to the right, causing the death of the single workman.

Is it appropriate for you to hit the switch to avert the deaths of the five workmen?

In the second scenario, a runaway trolley is heading down the tracks toward five workmen who will be killed if the trolley proceeds on its present course. You are on a footbridge over the tracks, in between the approaching trolley and the five workmen. Next to you on this footbridge is a stranger who happens to be very large.

The only way to save the lives of the five workmen is to push this stranger off the bridge and onto the tracks below, where his large body will stop the trolley. The stranger will die if you do this, but the workmen will be saved.

Is it appropriate for you to push the stranger onto the tracks in order to save the five workmen?

The majority of individuals respond "yes" to the first scenario and "no" to the second.

With either choice you will kill one person to save five. A similar example is in wartime. A group of 25 soldiers are in hiding as an enemy battalion is marching by. You are holding an infant that starts to cry. Do you smother the infant and protect the lives of the greater number or do you let the infant cry and risk being detected by the enemy troops?

We tend to make completely different decisions depending on the emotional context of how a problem and solution is presented. If you're holding the baby your thoughts would perhaps be different then your neighbor who is not. Most people will pull the lever, but not throw the man in front of the trolley.

When a person is thinking of pulling the lever, the frontal cortex activates. But when the person is thinking of pushing someone off the trolley to his death, the limbic system activates. Cortical versus limbic activation is identified depending on how emotional a problem and solution is presented. Depending on how it's framed.

Do you save five by sacrificing one by pulling a lever or pushing a button or by pushing someone on the track? Different areas of the brain are engaged although the math is the same. It depends on the emotional content.

Behavioral contracting, making commitments with consequences for non-performance, taps into this principle. You will have a cortical limbic loop whether you use a behavioral contract or not. It's the nature of the loop that you can influence. The stated commitment activates the outer cortex; "I'm going to the gym four times this week". The limbic area will be activated as well but the question is how? If you don't have a consequence, "pay a $10 fine", then the activation will be a neural network of the memory of past experiences, of how hard and uncomfortable it is to go to the gym and exercise. This will lead to avoidance and a justification of the avoidance with rationalizations.

If you do have a consequence that is strong enough, a high enough fine for example, (see conversation about the threshold of stimulation of the Axon Hillock), then your limbic system is still activated and you will still avoid, but you will be avoiding the consequence by doing the activity.

Beware. Imagine that you agree with everything I've researched and reported in this book. Imagine further that you intend to take action, to make changes, to be responsible and accountable.

It doesn't matter. Your intentions are not strong enough. To use the analogy presented here, your intentions will not be intense enough to pass the Axon Hillock's threshold to generate the action potential or results.

You've got one move. Dive into planning and making weekly commitments and have an outside source hold you accountable with consequences for non-performance. If you do that then you will be very competitive in this never-ending battle versus mediocrity.

Chapter 21

Is it Time Yet?

Time

Before a summary and conclusion of this book, I want to take a look at the fabric for which you will be executing into, namely time.

There are two distinct views on the meaning of the word time.[85]

(Sourced from Wikipedia) *One view is that time is part of the fundamental structure of the universe, a dimension in which events occur in sequence, and time itself is something that can be measured. This is the realist's view, to which Sir Isaac Newton subscribed, and hence is sometimes referred to as Newtonian time.*

An opposing view is that time is part of the fundamental human intellectual structure, (together with space and number), within which we sequence events, quantify the duration of events and the intervals between them, and compare the motions of objects. In this second view, time does not refer to any kind of entity that "flows", that objects "move through", or that is a "container" for events. This view is in the tradition of philosophers Gottfried Leibniz and Immanuel Kant, in which time, rather than being an objective thing to be measured, is part of the measuring system used by humans.

In physics, time and space are considered fundamental quantities (i.e. they cannot be defined in terms of other quantities because other quantities — such as velocity, force, energy, etc — are already defined in terms of them). Thus the only definition possible is an operational one, in which time is defined by the process of measurement and by the units chosen.

Periodic events and periodic motion have long served as standards for units of time. Examples are the apparent motion of the sun across the sky, the phases of the moon, the swing of a pendulum, heartbeats, etc. Currently the unit of time (the second), is defined as a certain number of hyperfine transitions in Cesium atoms.

Time has long been a major subject of science, philosophy, and art. Its measurement has occupied scientists and technologists, and was a prime motivation in astronomy. Time is also of significant social importance, having economic value ("time is money"), as well as personal value, due to an awareness of the limited time in each day and in human lifespans.

Time has been considered to be a fourth dimension, added to length, width and depth. "It's not so much that there's something strange about time," said Dr. John A. Wheeler, the famous Princeton cosmologist, "the thing that's strange is what's going on inside time. We will first understand how simple the universe is when we recognize how strange time is."

Time as a variable frequently appears in most of the mathematical equations used to describe the known physical world. However, whether time flows backwards or forwards usually makes no difference in the math. But in our everyday world we never see this happening. Time is experienced as always flowing forward, from past to present to future, and this is known as "Times' Arrow".

Time is how we view the passage of events. Our fundamental human drives have not changed from the Paleolithic era, hundreds of thousands of years ago. Much of what we are about still centers on the same impulses to eat, pass on our genes, and fight or flight that motivated cave man. Despite the constancy of these primal urges, human culture has experienced upheavals in the period since our hunter-gatherer ancestors roamed. Perhaps the most profound change in the transition from the Stone Age to the Information Age revolves around our subjective experience of time.

Keeping time is a practice that may go back more then 20,000 years, when hunters of the ice age notched holes in sticks or bones, possibly to track the days between phases of the moon. Only 5,000 years ago the Babylonians and Egyptians devised calendars for planting and other time-sensitive activities.

Early experts tracked natural cycles, the solar day, the lunar month and the solar year. Beginning in the 13th century, the mechanical clock initiated a revolution equal in impact to the later invention of the printing press. Time no longer flowed as it did literally in an early water clock; rather it was marked off by a mechanism that could track the beats of an oscillator. When refined, this device allows time to be counted to fractions of a second.

This technology changed our perception of the way society was organized and structured. It was a measurement that enabled one person to coordinate activities with another. "Punctuality comes from within, not from without," writes Harvard University historian David Landes in his book, "Revolution in Time: Clocks and the Making of the Modern World." It is the mechanical clock that made attention to the passage of time a common event.

Time has been measured in the following increments[86] (really, I'm not kidding!):

1. **One Attosecond**- a billionth of a billionth of a second. Researchers have created pulses of light lasting just 250 attoseconds using sophisticated high-speed lasers. Although this interval seems unimaginably brief, it is large compared with the Planck time-about 10 to the minus 43 seconds, which is believed to be the shortest possible duration of time.

2. **One Femtosecond**- a millionth of a billionth of a second. An atom in a molecule typically completes a single vibration in 10 to 100 femtoseconds. The interaction of light with pigments in the retina, the process that generates vision, takes about 200 femtoseconds.

3. **One Picosecond**- a thousandth of a billionth of a second. The fastest transistors operate in picoseconds. The bottom quark, a rare subatomic particle created in high energy accelerators, lasts for one picosecond before decaying.

4. **One Nanosecond**- a billionth of a second. Perhaps this is a more familiar term that you've heard of. A beam of light shining through a vacuum will travel only 30 centimeters, not quite one foot, in this time. The microprocessor inside a personal computer will typically take two to four nanoseconds to execute a single instruction, such as adding two numbers.

5. **One Microsecond**- a millionth of a second. That same beam of light will now have traveled 300 meters, about the length of three football fields.

6. **One Milisecond**- a thousandth of a second. The shortest exposure time in a typical camera. A housefly flaps its wings once every three milliseconds. The moon travels around Earth two milliseconds more slowly each year as its orbit

gradually widens. In computer science, the interval of 10 milliseconds is known as a jiffy.

7. **One Tenth of a second**- a hummingbird can beat its wings seven times. A tuning fork pitched to A above middle C, vibrates four times.

8. **One Second**- now we're talking in familiar terms. Your heartbeat lasts about this long. Earth travels 30 kilometers around the sun in one second. It is not quite enough time for moonlight to reach Earth, 1.3 seconds.

9. **One Minute**- the brain of a newborn baby grows one to two milligrams in one minute. The average person can speak about 150 words or read about 250 words in this time. Light from the sun reaches Earth in about eight minutes. When Mars is closest to Earth, sunlight reflected off the planets surface reaches us in about four minutes.

10. **One Hour**- cell reproduction takes this long. Light from Pluto, the most distant planet (not officially a planet, it's been downsized), reaches Earth in five hours and 20 minutes.

11. **One Day**- this is our most natural unit of time, the duration of Earth's rotation around the sun. Currently clocked at 23 hours, 56 minutes and 40.1 seconds, the planet's rotation is constantly slowing because of gravitational drag from the moon and other influences. The human heart beats about 100,000 times in a day.

12. **One Year**- Earth makes one trip around the sun and spins on its axis 365.26 times.

13. **One Century**- the moon recedes from Earth by another 3.8 meters. Baby boomers have only a 1 in 26 chance of living to the age of 100, but giant tortoises can live as long as 177.

14. **One Million Years**- a spaceship moving at the speed of light would not yet be at the halfway point on a journey to the Andromeda galaxy (2.3 million light-years away).

15. **One Billion Years**- it took approximately that long for the Earth to cool, develop oceans, give birth to single-celled life, and exchange its carbon dioxide rich early atmosphere for an oxygen rich one.

No one keeps track of time better than Ferenc Krausz. In his lab at the Max Planck Institute of Quantum Optics in Garching, Germany, he has clocked the shortest time intervals ever observed. Krausz uses ultraviolet laser pulses to track the brief quantum leaps of electrons within atoms. The events he probes last for about 100 attoseconds. For some perspectives, 100 attoseconds is to one second, as a second is to 300 million years!

There is a temporal realm called the Planck scale, where even attoseconds drag by like eons. It marks the edge of known physics, a region where distances and intervals are so short that the very concepts of time and space start to break down. Planck time, the smallest unit of time that has any physical meaning, is 10 to the minus 43 seconds, less than a trillionth of a trillionth of an attosecond. Beyond that, time is indistinguishable from matter and space.

The Planck scale has led scientist to even question the existence of time. If it doesn't exist, then what is time? This is known amongst physicists as the "problem of time". The laws of physics don't explain why time always points to the future. All the laws, whether Newton's, Einstein's, or the quirky quantum rules — would work equally well if time ran backwards. As far as we can tell though, time is a one way process. It never reverses, even though no laws restrict it. At least within the limits of human perception, we can't perceive a backwards arrow of time.

Einstein proved that time is part of the fabric of the universe. Contrary to what Newton believed, our ordinary clocks don't measure something that's independent of the universe. The question is, is time a fundamental property of reality or just the macroscopic appearance of things?

Einstein was comforted by these questions about time. In March of 1955, when his lifelong friend Michele Besso died, he wrote a letter consoling his family: "Now he has departed from this strange world a little ahead of me. That means nothing. People like us, who believe in physics, know that the distinction between past, present and future is only a stubbornly persistent illusion."

For most of us however, time is not only real, but it is the master of everything that we do. Our clock watching may be related to a basic biological reality. Our bodies are full of living clocks.

Scientists are honing in on areas of the brain that produce the sensation of time flying when we are emotionally engaged in an activity like a good movie or book, and the slow paced torment of sitting through a monotone lecture on the U.S. interest rate policy. Scientists are beginning to understand the connections between different kinds of memory, and how events are organized and recalled chronologically.[87]

Neither scientists nor philosophers really know what time is or why it exists. The best thing they can say is that time is an extra dimension like, but not identical to, space. For example, the two dimensional orbit of the moon through space can be thought of as a three dimensional corkscrew through space-time.[88]

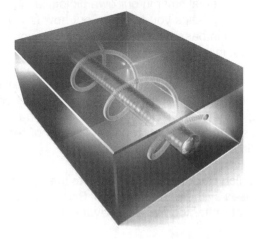

Einstein proposed that the measured interval between two events depends on how the observer is moving. Two observers moving differently will experience different durations between the same two events.

This effect is often described using the Twin Paradox. Imagine a set of twins, A and B. A boards a rocket ship and travels at a high speed to a nearby star, turns around, and flies back to Earth, while twin B stays home. For A, the duration of the trip might be one year, but when A returns and exits the spaceship, he will find that 10 years have gone by on earth. His twin is now nine years older then he is. A and B are no longer the same age, despite the fact that they were born on the same day.

Jet Lag

The effect known as Time Dilation occurs whenever two observers move relative to each other. Atomic clocks are accurate enough to record the shift and confirm that time really is stretched by motion.

Speed is one way to jump ahead in time. Gravity is another. Einstein predicted that gravity slows time. Clocks run faster in the attic than in the basement, which is closer to the center of the Earth and therefore deeper down in the gravitational field.

There is an interval timer in our own biological clocks. This sense of time and timing, helps you to figure out how fast you need to run to catch a fly ball in baseball, or how fast to clap your hands to keep up with the beat in music.

Interval timing uses the higher powers of the cerebral cortex, the brain center that governs perception, memory and consciousness. Stephen Rao of the Medical College of Wisconsin has used functional Magnetic Resonance Imaging to isolate areas of the brain that are engaged in time recognition and sensation.

The circadian clock tunes our bodies to the cycles of sunlight and darkness caused by the Earth's rotation. Body temperature regulation peaks in the late afternoon or early evening and bottoms out a few hours before we rise in the morning. Blood pressure typically starts to surge between 6:00 and 7:00 am. Secretion of the stress hormone cortisol is 10 to 20 times higher in the morning than at night. Urination and bowel movements are generally suppressed at night and pick up again in the morning.

Circadian patterns persist even in the absence of light and they are expressed in every cell of the body. Neurologists have made progress in understanding how daylight sets the clock. Two clusters of 10,000 nerve cells in the hypothalamus of the brain have been considered the clocks center.

Modern day humans in developed countries have a life expectancy of more than 70 years. The life expectancy of your average Mayfly, in contrast, is a day. Different species have different life expectancies. If your days are numbered, what's in control?

Genetics are important. A single gene mutation in mice can produce a strain that lives up to 50% longer then usual. High metabolic rates shorten life span. So far the closest thing to a timing mechanism is called the Mitotic Clock. The clock keeps track of cell division, or mitosis, the process by which a single cell splits into two.

There seems to be a ceiling on how many times normal cells of the human body can divide. In cultures they will undergo 60 to 100 mitotic divisions then distort or die. "All of a sudden they just stop growing", says John Sedivy of Brown University. What the cells are counting is not chronological time, but the number of cell divisions. It seems that each time a cell divides a bit of the non-coded DNA is lost. When the cells shrink below some type of specific length this would be the marker for aging.

There is another type of time altogether called "mind time". This is how we experience the passage of time. This clock is located in the brain's hypothalamus. Mind time is determined by the attention we give to events and the emotions we feel when they occur. The processing of time and certain types of memory share some common neurological pathways.

The ability to form memories is an indispensable part of the construction of a sense of our own chronology. Studies of brain-damaged patients suggest that structures in the temporal lobe of the brain, and in the basal forebrain, play important roles in laying down information about when events occurred and in what order.[89] The memory of one's wedding bears a time stamp.

Finding Time

Basal Forebrain
Injury to this area impairs recall of when events happened - this area identifies the chronology of pase events.

Hippocampus

Damage to this causes anterograde amnesia - an impaired ability to form new memories.

Temporal Lobe
Damage to this area can cause retrograde amnesia, where past memories cannot be retrieved.

It seems that humans are psychics after all. There is a strange mental time lag, a phenomenon first brought to the forefront in the 1970's by neurophysiologist Benjamin Libet of the University of California at San Francisco. Libet documented a gap between the time a conscious individual decided to flex his finger, and the time that his brain waves indicated that a flex was imminent. The brain activity occurred a third of a second before the person consciously decided to move his finger. This has also been observed in trials with monkeys that were trained to pull a lever to receive food.

One general fact is concluded from Libet's work. There exists a lag between the beginning of the neural events leading to consciousness and the moment one actually experiences the consequence of those neural events.

It takes time for the electrochemical modifications to be transmitted as signals to the central nervous system. It takes time to generate the neural pattern in the brain's sensory map to the event and the nervous system for action. This is nothing more then a few milliseconds, but there is a delay nonetheless.

We are all late for consciousness and we never know it. There is the illusion of continuity of time and space. John C. Rothwell of the Institute of Cognitive Neuroscience in London, suggests that the brain predates the perception of the target by as much as 120 milliseconds, thereby giving us all the perception of seamless viewing.[90]

Applications:

So what does this mean to you? It means that time is a moving target. It's a concept that has been invented by mankind to help organize agreements and to give pace, order and predictability to human interactions.

As we look at what science tells us, we can translate it into some ideas that will make life easier for you in your life. First, let's examine the concept that time is different for different observers. Imagine you are standing on a street corner and all of a sudden you hear a loud sound. You look up and see an SUV speeding around the corner, hit the curb, and jettison off the curb as it flips into the air making a solid rotation, until hit hits the ground and skids to a halt on the opposite side of the street.

Here is what you experience. As soon as you hear the vehicle you see in actual time the rotating and sliding vehicle. It seems to take about 10 seconds total. Here is what the occupants inside the vehicle experience. They are on the same time experience as you are until they hit the curb and begin the flip. Then they are on an altered state of dilated time. Time seems to slow down. It seems like slow motion as they slowly flip over and start a skid on the pavement. One of the occupants reaches out in slow motion grabbing an infant protecting it from going through the windshield. Finally after what seems like 30 seconds, the vehicle comes to a stop and then the occupants are on the same time experience as you are.

What happened in the brain to cause this distortion of time is not fully understood. If there was a time keeper with a stopwatch in the vehicle and outside, both clocks would read the same, even though the inside occupants experience time differently.

Our confusion or state of not understanding doesn't matter. The question is how can this be of benefit to you? Before I answer this, consider another scenario.

You are standing in line at the grocery store and the person in front of you pulls out a bag of coupons. The check stand cashier can't find one of the items that this person has a coupon for and needs to go through the entire receipt and rescan several items, and this goes on and on and on.

What happens to your perception of time, it drags doesn't it? One more scenario:

You are watching a great movie and eating popcorn. Finally the movie is over and you notice that all of the popcorn is gone and it's been two hours and thirty minutes. Time sure did fly by.

Here is how this impacts you. When you are conscious of time, time slows down. When you are not conscious of time, it speeds by. So when would it be in your best interest to slow down or speed up time? Let's first look at advantages of speeding time up.

Imagine you're on the Stairmaster and you plan to exercise for 45-minutes. This is an example of an instance where you would want to speed time up. Get yourself into a disengaged state with time. Get yourself to be non-conscious of time. How? By distracting yourself. Read a book, watch television, listen to music or talk with your neighbor. Do anything but look at the clock.

When you are conscious of time — time slows down. When would it be in your best interest to slow time down? How about if you're marketing from the west coast Pacific Time, to the east coast and it's 12:00 pm PST. You've got about two hours of marketing time before the close of the business day at 5:00 pm EST. Here is the technique to slow down time: become conscious of time by looking at your clock. Keep glancing at your clock and you will maintain the consciousness of time, thereby slowing it down. You will get more done by doing this.

You know by now that my mantra is to measure, report, review, and to execute the rewards or consequences. This is no different with time. Measurement again is the key. As a football coach I can remember that our staff would take 2 ½ hour practices and break them into 5-minute intervals. A manager would blow a foghorn and put a big sign on a large stand indicating which 5-minute time period we were in. I would hear the horn and look up and see 22 for example. This means that we were 22 5-minute periods into practice, or one hour and forty minutes into practice. I would even have the 5-minute periods broken down into segments, some as small as 30-seconds to run a bag drill, then two minutes to practice a curl drop, etc.

Once again the observation changes the perception and the reality, just like quantum physics and the double slit experiment. When you don't observe light, it acts like a wave. When you do observe it, it acts like a particle. Likewise time reacts differently depending on whether it is being observed or not. When you observe time, it slows down. When you don't observe time, it runs faster. How does it know?

An exercise I often give my coaching clients is to track and record all of their stops and starts. In other words, record time. Every time they start an activity they record the time and what they are doing. If they stop to change activities, such as to go to the bathroom they simply record the stop and the start time of the new activity. Even if their start is recreation, rest, or nothing — they still record a start and a stop time for the rest period

One client said that they were amazed at how much time they wasted when they became accountable for how they spent their time. Another client said they have cut their time on their cell phone in half because of this awareness. Another client had all of her sales people do this exercise for an entire week and report their findings to the entire group at their next meeting. Once again, the quantum world prevails because the act of measurement and accountability will change how you spend your time, and the activities you decide to pursue. We are back to the double slit experiment where the observation changes the wave to a particle; the act of measurement changed the outcome.

Another conversation I have with my live coaching clients is what I call the Wormhole effect.

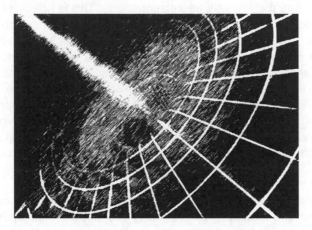

If you pay attention to it you will see that time really can speed by. I got tired of chronological time and before I knew it my wife was putting up the Christmas tree. It seemed like January had just been around the corner and it was the turn of the year again. I decided that I had had it with chronological time. I had enough of getting older so I decided to practice what I'd been preaching, and figured since there are multiple potentials for realities, that I would choose the one that suited me best. I decided that I would be younger at the end of the year rather than older.

Next, and this is my assignment to you, I decided to create the criteria, inspect and verify, of what would need to happen by the end of the year, so when the end of they year arrived, I would indeed be better off — younger in fact — than I was at the beginning. What are the criteria, or proof? I can't do anything about chronological time, but I sure can influence experiential time. How do you influence time? By observing it! Another word for observe is measure.

I decided that I would need to weigh a certain weight by the end of the year for one criterion. Good old gravity prevails again. A second item of proof would be that the first draft of this book would be complete. So my challenge to you is to do the same. Put an end to being helpless with time, and refuse to participate with getting older. Decide and declare what would be the proof that you are better off at the end of the year, and what the criteria would be for you to actually be experientially younger at the end of the next year. Make yourself an appreciating asset, not a depreciating one.

I also put a hefty $1000 fine on not accomplishing those two items just to speed things along! I'd recommend that you do the same. Next, put this into your business and life plans. Make sure you break down the activities necessary, into weekly commitments that you make in your behavioral contract.

Chapter 22

What Does the
Future Hold?

"Success will never be a big step in the future,
success is a small step taken just now."
— Jonathan Martensson

The future is very exciting. There is a wave of new discoveries that are happening on a daily basis. Scientists have found as recent as 2007 that neurogenesis, new neuron growth, increases after physical exercise. The latest research shows that new neurons are growing in one of the most important brain areas, the hippocampus, the seat of declarative and spatial memory. These discoveries raise the prospect that we might learn to manipulate neurogenesis to relieve ailments such as stroke and cognitive decline.

It has also been found that new neurons do connect with the existing circuitry. A recent paper by neuroscientists Nohjin Kee, Catia Teixeira, and their colleagues at the University of Toronto, contributes a key piece of evidence. It shows that new neurons do integrate themselves into functional networks in the hippocampus, and that these new circuits actually boost memory.

Brain Neurons

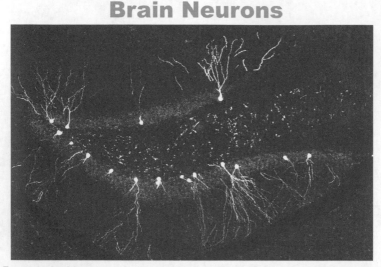

Four-week-old neurons in the hippocampus of a mouse, reveal themselves by expressing a fluorescent marker protein (shown in white).

Memories are not held inside neurons, the brain's cells. Rather, they are set in the connections between neurons called synapses, the tiny gaps across which the signal emitting axon of one neuron sends a message to the signal receiving dendrite of another. Memories, habits and learning are created, when nerve cells in a circuit increase the strength of their connections or form new connections.

Mice learn to find a submerged platform in a water maze, a standard memory test.

To make memories or learning stick, neurons must turn on genes to manufacture proteins that will cement more strongly the synapses shared among them. After training mice in this water task, Kee and his colleagues looked to see if the task switched on learning-associated genes in new hippocampal neurons. They knew they were looking at new neurons because they had injected the mice with a marker for dividing cells. They indeed found the genes were turned on.

Application:

Again, the evidence keeps mounting that you can make a decision about what habits to extinguish and what new habits to create. Once you've made that decision you can create the neurological pathways to cement the habit into an automatic status, in other words, you can change and keep the change as an automatic behavior. Remember, neurons that fire together, wire together. You can be the architect of your personality, habits and results. You are not a victim to, or limited by, your genes or to your environment[91]. The key is to get M.A.D., make a decision. What decisions are you avoiding?

More on Exercise

I've always said that you want to make your lifestyle an asset not a liability. You want to thank yourself twenty years from now for the decisions you've made and actions you've taken today. Health has always been my number one value and I recommend it for you as well, yes above family and above business.

Research confirms that regular cardiovascular exercise improves your memory and cognitive function. In fact, science shows that a sedentary lifestyle impairs brain function. The latest study exploring how exercise enhances cognitive ability was presented at the 2007 Annual Meeting of the American College of Sports Medicine in New Orleans.

Researchers from Miami University located in Oxford, Ohio, placed 108 rats in three different exercise categories: 1) no activity outside of standard cage living, 2) twice-weekly exercise in a large box, and 3) daily exercise on a running wheel. Scientists monitored the rats spatial maze performance over a 23-month period, and

271

reported that the group that exercised daily completed the maze in significantly less time, (more than 20% faster), and made far more correct choices in the maze than the other groups.

More is Better

This graph shows that rats exercising daily completed the maze in a significantly faster fashion, compared to rats that exercised less regularly and those that did not exercise at all.

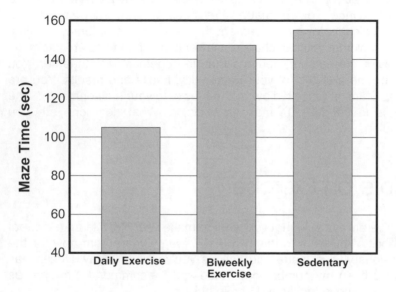

Once again this graph also gives credence to the S.A.I.D. principal that asks you to look at the intensity of your level of activities. It begs the question, are you doing enough to have an effect? As you can see here, the twice-weekly exercise sessions just aren't intense enough to have an impact. A low level of exercise is almost the same as not exercising at all, so why bother?

Neurobiologists Frank LaFerla, of UC Irvine, did a similar study with mice locating and remembering the position of a platform while they were swimming. He declared that such things as memory and learning exercises could be an important supplement to fighting Alzheimer's, a disorder that afflicts about 4.5 million Americans.

He also stated that exercise and mild learning tasks such as learning a maze had prevented the formation of brain amyloid beta plaque, one of the main causes of Alzheimer's. The mice also had less tangles, the other lesion that causes the disease.

The brains of the mice that went through the exercises and learning tasks, did not age as fast as the mice that didn't.

Learning to Remember

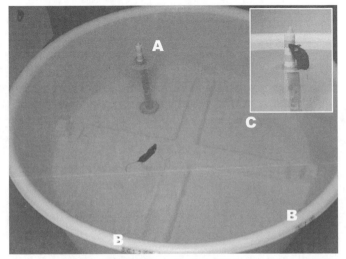

USC scientists discover that putting mice through mental activity delayed the onset of Alzheimer's disease. The mouse had to repeatedly remember the location of the small platform located at A. The mouse, released from B, had to find safety (shown in C).

The future indeed is exciting and you and I will benefit from future discoveries in our lifetimes.

Chapter 23

Some Thoughts to
Help Your New Beginning

"Mind is everything. Muscles — pieces of rubber.
All that I am I am because of my mind."
—Paavo Nurmi

I hope that after having read this book that you come to some of the same conclusions that I have after having done all of the research. One of those conclusions is that you and I are the inventors of our own reality. So this really is the beginning and not the ending. Do you recognize this?

"I'm starting with the man in the mirror. I'm asking him to change his ways. And no message could have been any clearer: if you want to make the world a better place, take a look at yourself and make the change." — From "Man in the Mirror", by Siedah Garrett, Glen Ballard & Michael Jackson.

Remember the quantum conversation; light acts like a particle sometimes and like a wave at other times. When you observe the electrons, the distribution of them on a screen is different, then when you do not look. The world you see and experience depends on you. You cannot observe the subatomic world without disturbing it. No one knows for sure how simply looking at a wave turns it into a particle. However, even though this is beyond the human capacity to understand, it nonetheless describes the phenomenon that reality isn't real until it is observed, and that you have a choice over that observation.

The fact that light is either a wave of energy if we do not observe, or a particle of physical substance if we do, means that it is up to us to use our control over our own observations. This wave particle duality, one of the foundations of quantum physics, points to an astounding truth. Just as with the particles of light, whatever we pay attention to will happen in our own world. What you focus on is what you get. It's all about taking responsibility and owning what you choose to observe.

The problem is that we don't exercise this choice. We forfeit our control. I love the scene from the movie "Instinct" with Anthony Hopkins and Cuba Gooding Jr., when Cuba's character, Theo Caulder a psychiatrist, is interviewing Anthony Hopkins' character Ethan Powell, who is in prison for the criminally insane.[92] Powell grabs Caulder by his neck and asks, "Who's in control?"

"So who is in control? Are you? Am I? Is it the guards outside?" As he has Caulder in a life threatening headlock, he commands him to write on a pad what he has taken from him. "What have you lost?"

Caulder's first response is "CONTROL." Hopkins (Ethan Powell) says "WRONG! You never had control; you only thought you had it. It's an illusion…what do you control, for sure? The volume on your stereo, the air conditioning in your car. What else? …Try again, what have you lost? What did I take?"

This time Cuba (Caulder) writes down "FREEDOM" to which Hopkins replies, "Do you think you are free? Where were you going at 2:00 pm today, to the gym right? In the morning you'll have your wake up call, you'll wake up in the middle of the night with your heart pounding. What is it that has you all tied up? Tied up in little knots? Is it ambition? You're no mystery to me boy, I used to be you. Ok, last try, what have you lost, what did I take from you?"

Cuba finally gets it right with his response, "MY ILLUSIONS".

This certainly makes sense in the context of this book. After all, reality is in the mind of the observer and it's all an illusion! The exciting thing about wave-particle duality is you can change what you choose to observe, and by doing so, you can change what happens. It is the very act of your observation, your focus that produces the result. Until you manifest it, your universe, like light, exists only as waves of energy, as waves of potentials and probabilities. The magical part of all of this is that you can cause whatever you want to appear in your life by your thoughts and actions.

So who is really in control? At the moment of your decision to make a choice you feel as if you are acting freely, selecting at will from an infinite number of options. However, recent research suggests this sense of freedom is merely an illusory byproduct of the way the human brain operates.

"An inexplicable but plainly measurable burst amount of activity occurs in your brain prior to your conscious desire to act. An outside observer monitoring electrical fluctuations in your brain can anticipate your action about a third of a second before you are aware that you have decided to act. That sequence was observed by Benjamin Libet, a neurophysiologist at the School of Medicine of the University of California at San Francisco.[93]

Consider these statements from Dr. Joseph Dispenza.[94]

"Is it possible that we're so conditioned to our daily lives, so conditioned to the way we create our lives, that we buy the idea that we have no control at all? We've been conditioned to believe that the external world is more real than the internal world. This new model of science says just the opposite. It says what's happening within us, will create what's happening outside of us"

We have been conditioned by society to be average with linear thinking. We simply wander through our lives in semiconscious states, neurologically wired to default to being a victim and blaming others. Remember my coaching commandment, no judgments, it's not good or bad, it just is.

I do this exercise in my live programs in response to the question, are you in control? I tell the audience that when I give them this cue, "ready, set, go", I challenge them to scream as loud as they possibly can these four words, "Fear is a lie". I get their agreement to do so. Then we test.

"Ready"

"Set"

"Go"

The room screams, oftentimes very loud. However, 100% of the time there is withholding in 100% of the audience. I have never had a person scream those four words as loud as they could like their life depended on it. I've had several instances where people thought that they did, but they were deceived. Perhaps they were louder than anyone else in the room but they still held back. Otherwise they would still be standing on their chairs screaming until they ran out of breath.

What held them back? What CONTROLLED them? Their human wiring held them back. Their past experiences of wired memories of being embarrassed held them back. Their wired in mechanisms and pattern recognition of avoiding pain or looking bad, compelled them to avoid an all out performance and then justify what they did. So I ask you again, who's in control?

Consider the neuroscience of economics. A colleague is promised $10 on the condition that he shares this amount with you. If you agree to accept the offer, both of you receive your shares; if not, both of you receive nothing. Your colleague offers you $5 and you go home happy. What if your friend only offers you 50 cents and keeps the other $9.50 for himself? Would you accept?

Most people refuse because they see it as unfair. These types of experiments have been done all over the world with the same results. Refusing even 50 cents is not rational. The offer of 50 cents may not be fair, but the alternative — going home empty is worse still. Why do people behave irrationally? They are not in control; it's their internal dialogue and past programming that controls them.

This is called the ultimatum game. Economic decisions are firmly based on rational thought processes. A decision maker calculates the costs and benefits of his actions, weighs the probabilities of certain scenarios, and then makes the optimal decision. This is the fundamental assumption on which economic theory is based. As you can see, the very premises of economical thoughts are flawed.

As it turns out, humans make decisions not only on the facts, but also on their emotional interpretation of them. Researchers at Princeton University investigated the physiological processes that take place in the brain, looking purely at the chemical and mechanical interactions between neurons, axons, synapses, and dendrites, using MRI's.

According to a report in the Journal Science, their study identified the regions in the brain that were activated during the ultimatum game. Somewhat to their surprise, not only the regions that are usually activated during thought processes, the prefrontal dorsolateral cortex became busy, a region that is associated with negative emotions, the limbic system, and the amygdala became activated as well. The more insulting the financial offer, the more intense the activity in the nerve cells became.[95]

All of the science points to purposeful thoughts and actions. A question might be, can you have a purposeful thought given that it seems that wired in neurological patterns of survival take hold. The answer is yes you can.

So do we have control? A study of babies addresses the impact of a lack of control. One group of babies had strings tied to their arms that turned on a short period of music when pulled. The other group had a similar set of strings attached, but pulling the strings did nothing. Instead, music came on and off at random intervals. The researchers found that there was a much higher level of interest, smiling, and engagement among babies in the first group, while babies in the second group remained blasé, not reacting much to the music that surrounded them.[96]

Application:

Even at an early age, the very beginnings of life, we are happy to learn that what we do makes a difference. When we feel in control, we enjoy things that resulted for our own actions more fully, then if they just happen without any input from us.

There is a powerful connection between the ability to maintain the illusion of control and the capacity to sustain a positive mood. Psychologist Martin Seligman studied dogs' responses and the anatomy of despair.[97]

I've previously talked about the concept of "learned helplessness", and related it to the rats that were shocked if they chose to run over a metal grid to get food. Seligman took three groups of dogs and gave one group shocks from which the dogs could escape by pushing a panel with their noses. The second group was given shocks that they could not escape, no matter what they did. The last group received no shocks at all.

All three groups were next tested in a cage with a low wall, in which one compartment was electrified and the other was not.

The dogs from the first group, who had been able to escape the shocks in the previous study, and the dogs that had never been shocked, quickly learned to jump the barrier and escape the shock. But the dogs in the second group, who had learned that nothing they did mattered and that they could not escape the shock, simply sat down and waited for the shock to end. They never learned to jump over the wall to escape. They never even tried. They simply resigned to the thoughts that they just were helpless. Their sense that they lacked control persisted, even when the reality of the situation shifted and they could have changed their outcomes through their actions. Seligman taught his helpless dogs a new move. He dragged each helpless dog over the wall between the compartments until the dogs "got it!" Once they realized that what they did mattered and that they did have control over the situation, they were depressed and passive no more.

There is a power and an autonomy that comes with self-regulation. You can self regulate. That's what the on-line coaching and accountability program is.

You have control, but most people forfeit this control by listening to the experts or the authorities that are very happy to set our limits for us. Social science research says that as a child you heard the word "No" about 40,000 times by the age of five, before you even started first grade. How many times had you heard the word "Yes", about 5,000?

All it takes is belief, proper expectations, proper planning and a heavy dosage of behavioral contracting with an extra helping of accountability.

Society tells us that there must be winners and losers. The reality is that this is not correct. I often do an exercise in my programs where I have people partnered and sit across from each other at a table. They lock hands in an Indian arm wrestling configuration. I explain that the objective of the game is to get their opponents back of the hand on the table as many times as possible in thirty seconds. I then start the clock.

After 30 seconds I go around the room and ask people to give me their numbers. I'll get a lot of ones, a winner and a loser, a lot of zeroes, a tie, and every so often I'll hear a number like 30. Wow! What does this mean? It means that they got it. Economic development is not a zero-sum game. The world does not need poor countries in order to have rich countries, nor must some people be poor in order for others to be wealthy. We live in a world of abundance. The keys remain your perceptual choices and the actions that you do or do not take.

In the arm wrestling game remember what the objective was, get the back of your opponent's hand on the table as many times as possible. This calls for win-win co-operation, not win-lose competition. The correct response is to have absolutely no resistance at all and to go for speed. You allow your hand to touch the table and your opponent allows theirs as well. You both win. That's getting it!

An extraordinary teacher, Annie Sullivan, had just come into a little girl's life. She was attempting to teach Helen Keller, who had up to this point in time been deemed to be unreachable. For months Sullivan had been spelling out the names of familiar objects into Helens' hand using the deaf-mute alphabet. Her task was to get Helen to realize that the cake she loves so much, or her favorite doll, had names of their own. They can be asked for by spelling out their names with her fingers, that specific words have specific agreed-upon meanings that don't change and that words are the tools of communication. She could open up little Helen's dark world with language. D-O-L-L. C-A-K-E. W-A-T-E-R. Over and over again Annie spelled the words for Helen. Helen had not made the connection between fingerspelling and the name of the object.

Finally, there was a miraculous moment when Annie grasps Helen's seven-year-old hand and again puts it under the pump and spells out W-A-T-E-R. But this time, Helen makes the connection. She understands. This spells water and this is what water feels like. From Helen Keller's own autobiography, "The Story of My Life":

"As the cool stream gushed over one hand, she spelled into the other the word water, first slowly, then rapidly. I stood still, my whole attention fixed upon the motion of her fingers. Suddenly I felt a misty consciousness as of something forgotten — a thrill of returning thought: and somehow the mystery of language was revealed to me. I knew then that W-A-T-E-R meant the wonderful cool something that was flowing over my hand..."

At this point Helen Keller's intellect had a higher ground then her instincts. She had made the connection.

How about you? Do you "get it?" Do you get how important having a system of accountability with a consequence for non-performance really is? Of course you need to have it matter to you that you do accomplish more then you would without it. Performance improvement needs to be important to you and no one else can give that to you. So if that is not your current state of mind, then put this book on the shelf, but remember where it is. Come back to it when you have an area in your life where you are not "satisfied" with the results you are currently experiencing. Come back when you are ready to make some significant progress.

Chapter 24

Some Thoughts
on Change

"Talk doesn't cook rice."
— Chinese Proverb

There is a principle in physics that states that every system becomes more disordered with time. This is called Entropy. The second law of thermodynamics that we discussed focused on the behavior of heat energy: heat flows spontaneously from warmer to cooler objects and all engines that convert heat to work are less than 100% efficient. These ideas are helpful, but the second law has a much wider meaning in its most general form, the degree of disorder, or entropy, of any system tends to increase with time. All systems left to themselves tend to increase their disorder.

If you shuffle a brand new deck of cards, one with all the cards in perfect order, it becomes disordered, never the other way around. In order to maintain an order there needs to be an energy input. You can get the deck of cards and physically input energy to rearrange the cards back to perfect order. Life on Earth is possible because the Sun provides a steady source of energy.

Another way of saying this is that the energy of an intervention is necessary to prevent entropy from happening to the systems of your life. If you exercise you prevent, or at least slow down, the cells march to disorder, chaos and destruction.

The maid comes on Friday and cleans our house. By Friday evening our daughter's rooms is a mess, unless energy is applied, meaning someone picks up the items immediately.

I'm looking for you to have an intervention in the battle against mediocrity. Rational thinking isn't going to tip the scales for you. We are more afraid of catastrophic events such as an airplane crash then of everyday risks like cancer. It's partly because of media coverage that makes the danger appear greater than it is and partly because the more grisly the prospect, the more it frightens us. The result is illogical behavior. I have over 1700 skydives. People who don't know the sport think I'm crazy, they constantly tell me how dangerous it is. I tell them I agree, the most dangerous aspect of this sport is the drive to the airport. So I fly in myself!

Take a look at how illogical our fears are:

Your risk of dying[98]:
* From a shark bite: 1 in 3,700,000
* In an airline accident: 1 in 40,000
* In a tornado or by lightning: 1 in 39,000
* In a car wreck: 1 in 88

It's logical and reasonable simply to be satisfied and comfortable. Remember my statement; being reasonable is the lowest level of human consciousness. This book is not for the person who is satisfied. I'm looking for you to be unreasonable.

It's going to take a vision, a desire and action on your part. It's going to take planning every week, making commitments, and being in an accountability system.

Keep in mind this thought, how could God help us if we won't help ourselves?

Consider this old joke:

A preacher had a deep faith in God. He would tell his friends that his life would work out because God would take care of him. One day a serious storm caused severe flooding in the town he lived in. While his neighbors packed up and left this man stayed put, believing that God would take care of him.

The waters began to rise into his house. His remaining neighbors came by in a large truck and said, "Preacher, get in, we'll take you to safety." The preacher's reply, "No thank you son, God is going to save me."

The water continues to rise. He runs upstairs. He's looking out the window and more neighbors came by in a boat. "Preacher, get in the boat, we'll take you to safety." Preacher, "No thank you, God's going to save me."

The water kept rising so he climbed up on the roof. Then the safety patrol came in a helicopter and yelled, "Preacher, get in." Preacher, "God's going to save me."

And the preacher drowns. At the pearly gates of heaven, the man had felt betrayed. "My God," he said, " I put my faith in you and prayed to you for my rescue. You said you would always take care of me, yet when I needed you most you were not there.

God replied, "What do you mean? I sent you a truck, a boat, and a helicopter. What more do you want?"

There is nothing wrong with faith, you must have faith. It is a part of right thought that generates an electrical-chemical response that begins your reality. However, you must take the next step and the purposeful action. Make a commitment to have what you want in life and then make a plan to get it. Put it into a weekly behavioral contract with a heavy dose of accountability, and then make choices throughout the week about what you pay attention to and the reality you create. Be competitive and be in action.

Debbie Ford in her book, "The Dark Side of the Light Chasers", mentions something I'll quote here and apply to my concepts. She doesn't make a scientific application but I will. She states:

"Whether your goal is to diet, to make more money, or to have a better relationship, you need to go back and discover your underlying commitments and beliefs. You don't need to suppress these beliefs. You need to allow them to exist, so you can choose ones which empower you and leave the rest behind."

I see this as another quantum call to choose your own reality. According to quantum mechanics, the universe works on the most fundamental level in terms not of fixed scientific certainties, but of probabilities and uncertainties. Physics could no longer predict what was going to happen; rather, all physics could determine were the probabilities that various outcomes would occur. However, natures' randomness is confined to the incredibly small.

Quantum mechanics tells us that the law of large numbers says that a ball consists of billions of billions of molecules, each of which behaves randomly, but which taken together are entirely predictable. So natures' randomness is not significant at sizes that we can see and experience. The key factor is you, your choices, your observations, and your created reality.

Successful entrepreneur and also a former football coach, Art Williams says that a key to success is to keep it simple. He gives three keys to keeping it simple.[99]

His keys:

1. **Manage activity**. You can't sit in a chair and analyze what's wrong with your business. You'll never generate any income. Activity is the key for any business.
2. **Create little successes**. Sometimes when you look at a business goal it can be overwhelming. To prevent yourself from giving up you need

more bite-sized parts. Even if you only do one positive thing a day your confidence gets a boost.

3. **Don't get bogged down in paperwork.**

"It was a critical point during World War II. General Mac Arthur and his troops were camped at the side of a big river, and they had to get across. Mac Arthur called in his engineer and said, "Soldier, how long will it take you to throw a bridge across that river?" The engineer replied, "Three days." Mac Arthur said, "Good, have your draftsman draw up plans immediately." Three days later Mac Arthur called the engineer back into his office to ask how the plans were coming along. "Sir," replied the engineer, "the bridge is finished, and you can take your troops across now provided you don't have to wait for the plans. They're not done yet."[100]

Art and I would both agree with precise, previous planning prevents poor performance, but we would never use it as an excuse to delay action.

Thomas Edison once said, "Opportunity is missed by most people because it is dressed in overalls and looks like work." Here's an interesting question that I often ask my clients,

"What action do you not have the courage to take?" Think about that one.

I say that a fundamental core ingredient for success is my third core principle, "I am the source of all that I experience versus playing victim and blaming people." We must take responsibility for the way that we think and for all of the corresponding chemistry that follows.

Dr. Candance Pert in her book, "Molecules of Emotions"[101] states:

"We must take responsibility for the way that we feel. The notion that others can make us feel good or bad is untrue. We are choosing how we feel at every single moment. The external world is in so many ways a mirror of our beliefs and expectations. Why we feel the way we feel is the result of the symphony and harmony of our own molecules of emotion that affect every aspect of our physiology, producing blissful good health or miserable disease."

It's going to take persistence. Angela Duckworth, a graduate student at Penn State who has conducted several key studies on grit, studied neurobiology in college and eventually went on to teach. "It became obvious to me that IQ didn't explain why so many of the kids had reading skills that were four grade levels below the average" she says. Duckworth was intrigued enough to return to school for a Ph.D. She worked alongside of Martin E. P. Seligman, director of the University of Pennsylvania's Positive Psychology Center, and began identifying high achievers in various fields, interviewing them, and describing the characteristics that distinguished them.

"There were certainly people who were brilliant, but also a lot who were not a genius in any way but were really tenacious," they reported. They began to refer to this tenacity as grit. This common trait was the determination to accomplish something ambitious and long-term despite the inevitable obstacles.

Perseverance is purely a state of mind. Almost all of the greatest leaders are passionate. Look at the word passion. Pass-I-on. Leaders live with Passion. They are excited about what they do and they pass that on with energy and preparation. The best way to predict the future is to invent it!

Chapter 25

And the Issue of Change Itself

"People seem not to see that their opinion
of the world is also a confession of character."
— Ralph Waldo Emerson

John is the CEO of an ever-expanding personnel staffing firm that has a history of growing through the increased penetration of current accounts, increased new accounts, and the acquisition of competitors, thereby acquiring talent and new accounts.

John has a staffing issue. He needs to either fire a trainer from an acquired company or get that person to change her outlook and take on a sales mentality and sell training to outside organizations. They don't need more web based training initiatives created, they need her to bring in revenue. How can John change the way that she thinks and behaves every day?

Businesses everywhere face this type of a problem, changing the mindset of their employees. Despite all of the rhetoric, books, effort, and money thrown into change, efforts in organizations today mostly fail. Mega-consulting firms like Arthur D. Little and McKinsey & Co. have studied hundreds of companies that entered into Total Quality Management or Six Sigma programs, but about two thirds of them have "ground to a halt because of their failure to produce the hoped-for results." Peter Senge puts it quite literally in his book, "Dance of Change": "This failure to sustain significant change recurs again and again despite substantial resources committed to the change effort, talented and committed people driving the change, and high stakes."

Can people change? At first glance it might look like the answer is no. However, hold on, the answer is yes and I've been showing you how. First before I emphasize what our conversation all along in this book has been, let's look at what we're up against.

Imagine that a trusted figure, say your doctor, told you that you needed to change and it was a life or death matter. Would you change your lifestyle habits? Yes you say? Try again. You're probably deluding yourself. Here are the odds that the change experts are giving us: 9 to 1 against you.

The crisis is in health care, an industry that consumes $2.1 trillion a year in the United States alone, more than one seventh of the entire economy. Despite all of the economic outlay we aren't getting any healthier. We aren't preventing the three deadly diseases, heart disease, stroke and cancer.

A relatively small percentage of the population consumes the vast majority of the health care budget for diseases that are very well known and largely behavioral and preventable. They are sick because of how they choose to lead their lives, not because of genetic factors beyond their control. For years it has all boiled down to five behavioral issues:

1. Smoking
2. Drinking
3. Eating too much
4. Too much stress
5. Not enough exercise.

More than a half million people every year in the United States undergo coronary bypass graft or angioplasty surgery at a total price of around $60 billion. These surgeries are no more than temporary fixes. The bypass grafts often clog after about three years, and the angioplasties in only a few months. These procedures often cost the individuals upwards of $100,000 of that $60 billion.

Doctors tell their patients that they will have to switch to a healthier lifestyle or they will die, but very few do.

In 1993, Dr. Dean Ornish, a professor of medicine at the University of California at San Francisco, convinced the Mutual of Omaha insurance company to pay for an unusual experiment.

The researchers recruited 194 patients who suffered from severely clogged arteries and could have bypass grafts or angioplasties covered by their insurance plans. Instead they signed up for a trial. The staffers helped them to quit smoking and switch to an extreme vegetarian diet that derived fewer than 10 percent of its calories from fat. In places like Omaha, they shifted from steaks and fries to brown rice and greens. The patients got together for group conversations twice a week, and they also took classes in meditation, relaxation, yoga, and aerobic exercise, which became parts of their daily routines.

The program lasted for only a year, after that they were on their own. But three years from the start, the study found, 77 % of the patients had stuck with these lifestyle changes — and safely avoided the need for heart surgery. They had halted — or, in many cases, reversed — the progress of their disease.

If the medical establishment was resigned to the supposed fact that only one out of every nine people can change, even in a crisis, then how did Dr. Ornish's team inspire and motivate nearly eight out of ten of its heart patients to accomplish and sustain such dramatic transformations?

In 2002, the Justice Department published a study that tracked 272,111 inmates after they were released from state prisons in fifteen states. This was the largest study of criminal recidivism ever conducted in the United States. The results were alarming: 30 % of former inmates were rearrested within six months, and 67.5 %percent of them were rearrested within three years. Most of the repeat offenders were felons.

You would like to think that people would think rationally. They don't want to die. They don't want to be sent back to prison. But as we've discussed earlier, rational thinking does not carry the day and change behavior. Why is that?

Let's look at the neuroscience. Rational thinking occurs in the frontal cortex area of the brain. This has to do with "working memory" and conscious attention. This area is engaged when you encounter something new like driving a stick shift car or seeing a new product on the supermarket shelves. You will pay close attention to driving the stick shift, and rationally compare the benefits of the new product to one that you already use. It's your working memory that takes the new information and matches it against your old patterns. The pre-frontal cortex is an energy intensive area of the brain.

The basal ganglia on the other hand, are fired by routine, familiar activity like reaching for the known supermarket product and putting it in the cart without thought, or like riding a bike. This part of the brain, located near the core, is where the circuitry of long standing habits are formed and held. It requires much less energy to function than the cortex and working memory requires.

The basal ganglia can and do function very well without any conscious thought in your routine activity. This frees you up to pay attention to other more life threatening events like a tiger on the loose! In contrast, working memory fatigues easily and can hold only a limited amount of information at one time. So any activity conducted repetitively will get routed to the basal ganglia, the habit area of the brain.

Trying to change a hardwired habit requires a lot of energy, effort and attention. This often leads people to feeling uncomfortable, which of course they resist. It's not that they don't want to change, it's that they are hardwired to avoid being uncomfortable.

Another event that enters into the plan is what I've called "Cortical Limbic Loops". When the new or threatening or unfamiliar occurs, there is a direct neurological path to the amygdala or fear area of the limbic system. MRI's reveal a burst of "error" firing, caused by the fear stimulus. Just trying to change a routine behavior sends out strong messages in the brain that something is not right. These messages grab and stimulate the reticular activating system, alerting the individual of "danger" and readily overpowers' rational thoughts.

So, again the question, is change ever going to happen? Again, the answer is yes! It's going to take a tremendous amount of energy to change, at least that is what you may think. But hold on, not so fast.

Let's travel a bit more into another layer of science with the study of energy. Energy exists in many forms, such as heat, light, chemical energy and electrical energy. Energy is the ability to bring about change or to do work. Thermodynamics is the study of energy.

Although I've touched on this briefly, I'll introduce more specifically the three laws of thermodynamics. I will paraphrase and include a dialogue rather than just list the laws.

1. We experience many limitations on energy transfers. The amount of energy is constant. This is referred to as the law of conservation of energy. Energy cannot be created or destroyed. Restrictions are summarized in the second law.
2. Heat tends to diffuse evenly, spreading out from warmer to cooler objects. A hot bowl of soup becomes cooler, never hotter. Also a direction of time.

    Another more subtle statement of the second law is that an engine cannot convert heat energy completely into useful work. There is no perfect system. Entropy is increased over time. Entropy is the state of increased disorder.
3. If all the thermal motion of molecules, kinetic energy, could be removed, a state called Absolute Zero would occur.

I want to focus for now on law number 2. There is no perfect system. The next time you take a trip feel the hood of your car. You'll notice that it's hot. There is no reason for energy to be expended to heat the hood. The reason that this happens is because there is no perfect system, and it is simply wasted heat being released into the surrounding areas.

Let's look at the analogy of a built-in flaw in the airplanes that I fly. A single engine airplane has a propeller that spins violently to the right, generating Newton's third law of motion, for every action there is an equal and opposite reaction. Every single engine aircraft has the built-in flaw of a left-turning tendency.

Left-Turning Tendancy - Compensate

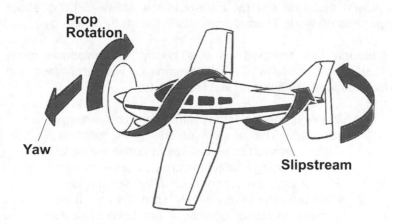

Prop Rotation

Yaw

Slipstream

As the slipstream produced by the propeller rotation wraps around the fuselage, it strikes the left side of the vertical fin. A left-turning tendency is created as the air "pushes" the tail of the airplane to the right and yaws the nose left.

This is a built-in imperfection or unintended consequence of the design of the aircraft. How can I fly? If I take off from John Wayne Airport in Orange County, California and want to fly to San Francisco, I'm going to wind up out over the ocean. Unless that is, I do something to compensate for the built-in design flaw. I need to have an intervention. The intervention is to press down on the right rudder pedal that turns the tail fin to the right to deflect the airflow, and keeps the aircraft going straight ahead. Here's a clue. We can get the aircraft to do what we want it to do, rather then what it is designed to do, but only if we have an intervention. Remember that. It is going to be a very important strategy to change, having an intervention.

Back to thermodynamics — which is not a perfect system. The human being is likewise an imperfect system. We all have direct-wired components that will be pushbacks to change. They are:

1. We resist doing activities that we don't feel like doing.
2. We resist doing activities that we perceive as being linked to pain. We avoid and justify the avoidance with rationalization, and never know that we are doing this.
3. We resist, avoid, and fear change.

This concept is called homeostasis. Homeostasis is the property of either an open system or a closed system, especially a living organism that regulates its internal environment so as to maintain a stable, constant condition. Multiple dynamic equilibrium adjustments and regulation mechanisms make homeostasis possible. The concept was created by Claude Bernard, often considered as the father of physiology, and published in 1865. The term was coined in 1932 by Walter Bradford Cannon from the Greek *homoios* (same, like, resembling), and *stasis* (to stand, posture).[102]

This is the driving non-conscious coding of all of life, to maintain the state of being that is currently present. It doesn't matter if the change is good for you or not. Your coding doesn't intrepret or judge. It is simply coded to stay the same.

You may remember years ago a famous basketball player had a kidney transplant. What is the body designed to do? It is designed to recognize the foreign tissue as "different" and to reject it. That is exactly what the body will do unless there is an intervention. That intervention is immunosuppresant drugs. You must stop the body from doing what it is designed to do with an intervention, forever! Change is possible, but not without an intervention.

Are you starting to see a theme here? Change is possible but only with an intervention.

Some of the greatest changes and breakthroughs in industry have emerged from the integration of separate fields. Electricity and magnetism became the science of electromagnetism. This gave us the electric motor and generator, which in turn lead to the industrial revolution. To understand how to better elicit change, we turn to another combination, this time between neuroscience and physics.

Neurons communicate with each other through an electrical chemical transmission across a gap or synapse. This is driven by the movement of ions such as sodium, potassium and calcium. These ions travel through channels that are a little more than a single ion wide. This means that the brain is in a quantum environment and is therefore subject to the laws of quantum mechanics.

One of these laws is the **Quantum Zeno Effect**, QZE. The quantum Zeno effect is a quantum mechanical phenomenon first described by George Sudarshan and Baidyanaith Misra of the University of Texas in 1977. It describes the situation in which an unstable particle, if observed continuously, will never decay from a high energy state to a low energy state. This occurs because every measurement causes the wave function to "collapse" to a pure eigenstate of the measurement basis.

As the concept is used here, an "observation" can be the absorption of a particle, with no observer in any conventional sense. As the number of measurements increased the probability of the energy transition fell off. The atom stayed longer in its excited state because the scientists, in effect repeatedly asked, "Have you decayed yet?" In the quantum world, the watched pot never boils. The very nature of quantum physics is counterintuitive to conventional thinking.

Among the many bizarre characteristics is the quantum Zeno paradox, an odd mathematical result that is being debated to this day. Assuming an unstable quantum state, intuition would dictate that eventually the system would irreversibly decay in a certain amount of time, defined as the Zeno time. However if the system is measured in a period shorter than the Zeno time, then the wave function of the system will repeatedly collapse before decay. In effect, constant measurements of the system will actually prevent its collapse!

Don't worry about understanding this. Let me apply to you. In a 2005 paper published in the Philosophical Transactions of the Royal Society (U.K.), physicist Henry Stapp and Jeffrey Schwartz, linked the QZE with what happens when close attention is paid to a mental experience.[103]

Having clearly annunciated his views on quantum mechanics, Stapp sets out to transform the brain from a classical to a quantum system. He chooses to attack this in a short surgical way by striking at the lowest level of physiological brain function. Drawing on a brief background discussion of cloudlike forms, harmonic oscillation, and the double-slit experiment to introduce the necessity of the brain's nerve terminals, and calcium ion channels being quantum in nature, Stapp goes on to argue that because these foundational components are best understood in quantum terms, the brain itself must be treated as a quantum system. Stapp next draws on many of the same points used in discussing the brain's ion channels to make his case from another angle. He introduces his action template theory involving microscopic brain states capable of producing particular actions if held for a sufficient length of time.[104]

Simplified, he states what happens when close attention is paid to a mental experience. The mental act of focusing attention, (as in a behavioral contract on Sunday night), stabilizes the associated brain circuits. Concentration attention on your mental experience, whether a thought, a plan, a weekly view, or even a fear, as you would in phase two of my four phase strategy for planning, maintains the brain state arising in association with that experience.

Over time, paying enough attention to any specific brain connection keeps the relevant circuitry open. These circuits will then become stable links; remember neurons that fire together wire together and eventually physical changes occur in the brains' structure.

The brain changes in relationship to where you place your attention, focus and commitment. What you focus on continuously reshapes the brain. The power is in the focus and commitment along with the emotional surge from the consequence for nonperformance.

To achieve a result (change), given the brains limited working memory, we need to use both right brain and left brain functions which you get from the behavioral contracting.

For a change to stick, certain protocol needs to be followed. There is a real problem with the amydgala and its fight or flight response. This is set off whenever you want to make a departure from your usual, safe routines. The brain is designed so that any new challenge or desire triggers some degree of fear. A solution lies in setting realistic, small step goals.

I've addressed this with my MLO's, or Minimum Level Objectives. This is the lowest level of results that you give your word that you will accomplish, and falling short does not exist. You would also have a stretch or superstar level, but this is the level that you are held accountable for.

Here is a visual showing the bypassing of the cortical limbic loop:

Limbic Loop

Large goal→Fear→Access to cortex restricted→Failure

Small goal→Fear Bypassed→Cortex engaged→Success

As your small steps continue and your cortex continues to lay down new circuitry, through repetition this will be regulated to the basal ganglia area and become a new habit. There you go; you now have change wired in.

A 1997 study by Baruch College researchers Gerald Olivero, K. Denise Bane, and Richard E. Kopelman found that a training program alone increased productivity 28%, but the addition of follow-up coaching to the training increased productivity 88%, so either hire a live coach or stay on the on-line coaching and accountability program.

Let's go back to John, our staffing company CEO. Rather than look at what his sales person/trainer did not do or accomplish, it would be more helpful to focus her attention on the new circuits she needs to create to achieve her objectives in the future. John could ask her, "What do you need to do to make more sales?" "What are the most productive and important indicators of success, activities, measurements etc?" John would help her to build this new sales circuitry by directing her attention towards the goal, by moving towards a strategy.

In a world of so many distractions new mental maps are constantly being formed every second in the brain. One of the biggest challenges is to be able to focus on one idea. This organization is right on target with their cultural theme that reinforces the brain circuitry necessary for maximum performances across the board. Their theme is:

Maximum Performance

Measure   Report   Review   Reward/Consequence

It has served them well in structuring the thinking of the masses. They have a built-in culture of making weekly commitments with a consequence for non-performance. They use behavioral contracting. In fact, I'm thrilled to be their corporate coach. They bring me in for my live training with each acquisition that they make to jump-start their culture of measurement and accountability.

When people are using behavioral contracting they are being taught how to learn. They are taking responsibility for being held accountable to do what they say is important to them, so the behavior is self directed, which has the highest brain impact.

So can you change? Science says you can.

Chapter 26

The Final Word

"I have always thought the actions of men the best interpreters of their thoughts."
— John Locke

I'm asking you to make one small change in your habits. That small change can make all the difference in the world in the quality of your life and your contribution to others.

In 1962, the Venus bound spacecraft Mariner 1 had to be destroyed because it strayed off course during launch. A mistake caused by the omission of a hyphen in the mission's computer programming. This single punctuation mark cost taxpayers $18 million. The small does impact the large.

Vince Lombardi, Hall of Fame football coach said, "Inches make a champion." Thomas Edison said, "Many of life's failures are men who did not realize how close they were to success when they gave up."

I have one last insight for you before you decide to take action on what you've read. Here is that insight:
It's just as easy to say no as it is to say yes.

I read a book titled, "The Slight Edge" by Jeff Olson. The one statement that is the essential element of his book is simply that phrase, it's just as easy to say no as it is to say yes.

It's just as easy to over-eat as it is to restrict your calories, and tomorrow you'll be just fine. It's just as easy to sleep in as it is to go to the gym, and tomorrow you'll still be fine. It's just as easy to read as it is not to read, and tomorrow you'll still have your routine and everything will be fine.

Like I said earlier, you want to be able to look back twenty or thirty years from now and be thankful about the choices you've made today. So what will you say yes to and what will you say no to. It's your choice. The law of accumulative effect will work for you or against you, but it will work. You'll either be thankful or regretful, your choice.

I'm only an e-mail away:

info@bobdavies.com or **www.bobdavies.com**.

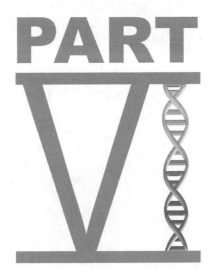

Coaching Commandments

Being Reasonable
is lowest level of
Human Consiousness

I've taken notes for you and captured the major coaching commandments or guiding questions or challenges that I've given you throughout the book. Here they are in the first person:

1. Challenge my way of thinking. Seek to understand the opposite point of view.
2. Where am I living my life in resignation?
3. No judgments, it's not good or bad, it just is.
4. Eliminate the phrase "I can't" and replace it with: "At my current state of mind a solution is not available."
5. Identify where I am making assumptions and challenge my assumptions.
6. I am an avoidance machine.
7. How can I play a bigger game and have a larger impact in the lives of others?
8. I am either growing or decaying; there is no middle ground.
9. What habits do I not currently have that would make life easier and more fulfilling?
10. Inspect and verify.
11. I don't get to not know.
12. Everything that can be measured must be measured.
13. What limits do I accept?
14. What lies am I buying into?
15. I turn frustration into fascination.
16. I look at all issues from multiple points of view.
17. I look for the essence of all things. I take the complicated and first investigate a simple reflection of it.
18. S.A.I.D. Principle. Are my actions intense and consistent enough to have an effect on the results that I seek?
19. I live the 3 core principles: I do what I said I would do, I am better as a part of a team than alone, I am the source of all that I experience versus playing victim and blaming others.
20. I am a meaning-making machine, so I choose interpretations that serve me.
21. Notice my fear-driven alien conversation.
22. Identify the stories that I tell myself.
23. Get M.A.D., make a decision and take action.
24. My lifestyle is an asset not a liability.
25. Health is my number one value.
26. Where am I holding back? From whom am I withholding?
27. Where do I need to say no, or yes?

28. I answer the questions: Why bother? What am I building? How much is enough?
29. I use the power of the ANDS, and then some.
30. Tell the truth faster. Where or to whom do I need to tell the truth?

Quotes — Reality

1. "There are no facts, only interpretations." Friedrich Nietzsche
2. "Reality is merely an illusion, albeit a very persistent one." Albert Einstein
3. "Everything you can imagine is real." Pablo Picasso
4. "An error does not become truth by reason of multiplied propagation, nor does truth become error because nobody sees it." Mahatma Gandhi
5. "Some things have to be believed to be seen." Ralph Hodgson, The Skylark and Other Poems.
6. "Wherever you go, no matter what the weather, always bring your own sunshine." Anthony J. d'Angelo, The College Blue Book.

Quotes — Attitude

7. "Attitude is a little thing that makes a big difference." Winston Churchill
8. "Happiness is an attitude. We either make ourselves miserable, or happy and strong. The amount of work is the same." Francesca Reigler
9. "If you don't like something change it; if you can't change it, change the way you think about it." Mary Engelbreit
10. Every thought is a seed. If you plant crab apples, don't count on harvesting Golden Delicious." Bill Meyer
11. "To be wronged is nothing unless you continue to remember it." Confucius
12. "The greatest discovery of my generation is that a human being can alter his life by altering his attitudes." William James
13. "Everywhere is paradise; it's up to you." Author Unknown
14. "What counts is not necessarily the size of the dog in the fight- it's the size of the fight in the dog." Dwight Eisenhower, address to

Republican National Committee, 31 January 1958, also sometimes attributed to Mark Twain (unverified)

15. "No life is so hard you can't make it easier by the way that you take it." Ellen Glasgow

16. "I have learned to use the word impossible with great caution." Werner von Braun

17. "The human spirit is stronger than anything that can happen to it." C.C. Scott

18. "We cannot direct the wind but we can adjust our sails." Author unknown

19. "The block of granite that was an obstacle in the pathway of the weak became a stepping-stone in the pathway of the strong." Thomas Carlyle

20. "A happy person is not a person in a certain set of circumstances, but rather a person with a certain set of attitudes." Hugh Downs

21. "Some people are always grumbling because roses have thorns; I am thankful that thorns have roses." Alphonse Karr

22. "Become a possibilitarian. No matter how dark things seem to be or actually are, raise your sights and see possibilities-always see them, for they are always there." Norman Vincent Peale

23. "Surrounded by people who love life, you love it too; surrounded by people who don't, you don't." Mignon McLaughlin, The Second Neurotic's Notebook, 1966

24. "There are souls in this world, which have the gift of finding joy everywhere and of leaving it behind them when they go." Frederick Faber

25. "Be enthusiastic. Remember the placebo effect-30% of medicine is showbiz." Ronald Spark

26. "A loving person lives in a loving world. A hostile person lives in a hostel world; everyone you meet is your mirror." Ken Keyes, Jr.

27. "Mind is everything. Muscle-pieces of rubber. All that I am I am because of my mind." Paavo Nurmi

28. "Anywhere you go liking everyone, everyone will be likeable." Mignon McLaughlin, The Second Neurotic's Notebook, 1966

29. "People seem not to see that their opinion of the world is also a confession of character." Ralph Waldo Emerson

30. "People are not disturbed by things, but by the view they take of them." Epictetus

31. "I have found that if you love life, life will love you back." Arthur Rubinstein

32. "Those who wish to sing, always find a song." Swedish Proverb

33. "Excellence is not a skill. It is an attitude." Ralph Marston

Quotes — Action

34. "I have always thought the actions of men the best interpreters of their thoughts." John Locke
35. "Well done is better than well said." Benjamin Franklin
36. "Trust only movement. Life happens at the level of events, not of words. Trust movement. Alfred Adler
37. "A promise is a cloud; fulfillment is rain." Arabian Proverb
38. "Small deeds done are greater than great deeds planned." Peter Marshall
39. "A barking dog is often more useful then a sleeping lion." Washington Irving adapted from a verse in the Bible.
40. "Nothing diminishes anxiety faster than action." Walter Anderson.
41. "Remember, people will judge you by your actions, not your intentions. You may have a heart of gold—but so does a hard-boiled egg." Author Unknown.
42. "Talk doesn't cook rice." Chinese Proverb
43. "All know the way; few actually walk it." Bodhidharma
44. "Action is the antidote to despair." Joan Baez
45. "The great composer does not set to work because he is inspired, but becomes inspired because he is working. Beethoven, Wagner, Bach and Mozart settled down day after day to the job in hand with as much regularity as an accountant settles down each day to his figures. They didn't waste time waiting for inspiration." Ernest Newman
46. "Don't find fault. Find a remedy." Henry Ford
47. "Success will never be a big step in the future, success is a small step taken just now." Jonathan Martensson
48. "As I grow older I pay less attention to what men say. I just watch what they do." Dale Carnegie
49. "What you do speaks so loudly I can't hear what you say." Ralph Waldo Emerson
50. "The best way out of a problem is through it." Author unknown.
51. "We cannot do everything at once, but we can do something at once." Calvin Coolidge
52. "You see but do not observe." Sir Arthur Conan Doyle
53. "Nothing in the world will take the place of persistence. Talent will not; nothing is more common than the unsuccessful person with talent.
Genius will not; unrewarded genius is almost a proverb.

Education will not; the world is full of educated derelicts. Persistence and determination alone are omnipotent. The slogan "press on" has solved and always will solve the problems of the human race." Calvin Coolidge

54. "If there is no wind, row." Author unknown.
55. "Only those who risk going too far will ever know how far they can go." Author unknown
56. "If you're not on the edge you're taking up too much room." Author Unknown
57. "If opportunity doesn't knock, build a door." Author Unknown

Part VI

310

References

[1] Chaos theory has received some attention, beginning with its popularity in movies such as Jurassic Park; public awareness of a science of chaos has been steadily increasing. However, as with any media covered item, many misconceptions have arisen concerning chaos theory.
The most commonly held misconception about chaos theory is that chaos theory is about disorder. Nothing could be further from the truth! Chaos theory is not about disorder! It does not disprove determinism or dictate that ordered systems are impossible; it does not invalidate experimental evidence or claim that modeling complex systems is useless. The "chaos" in chaos theory is order--not simply order, but the very ESSENCE of order.
It is true that chaos theory dictates that minor changes can cause huge fluctuations. But one of the central concepts of chaos theory is that while it is impossible to exactly predict the state of a system, it is generally quite possible, even easy, to model the overall behavior of a system. Thus, chaos theory lays emphasis not on the disorder of the system--the inherent unpredictability of a system--but on the order inherent in the system--the universal behavior of similar systems.

[2] For more information go to http://www.bobdaviescoaching.com/introduction/

[3] The bridge-line call in number currently is 218-486-1300 access code 239172. Please call the High Performance Training, Inc. office to get the date of the next monthly call. Also, please verify that phone number is the current bridge line-number being used. The monthly date and number are both subject to change. The calls are usually held on the first Wednesday of every month but that may change due to holidays or Mr. Davies' speaking schedule. Call 866-262-3284.

[4] See Michael Shermer, publisher of Skeptic (www.skeptic.com) His latest book is "Why Darwin Matters".

[5] Author Bob Davies was named in the top 100 minds on personal development by Executive Excellence Publishing Leadership Excellence 2007, listing of the top 100 thought leaders.

[6] Author, Bob Davies, has the highest credential earned by coaches, Master Certified Coach, one of the first to receive the designation in 1998, and served on the board of the International Coaches Federation.

[7] Recommended book: "The Sky Is Not The Limit-You Are!" by Bob Davies. http://www.bobdavies.com/motivational_books.html#Limit

[8] The American Heritage Dictionary

[9] Walter Bradford Cannon -(born Oct. 19, 1871, Prairie du Chien, Wis., U.S. - died Oct. 1, 1945, Franklin, N.H.) A U.S. neurologist and physiologist. He was the first to use X rays in physiological studies. He also investigated hemorrhagic and traumatic shock during World War I and worked on methods of blood storage. He researched the emergency functions of the sympathetic nervous system and homeostasis and sympathin, an epinephrine-like substance released by certain neurons. With Philip Bard he developed the Cannon-Bard theory, which proposed that emotional and physiological responses to external situations arise simultaneously and that both prepare the body to deal with the situation.

[10] Robert Maurer, Ph.D. (2004) One Small Step Can Change Your Life. (22-25) Workman Publishing ISBN 0-7611-2923-5

[11] Donald McNeil Jr., New York Times, 2006.

[12] Select Family of Staffing Companies, Santa Barbara, Ca. 800-688-6162.

[13] Article "Eat a Spider For Success", By Bob Davies, appeared in Excellence Magazine, October 2006. www.leaderexcel.com
[14] Read more on entertainment versus impact and the development of the on-line coaching program by going to this link; http://www.bobdaviescoaching.com/introduction/
[15] Calls refer to logging onto the program www.bobdaviescoaching.com and completing the steps to the on-line coaching experience for the week.
[16] Brandreth, DiSpezio, Joyce, Paraquin, Optical Illusions, Main Street Publishing, ISBN # 1-4027-1064-X
[17] For more information the on-line program itself will walk you through how to use it. You can also purchase a two-cd plus workbook album, which is a detailed explanation of the program. To order go to: http://www.bobdavies.com/motivational_books.html#Online1
[18] Wheelan, Charles "Naked Economics" W.W. Norton & Co. page 6
[19] Do a search engine search on Google for the research on Rewards versus Punishment.
[20] Thaler, Richard H, 1992 "The Winner's Curse: Paradoxes and Anomalies of Economic Life".
[21] Kahneman, D. J.L. Knetsch and R.H.Thaler, 1990 "Experimental Tests of the Endowment Effect and the Coase Theorem." The Journal of Political Economy. [Cited by 505] (31.97/year)
[22] Reported by Barry Schwartz, a professor of psychology at Swarthmore College. He is the author of the "Paradox of Choice; Why More is Less" (Ecco, 2004).
[23] Scientific America, August/September 2007 issue, pg. 39.
[24] Kahneman and Tversky, "Choices, Values, and Frames", in American Psychologist, Vol. 39, No. 4, pages 341-150; April 1984.
[25] Dickinson, D.L., and Isaac, R.M. (1998). "Absolute and Relative Rewards for Individuals in Team Production." Managerial and Decision Economics. 19, 299-310
[26] David Dickinson, Department of Economics, Appalachian State University, Experimental Economics, 4:107-124 (2001)
[27] Cialdini, R. B. (2001) Influence: Science and Practice. (4th edition.) Boston: Allyn & Bacan.
[28] Ostrom, E., Walker, J., and Gardner, R. (1992). "Covenants with and Without a Sword: Self-Governance is Possible." American Political Science Review, 86, 404-417.
[29] A Quixtar.com powered organization.
[30] Nurnberger, J.I., & Zimmerman, J. (1970), Applied analysis of human behaviors: An alternative to conventional motivational inferences and unconscious determination in therapeutic programming. Behavioral Therapy1, pages 59-69.
[31] Walker EH (2000) The Physics of Consciousness: Quantum minds and the meaning of life. Cambridge MA: Perseus ISBN 078202347..
[32] Dispenza, Joe (2007) Evolve Your Brain, pg. 352-353.
[33] Amen DG (2000) Change Your Brain Change Your Life; The breakthrough program for conquering anxiety depression obsessiveness anger and impulsiveness. NY: Three Rivers Press ISBN 0812929985
[34] Davies, Bob (1994) The Sky is Not The Limit-You Are! High Performance Training, Inc. ISBN 1-881461-06-8 pg. 37.
[35] For more information on how to communicate effectively, the following is recommended by the author, Bob Davies: CD Albums "The Subconscious Aspects of Persuasion" and "Mission Accomplished" author, Bob Davies.
[36] Book by author, "The Sky is Not The Limit-You Are!" Page 42.
[37] Stanley, Thomas, Phd., "The Millionaire Mind", Andrews McMeel Publishing, ISBN 0-7407-0357-9, pg 34.

[38] Dr. Stanley, "The Millionaire Mind", page 137.

[39] Analogy of the 1.2% is that a small change will have a large impact in results. In this case the habit of making small commitments on Sunday night for the next seven days with a consequence for non-performance (behavioral contracting) is that small change that will lead to significant results over time.

[40] Larry Benowitz, Children's Hospital, Boston Ma. Reported in Science, Vol. 311: Jan. 27th, 2006.

[41] Candace Pert, Ph.D., "Molecules of Emotion", Scribner Publications.

[42] Mission Accomplished album, htttp://www.bobdavies.com/motivational_books.html#Mission

[43] Authors humor

[44] Brain Gate is a Trademarked name.

[45] http://www.cyberkineticsinc.com/content/clinicaltrials/braingate_trials.jsp

[46] For this Birbaumer was awarded the Leibniz Prize, the German equivalent to the Nobel Prize in medicine, in 1995.

[47] International Journal of Parapsychology, "Evidence of a Primary Perception in Plant Life," vol. 10, no. 4, Winter 1968, pp. 329-348

[48] Masaru Emoto, "The Hidden Messages in Water", Beyond Words Publishing.

[49] See end note #7, "The Sky Is Not The Limit-You Are!" page 26

[50] To watch a video of Jessie Sullivan: http://www.ric.org/research/accomplishments/Bionic.aspx

[51] More of the authors' humor.

[52] DISC is the four quadrant behavioral model based on the work of William Moulton Marston Ph.D. (1893 - 1947) to examine the behavior of individuals in their environment or within a specific situation. DISC looks at behavioral styles and behavioral preferences.

[53] For references and more information on neuroplasticity, see:
1. Drubach, D. (2000). The Brain Explained, Upper Saddle River, NJ: Prentice-Hall, Inc.
2. Gopnic, A., Meltzoff, A., Kuhl, P. (1999). The Scientist in the Crib: What Early Learning Tells Us About the Mind, New York, NY: HarperCollins Publishers.
3. John F. Kennedy Center for Research on Human Development, Vanderbilt University Staff. Brain Plasticity, Retrieved July 28, 2002 from http://kc.vanderbilt.edu/kennedy/research/topics/plasticity.html
4. Kandel, E.R., Schwartz, J.H., and Jessell, T.M. (2001). Principles of Neural Science. (4th ed.), New York: McGraw-Hill.
5. Kolb, B. (Winter 2000). Experience and the developing brain. Education Canada, 39(4), 24-26.
6. Neville, H.J. and Bavelier, D. (2000). Specificity and plasticity in neurocognitive development in humans. In Gazzaniga, M.S. (Ed). The New Cognitive Neurosciences. (2nd ed.), Cambridge, MA: The MIT Press, pp. 83-99.
7. Society for Neuroscience. (July 2000). Brain Plasticity, Language Processing and Reading, Retrieved August 3, 2002 from http://web.sfn.org/content/Publications/BrainBriefings/brain_lang_reading.html

8. Sousa, D.A. (2001). How the Brain Learns (2nd ed.), Thousand Oaks, CA: Corwin Press, Inc.
9. Tortora, G. and Grabowski, S. (1996). Principles of Anatomy and Physiology. (8th ed.), New York: HarperCollins College Publishers.
10. Tulving, E. and Craik, F.I.M. (Eds.) (2000). The Oxford Handbook of Memory, London and New York: Oxford University Press.

[54] D.Dobbs, "Fact or Phrenology?" Scientific American Mind, 16, no. 1 April 2005: 24-31

[55] Gerard Tortora and Sandra Grabowski, "Principles of Anatomy and Physiology, Control Systems of the Human Body, Vol. 3, 10th Edition.

[56] Candace Pert, Ph.D. "Molecules of Emotion", pp. 270-271

[57] Pert, "Molecules of Emotion", page 321

[58] For a complete description of this concept the author recommends his DVD album, Vol 3, "Attitude Interventions and Coaching Commandments". See http://www.bobdavies.com/motivational_books.html

[59] Gates, Bill, "The Secret Diary of Bill Gates"

[60] At some point in time there is a measurement where everything ceases to be separate entities and matter presents itself in a wave form that is indistinguishable from other matter, "entanglement", the Planck length atomic scale, string theory, and at that time you are not able to make another ½ cut. Suggested reading, Green, "The Elegant Universe: Superstrings, Hidden Dimensions, and the Quest for the Ultimate Theory".

[61] Johnson, George, New York Times, "How is the Universe Built? Grain by Grain" 1999

[62] Garland, Trudi Hammel, "Fascinating Fibonaccis: Mystery and Magic in Numbers"

[63] Cook, Theadore, "The Curves of Life"

[64] Recommended reading, Edward Burger and Michael Starbird, "The Heart of Mathematics: An invitation to effective thinking", Key College Publishing.

[65] Donald, T. S. (1986). The Geometric Figure Relating the Golden Ratio and Phi, Mathematics Teacher 79, 340-341. (Article)

[66] It is a very provable fact that our human bodies are phi-designed as the golden section template is intimately seen throughout our whole human form ratios. This absolutely proves that we like the macrocosm (the planets and stars) or the microcosm (of atomic and subatomic particles) all were created using the Creator's PHI design.

[67] For further explanation in the Monty Hall problem, see http://en.wikipedia.org/wiki/Monty_Hall_problem

[68] Edward Burger, Williams College and Michael Starbird, The University of Texas at Austin, "The Joy of Thinking: The Beauty and Power of Classical Mathematical Ideas", The Teaching Company.

[69] When you get on the scale in the morning, you may be hoping that it registers a smaller number than the day before -- you may be hoping that you've lost weight. It's the quantity of mass in you, plus the force of gravity, that determines your weight. But what determines your mass?

That's one of the most-asked, most-hotly pursued questions in physics today. Many of the experiments circulating in the world's particle accelerators are looking into the mechanism that gives rise to mass. Scientists at CERN, as well as at Fermilab in Illinois, are hoping to find what they call the "Higgs boson." Higgs, they believe, is a particle, or set of particles, that might give others mass.

[70] In chemistry and physics, an atom (Greek átomos meaning "the smallest indivisible particle of matter, i.e. something that cannot be divided") is the smallest particle still characterizing a chemical element.

[71] Quantum physics in named for the word quanta used by Max Planck to describe his discovery that energy is not a steady stream. Planck found that energy works in discrete clumps or packets which he called quanta.

[72] Natalie Reid, "5 Steps to a Quantum Life", Winged Horse Publishing ISBN -13:978-0-9792110-0-3

[73] See www.whatthebleep.com for additional resources and information on this topic.

[74] Natalie Reid, "5 Steps to a Quantum Life", Winged Horse Publishing.

[75] Placebo, a substance containing no medication. An inactive substance used as a control in an experiment.

[76] "Against Depression, a Sugar Pill Is Hard to Beat," By Shankar Vedantam, The Washington Post, May 7, 2002.

[77] Grasping the Intentions of Others with One's Own Mirror Neuron System. M Lacoboni et al. in Public Library of Science Biology, Vol. 3, No. 3, pages 529-535; March 2005

[78] Recommend product by the author, Bob Davies, "The Subconscious Aspects of Persuasion", www.bobdavies.com or http://www.bobdavies.com/motivational_books.html#Subconscious

[79] William Teller, Walter Dribble, Michael Kohane, "Conscious Acts of Creation", ISBN # 1-929331-05-3

[80] E. Kandel, J. Schwartz, and T. Jessell, T"The Foundations of Neural Science, 4th edition. Diagram and explanation by Robert Sapolsky, Ph.D., Stanford University

[81] Squire, "Memory and Brain".

[82] The Wright Exit Strategy, by Bruce Wright, pg 49.

[83] Walker, EH. (2000) "The Physics of Consciousness: Quantum Minds and the Meaning of Life", Cambridge MA.

[84] Joe Dispenza, D.C., "Evolve Your Brain" 2007 Health Communications, Inc.

[85] http://en.wikipedia.org/wiki/Time

[86] David Labrador, freelance writer and researcher, assembled this list.

[87] Recommended reading "Faster: The Acceleration of Just About Everything." James Gleick. Vintage Books 1999 and "Revolution in Time" Revised edition. David S. Landes. Belknap Press of Harvard University Press, 2000.

[88] Source: Scientific American, September 2002, page 41.

[89] Antonio R. Damasio, head of the department of neurology at the University of Iowa College of Medicine and adjunct professor at the Salk Institute for Biological Studies in La Jolla, Ca. He is recognized for his studies of neurological disorders of mind and behavior.

[90] Suggested reading: "From Physical Time to the First and Second Moments of Psychological Time", Simon Grondin in Psychological Bulletin, Vol. 127, No. 1, pages 22-44; January 2001.

[91] R.Douglas Fields, "Making Memories Stick", in Scientific American, Vol. 292, no. 2, pages 75-81; February 2005.

[92] Instinct, distributed by Buena Vista Home Entertainment, Inc.

[93] "The Brain Has a Mind of Its Own" by Richard Restak, MD. Crown Trade Paperbacks.

[94] From "The Little Book of Bleeps"., Quotations from the movie. Beyond Words Publishing

[95] Alan G. Sanfey, James K. Killing, Jessica A. Aronson, Leigh E. Nystrom, and Jonathan D. Cohen, "The neural basis of economic decision-making in the ultimatum game," Science, vol. 300 (2003), pp. 1755-1758.

[96] Lewis, M. Alessandri, S.M., & Sullivan, M.W. (1990). Violation of expectancy, loss of control, and anger expressions in young infants. Developmental Psychology, 26, 745-751.

[97] Seligman, M.E. (1990) Learned Optimism. Ney York: Pocket Books.

[98] Source: Estimated risk over a lifetime, from "Risk: A Practical Guide for Deciding What's really Safe and What's Really Dangerous in the World Around You", By David Ropeik and George Gray.

[99] A.L. Williams, "All You Can Do Is All You Can Do But All You Can Do Is Enough!" Ivy Books, N.Y.

[100] A.L. Williams, above, page 140.

[101] Dr. Candance Pert, "Molecules of Emotion", page 321. Scribner Publishing.

[102] Wikipedia definition.

[103] Jeffrey M. Schwartz, M.D. is a well known American scientist in the field of Neuroplasticity, and its application to obsessive-compulsive disorder (OCD). After receiving a bachelors with honors in Philosophy, he changed career directions to the medical sciences. Currently associate research professor of psychiatry at UCLA School of Medicine, he is also a fellow with the International Society for Complexity, Information and Design.
Schwartz is a seminal thinker and researcher in the field of self-directed neuroplasticity. He is the author of almost 100 scientific publications in the fields of neuroscience and psychiatry, and several popular books. His major research interest over the past two decades has been brain imaging/functional neuroanatomy and cognitive-behavioral therapy, with a focus on the pathological mechanisms and psychological treatment of obsessive-compulsive disorder (OCD).
For his book The Mind and the Brain: Neuroplasticity and the Power of Mental Force, Schwartz received collaboration from LBL physicist Henry Stapp (who is himself unaffiliated with the ICSID).

[104] Stapp, H. P., & Atmanspacher, H. (2006). Clarifications & Specifications. Journal of Consciousness Studies, 13(9), 67-85. Copyright © J. Martin & A. Combs

Index

D

E

F

G

H